C000199587

THE BOURNE SOCIETY

Village Histories

6. KENLEY

Editor: Grahame Brooks

Series Editors: Roger Packham and Gwyneth Fookes

ISBN 0 900992 57 3

Acknowledgements

My grateful thanks are due to the enthusiastic team of authors – John Bishop, Colin Burgess, John Carr, Gordon Newall, Roger Packham, Frances Perry, Jane Ruffle, Andrew Scott, Jill Tassera and Robert Warner, who have made the completion of the Kenley volume in the Society's Village History series a reality.

Without the support and encouragement of family & friends plus the help, advice and memories of many individuals it would not have been possible. Special thanks are due to the staff of Purley Library and the Croydon Local Studies Library, who have given much assistance in obtaining information and allowing us to copy and reproduce photographs from their extensive collections. Our thanks also to the skill and dedication of those Victorian & Edwardian photographers, who captured postcard views of the area in such detail.

Our Series Editors – Gwyneth Fookes and Roger Packham are to be warmly thanked for the many hours they have spent checking, amending and adding information from their comprehensive local knowledge. Without their help and the technical assistance of Robert Warner this volume would not have appeared.

Finally, to the residents of Kenley, for whom this book has primarily been published, we hope they will enjoy reading it and will not find too many errors and omissions!

Grahame Brooks

Cover photograph by Grahame Brooks

Kenley Station in 1989

CONTENTS

Illustrations

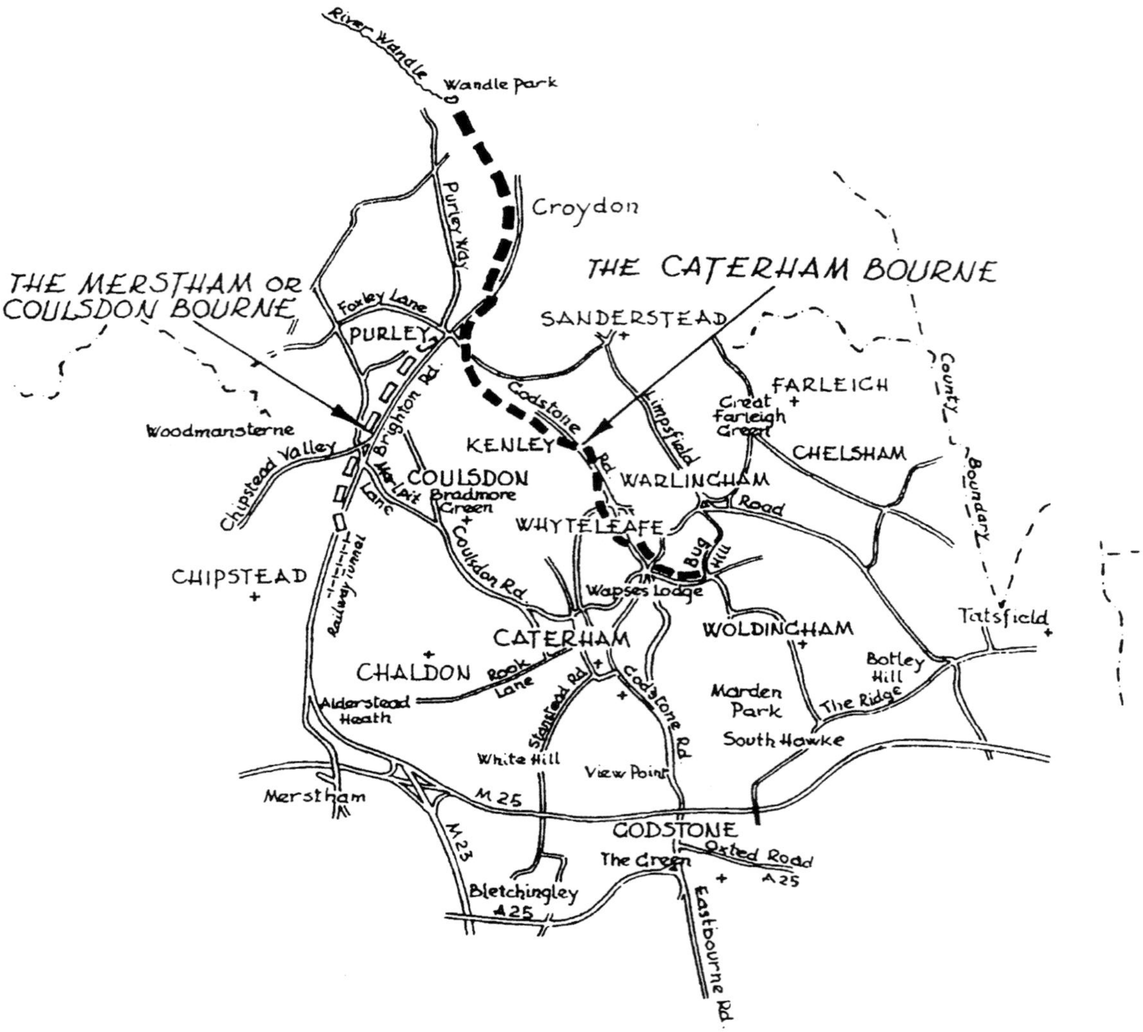

The Bourne Society Area

Introduction

We present volume six of the Village History Series – a series that becomes more exciting as it progresses. Little did we realise when we started on volume one how different each village would be — communities so near to one another and yet each with a unique development. Kenley, seemingly a product of the building of the Caterham railway in 1856, proves to have a pedigree as long as any other ancient community – a name change certainly, but nevertheless Watendone was in Domesday, and was actually larger than Coulsdon at that time.

The isolated community of Watendone can be traced back to the 7th century. The original names of the farms have survived to the present day. The name Kenley first appeared in the 13th century.

The team researching Kenley headed by Grahame Brooks has been working since the earliest days of the project. Such was their enthusiasm that several of the contributors gathered their material as long ago as 1994 and became rather frustrated that the Kenley volume had to wait so long to come to completion. Their fields of interest often overlap and they have contributed to a variety of chapters apart from those under their names.

It has been particularly pleasing to include the reminiscences of a number of elderly ladies and gentlemen who lived in Kenley many years ago, and some of whom still live there.

That natural phenomenon, the Bourne, has been flowing since the first days of December 2000. It has created havoc this year, as it has traditionally every seven years for hundreds of years. It must have been a decisive factor all those years ago in the siting of the original farms.

The team is to be congratulated on a magnificent effort in gathering such a wealth of information. There is always more to be gleaned and if readers can add to the story we will be very pleased to hear from them.

Gwyneth Fookes

Roger Packham

May 2001

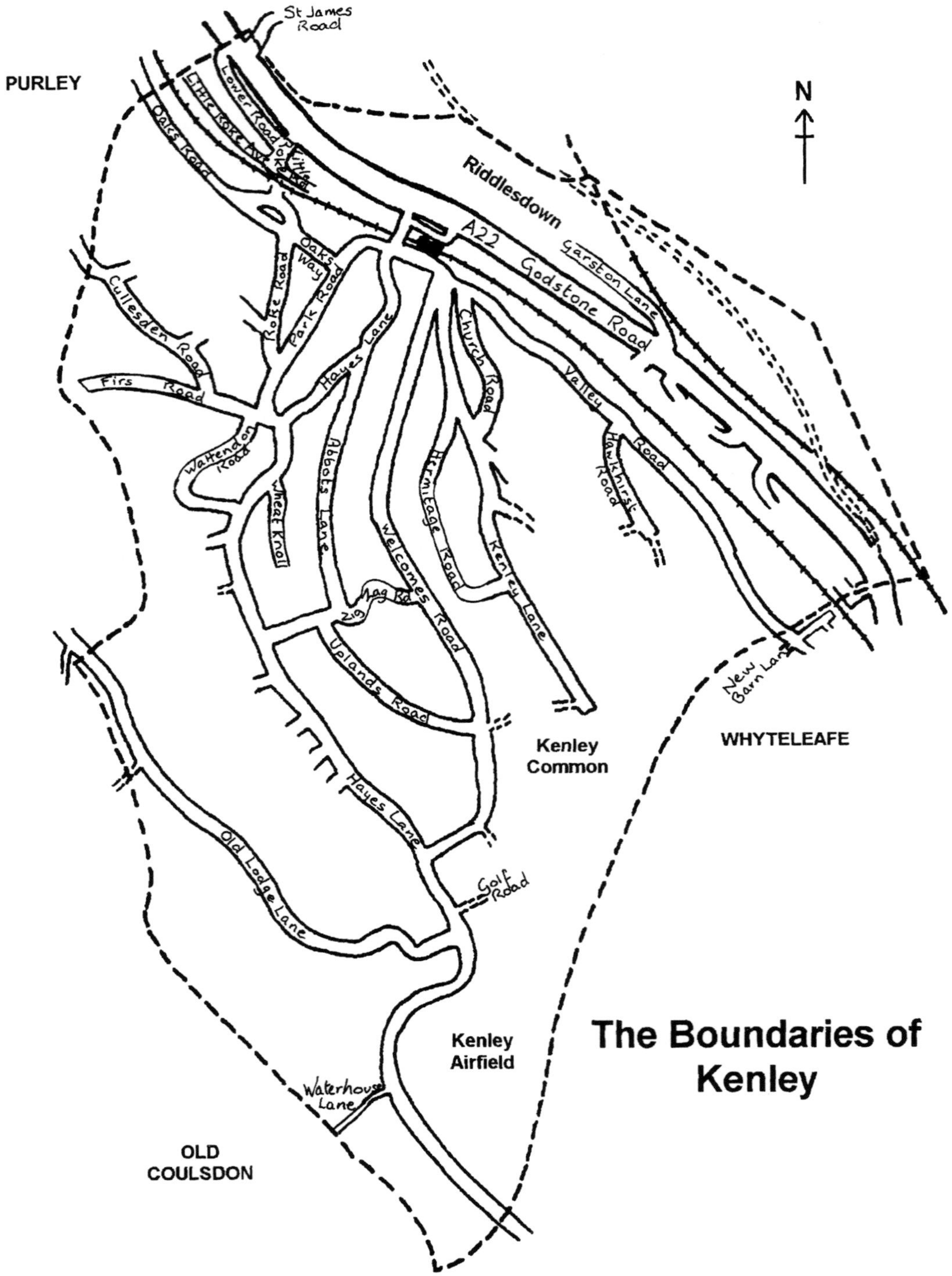

The Boundaries of Kenley

Chapter 1

Chronology

by Grahame Brooks

c.100,000 BC **Mammoths and hippopotami** roamed the region – fossils found in Purley and Whyteleafe

c.3,500 BC Evidence of **early man** from the discovery of flint axe in Hayes Lane

c.100 BC Possible evidence of **Celtic fields** on Riddlesdown – Hope-Taylor

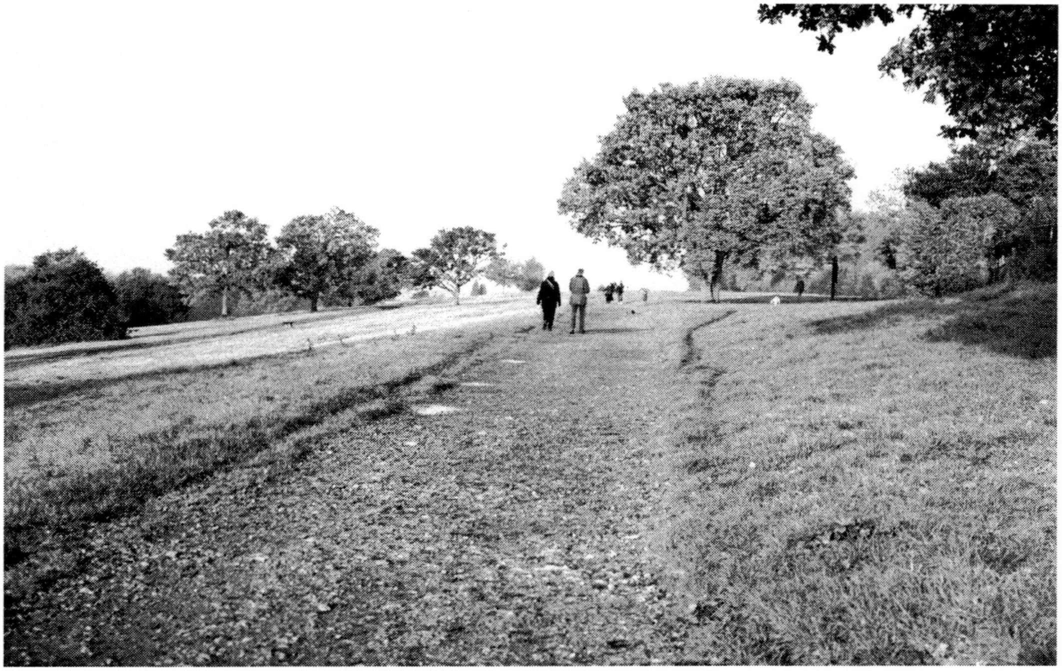

The Roman road over Riddlesdown is still well-used

Photograph: Gwyneth Fookes, 2001

c.AD 100 Construction of **Roman Road** over Riddlesdown

675 Probable date of grant of **Watendone** to **Chertsey Abbey** by Surrey sub-king Frithwald

The former Watendone manor covered the whole extent of modern Kenley and part of Whyteleafe

c.700 **Anglo-Saxon cemetery** – found at the corner of Riddlesdown Road and Mitchley Avenue in 1927

A HISTORY OF KENLEY

880	**Watendone** – Hwaetedune – The Wheaten Down named in a deed
1086	Domesday Book refers to **Watendone**, which had a church, 17 villagers and 2 cottagers
1150/1350	**Pottery** from this period found in 1966 excavations at 'Watendone Manor'
1255	Earliest known record of the name **Kenley** as Kenele – probably derived from Coena's leah
1269	**Watendone manor merged with Coulsdon** and formation of **Garston** manor
1279	Earliest known record of **Fox(e)le** in Chertsey Abbey records
1300	Charter gave freehold of estate to Purlee family in **Standene (Roke)** at 10s. 0d per annum rent
1300	Present thinking dates **The Roke Oaks** and **The Kenley Oak** to about this time
*c.*1320	**Charter** describes local boundaries
1329	Earliest known record of **Roke –** Thomas atte Rok
1330	Earliest mention of **Waterhouse –** Wereghtehaghe
1331	Earliest known record of **Riddlesdown –** Ridelesdoune
1339	**John de Cattesfeld** parson of Watendone Church
1349	The **Black Death** (population of England 4-5 million before – 100 years later the population estimated to be still only about 2¼ million)
1389	Thomas de Purlee failed to pay rent on **Standene** (Roke)
1395	First mention of **Welcomes** – Thomas Bassett passed the freehold to his son, Thomas
1403	Hugh Quecche died, owner of a tenement called **Kenley,** leaving it to Joan Quecche. She married John Norton
1406	John Norton granted the tenement of **Kenley** to the Chantry chapel of St Mary in Steyning
1414	William atte Hall held **Garston** in partnership with John Pertenhall, Thomas Sharpe & John Barton
1443	**Standene** estate conveyed to John Stopynden and John Kyriell
1450	Thomas and John Bassett of Welcomes pardoned after **Jack Cade's rising** in Kent.
1453	Henry Gerbregge rector of Coulsdon and the **chapel at Watendone**
1536	Dissolution of **Chertsey Abbey** and lands in Watendone, along with Coulsdon, annexed to Hampton Court
1549	The church described as 'the former **chapel of Whattingdon** in Coulsdon'
1549	**Standene** land (Roke) was held by Henry Polsted of Purley, who passed it on to the Covell and Walter families
1553	**Watendone** granted to Sir Francis Carew
1617-61	**Standene** conveyed to Matthew Bedell; Ralph Hawtry; Lewis Audley and Harman Atwood

CHRONOLOGY

1723	Original ***Rose (& Crown) Inn*** built
1743	**Milestone** erected near *The Rose & Crown* – extant
1762	Isaac Messeder commissioned to draw up an **estate map** by Joseph Hodgkins of Kenley Farm
1780	**Watendone church**, which had been used as a barn, burned down
1782	**Thomas Byron** purchased Coulsdon Manor
1785	**Bainbridge Map** of Coulsdon prepared for Thomas Byron
1795	Construction of the present **Godstone Road** along the Bourne valley
*c.*1800	**Riddlesdown Lime Quarry** in operation
*c.*1823	**'Kenley House'** built on the site of Kenley Farm
1851	There was a **beerhouse** at Waddington, later recorded as ***The Pig & Whistle***
1856	On 4 August formal opening of **Coulsdon Station,** renamed **Kenley** before the end of the same year
1865	**'Oaklands'** at the bottom of Hayes Lane was built for James Hall
*c.*1865	A number of other **mansions** were in course of construction at this time

Milestone dated 1743, re-sited on the 'new' Godstone Road (opposite Devon Close) some time after 1795.

The indistinct inscription states 'XIV Miles from Westminster Bridge'.

Photograph: Grahame Brooks

1869	**Caterham & Kenley Gas Company** mooted at 'Kenley House', home of John Young
1869	**Kenley Waterworks** first supplied water in the area
1869	***The Kenley Hotel*** built
1870/71	**All Saints' Church** built, designed by J W Fowler of Louth, Lincs and built by G W Booth
1871	**Riddlesdown National School** opened at the bottom of Downs Court Road
1872	First **shops** on record, comprising a butcher's, a grocer's and a haberdasher's, near *The Kenley Hotel*
1880	**Kenley Cricket Club** formed
1881	**Kenley Waterworks** established
1882	**St Winifred's School** for boys founded
1883	**Kenley & Riddlesdown Commons** dedicated to the public by the Corporation of London

An aerial view of Riddlesdown Quarry, and Riddlesdown, *c.*1954, looking north west and showing Godstone Road on the left

CHRONOLOGY

1884 **Kenley & Coulsdon Horticultural & Cottage Garden Society** formed

1885 **Kenley National School** opened on Riddlesdown opposite Kenley Waterworks

1888 **Kenley ecclesiastical parish** formed

1889 **'Shord Hill'** built for Benjamin Blenkinsop JP – it was demolished in 1964

1891 **'Worton Cottages'** in Hayes Lane built, one of which was used as the forge by Austin Killick

1891 Population of Kenley 918

1892 **Gardner's Pleasure Resort** opened to the public

1896 **Kenley Police Station** opened, forming part of 'W' or Clapham Division

Kenley Police Station July 1989
Photograph: Grahame Brooks

1897 **Commemoration Hall** built by Sir Joseph Lawrence to celebrate Queen Victoria's Diamond Jubilee

*c.*1900 **'Watendone Manor'** built in Hayes Lane for Carleton Fowell Tufnell

1901 At the turn of the century the population was 1299

1902 **Wickings Stores –** which still exists as The Village Stores – opened near Kenley Police Station

1903 Original **St James' Church** (now the hall in Little Roke Avenue) dedicated

1904 A serious accident at **Gardner's Pleasure Resort** injured nine children

A HISTORY OF KENLEY

1905	**Lloyds Bank** opened a sub-branch in Godstone Road
1906	The **Methodist Church** was built in Sylverdale Road
1907	**Roke County Primary School** built in Purley Vale
1912	The first **motor bus service** ran – Sundays only – from Brixton to *The Whyteleafe Tavern*
1914	The first sod was cut for new **St James' Church**, St James' Road
1915	**Coulsdon & Purley Urban District Council** formed
1916	**Zeppelin** drops bombs over Kenley in the Downs Court Road/Hall Way area, injuring two people
1917	**Aircraft Acceptance Park** established on Kenley Common
1918	**Revd L Harding Squire** died. He was the first vicar of the parish, serving for 29 years
1921	**Edmund Byron**, the last resident squire of Coulsdon Manor, died aged 77
1921	**Kenley Memorial Hall** built
1921	**Kenley Recreation Ground,** now Bourne Park, was laid out by Coulsdon & Purley UDC
1922	**'The Welcomes'** house & racing stables destroyed by fire
1923	Aircraft crashed on **'Colescroft'** in Firs Road
1928	'Third rail' **electrification** of the Caterham railway line completed
1929	***The Rose & Crown*** rebuilt
1929	**Whyteleafe and Kenley Estate Residents' Association** formed
1930	**Green Line** Coach Service from Godstone to Oxford Circus inaugurated
1931	Pilot Officer **D R S Bader,** flying from Kenley in a Bristol Bulldog, had a flying accident at Woodley
1936	**Kenley County Primary School** rebuilt in New Barn Lane
1936	**Kenley Library** built in Beverley Road – it was closed in 1975
1938	**New Barn** opposite *The Rose & Crown* burned down
1939	**Waterhouse Farm** demolished when RAF Kenley was extended
1939	**Hayes Lane** diverted around the airfield
1940	**RAF Kenley** suffered a serious bombing raid on 18 August
1944	On 3 August, ***The Rose & Crown*** was hit by flying bomb
1944	**RAF** control of Kenley sector transferred to Biggin Hill
1945	**Roke & District Residents' Association** formed, changing to Roke & East Purley Residents' Assocation in 1952
1955	**'Reach for the Sky'** filmed locally

CHRONOLOGY

1958 **The Hayes County Primary School** officially opened

1964 **Coulsdon & Purley Urban District Council** ceased to exist and Kenley became part of the London Borough of Croydon

1966 Bourne Society excavation of **Watendone Manor** site

1967 Closure of **Riddlesdown Lime Quarry**

1968 **Wattenden Primary School** in Old Lodge Lane opened

1970 **Kenley & District Residents' Association** established from Roke & East Purley Residents' Association and Whyteleafe & Kenley Residents' Association

1975 Re-opening of **Memorial Hall** on 8 November

1976 **Shaftesbury School** opened at former Roke Senior School

1979 **Observatory** off Waterhouse Lane opened on 30 June

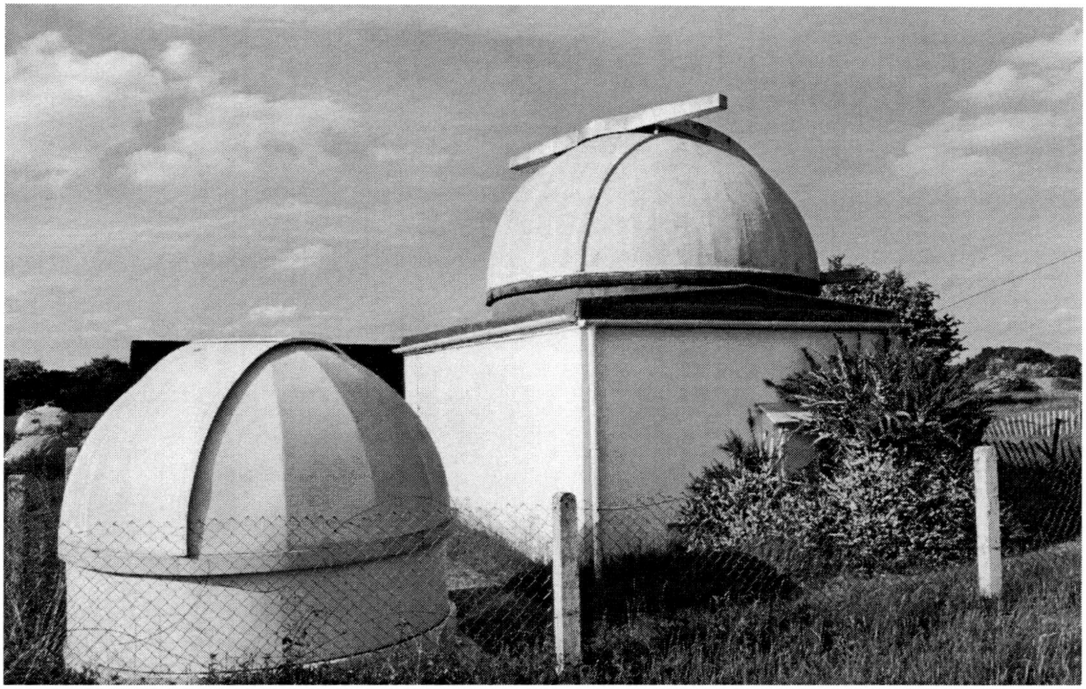

The Observatory (off Waterhouse Lane) was opened in 1979

Photograph: Grahame Brooks May 2001

1979 **South London Gliding Centre** established

1981 **Population** 9,260

1989 **Kenley Waterworks** was rebuilt

1994 The new **Roke Primary School** opened – the old school closed and was converted to housing

2000 **RAF Kenley Memorial** unveiled on 19 August

RAF Kenley Tribute
The inscription on the centre panel reads–
'IN HONOUR OF ALL PERSONNEL WHO SERVED HERE 1917-1950'
Photograph: Grahame Brooks

2000 Severe flooding by the **Bourne** in December

2002 Publication of ***Kenley Village History***

SOURCES

Bourne Society Bulletins & *Local History Records*

Caterham Mirror

Coulsdon & Purley Advertiser

Croydon Local Studies Library

FLINT, Peter (1985) *RAF Kenley* Terence Dalton

HARRIS, G E *1929-1979: 50 Years of Service to Kenley & District*. Kenley & District Residents' Association

MALDEN, H E (Ed) (1902-1912) *Victoria County History of the County of Surrey*

PILKINGTON L (1997) *Surrey Airfields in the Second World War*

Purley Library

Chapter 2

Chalk, Flints and Clay

by Frances Perry and Jane Olver

The story of Kenley began almost a hundred million years ago, in a warm, quiet, shallow sea, where the skeletons of countless tiny planktonic creatures called diatoms sank through the clear water and collected on the sea floor, layer upon layer, to form what we now call chalk. More recently, the forces that created the Alps pushed the chalk up to form the Wealden dome which eroded to leave the Downs. From the middle of the airfield, Kenley appears to consist of nothing more than flat grassland stretching to a circular horizon.

Of course there are other, older, rocks than chalk far beneath our feet. The deep coal mines of Kent tell us that somewhere below us there may still lie the remains of great, swampy fern forests. They eventually vanished beneath a huge desert, where dunes later trapped gas from the rotting forests. The gas flares at Godstone remind us of other rocks under the chalk – Jurassic rocks from tropical flood-plains where dinosaurs once walked and where mighty rivers deposited the sands that later trapped both gas and oil.

Kenley has been explored for oil. One day in the summer of 1988 a convoy of four surveying lorries worked its way ponderously up Park Road and along Hayes Lane, pausing every hundred yards to shake the ground with four huge suction pads so that a mobile instrument room on the airfield could record the echoes of the vibrations from rock layers underground. If the seismic survey had shown domes or faults that might have trapped oil, drilling would have followed, but the discreet little oil pumps would have had to be located over the boundary, in Whyteleafe or Caterham-on-the-Hill, because Kenley is in the Greater London area.

No oil traps were found, so Kenley's only underground products – water and optical lenses – continue to be based in the chalk.

The chalk was formed in the Cretaceous period that followed the Jurassic. This was a time when the air was richer in oxygen even than today. The world's plants flourished, and the sea levels were higher, as the waters of the world's oceans were pushed up on to the skirts of the continents by hot rock welling up along the central ridges of the newly opening Atlantic, Indian and Antarctic oceans. Kenley, with the rest of Europe, was still drifting northwards from the equator as the sea flooded over the Jurassic rocks until no current from the far-off land brought silt or even clay to muddy the waters. Over the ages the white chalk built up until it was hundreds of feet deep, disturbed only by nodules of flint in the upper layers where the siliceous skeletons of sponges had dissolved and reprecipitated. Most are irregular or formed as flattened lumps along the surfaces between the beds of chalk, but some filled the shells of the heart-shaped or conical sea urchins that now adorn the shelves of Kenley residents, or act as paper-weights on their desks.

Fossil Sea Urchin

Micraster coranguinum

Photograph: Grahame Brooks

Because the beds have since been domed and now dip gently (3-5 degrees) northwards, the oldest chalk exposed in Kenley is in the valley bottom from the railway station southward towards *The Rose and Crown*, where the hard, greyish Middle Chalk forms the lower 50 ft of the quarry. The small shells of *Terebratulina lata* are used to identify rocks of this age. The white Upper Chalk has several zones: the lowest, around 80 ft thick and exposed in the quarry opposite *The Kenley Hotel*, used to be identified by ammonites (coiled shells that once held octopus-like creatures) called *Hyphantoceras reussianum* and are now officially distinguished by the sea urchins called *Sternotaxis plana* (formerly *Holaster planus*). More familiar to Kenley residents living higher up the slopes is the *Micraster* sea urchin *Micraster cortestudinarium*, which is the zone fossil for the next 90 ft or so, and its successor the heart-shaped *Micraster coranguinum*, which continued to inhabit the seas while another 200 ft of chalk were laid down. The youngest beds of the Upper Chalk have been worn away from above Kenley but are still present where they dip down in the Purley area.

Lateral section through the Middle and Upper Chalk at Kenley Station

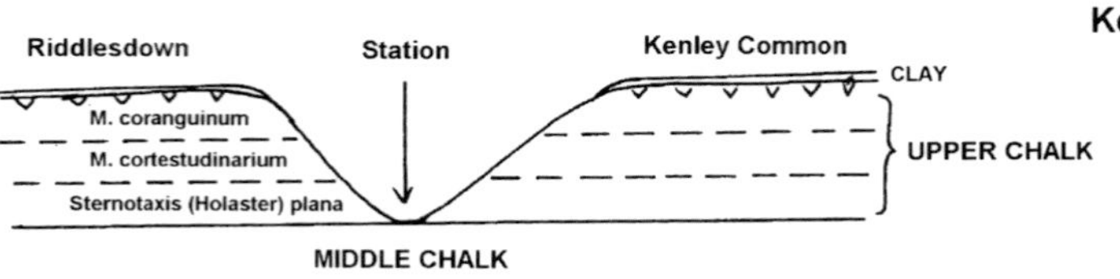

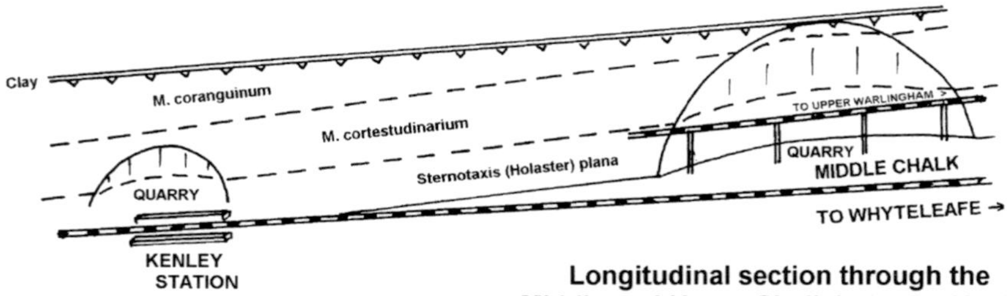

Longitudinal section through the Middle and Upper Chalk between Kenley Station and the 'Rose and Crown'

When Italy was pushed into Europe and the Alps began to rise, a ripple – its remnants we call the North and South Downs – was pushed up into a high dome, the centre of which has since been eroded to expose the older rocks of the Weald. As the chalk above Kenley was worn away over millions of years, numerous vertical pipes were formed by flowing water dissolving the chalk down lines of weakness. These pipes, which are very common, are similar in origin to the swallow holes seen today in the Peak District and eventually became filled with whatever deposit lay above them. Along the top of *The Rose and Crown* quarry, pipes filled with red clay stand out clearly against the white chalk on either side, and have been thought by some local people to be the remains of old flint mines – but similar holes elsewhere in the North Downs contain old rocks that were worn away from the surface of the chalk long before humans existed.

Although the beds of the chalk at Kenley are only gently inclined northwards, the surface of the land has been eroded into valleys over the last million years or so. Kenley Station and Godstone Road lie near the bottom of a

Clay-filled pipes exposed in the top of Riddlesdown Quarry
Photograph: Grahame Brooks

main valley running roughly northwards from Caterham to Purley. This must originally have been cut by a river flowing down the dip slope of the chalk, at a time when water tables were much higher or when the ground was frozen so that water could not penetrate it. Side-streams, such as the one which cut the Welcomes Road valley, fed into it. There are river gravels in Godstone Road at the bottom of Foxley Hill Road (an area formerly known as Standene or Stoney Dene) and water-worn pebbles have been found on the valley bottom on Welcomes Road. Now the river is represented by the Bourne, which usually flows underground and is only seen when water tables rise after a period of high rainfall.

The Bourne flowing down 'Axell Hill' – Little Roke Road, at the junction with the Godstone Road, where today it can still be heard in its underground conduit

From a postcard dated 1904
Courtesy of Roger Packham

The origin of the clay-with-flints, which often overlies the chalk in Kenley and is the basis of the thicker soils, has been much debated. In 1889 it was suggested that clay-with-flints was the residue left when chalk had dissolved slowly away over the millennia, while in 1933 Dines & Edmunds pointed out that some clay-with-flints appears to be a mixture assembled under glacial conditions, perhaps under a local ice-cap or snowfield. On the flat hilltops it is thick and fertile, and has had an important influence on the history of Kenley – the old village of Watendone was named for the wheat that grew on the top of the down. There is also some on the shallower valley sides and floors, which must have moved down the slope or have been blown for a short distance as dust during the glaciations when cold-desert conditions prevailed; the name of Roke farmstead records the oak trees that grew on the thick clay near the valley bottom.

One of the Roke Oaks – an ancient oak tree growing on slumped clay in the valley bottom at Roke. The level crossing has been replaced by a footbridge

From an old postcard dated 1906 ***Roger Packham collection***

On the steeper slopes, there is little or no clay-with-flints, and the soil is only a few inches thick with a high component of chalky rubble. Here the chalk has been quarried extensively, mainly for use in cement but in earlier times for agricultural use to 'sweeten' acid soils. The tunnels of the disused quarry opposite *The Kenley Hotel* have also provided shelter from air raids, and the uniform temperatures needed for the precision grinding of optical lenses.

There is a sharp contrast between the two sides of the valley. The west-facing slopes such as the side of Riddlesdown tend to be steep, with very little soil over the chalk, while the east-facing slopes are gentler with much more soil. This has been explained by a hypothesis that gives us a picture of Kenley in the Ice Ages. There were never glaciers this far south, but for long periods the land would have been tundra, with little vegetation and the ground permanently frozen apart from the surface few inches. Where the afternoon sun warmed one side of a valley for a few hours a day in summer, it thawed the surface of the chalk, while the heavy night frosts froze it again; this process gradually shattered the chalk. At times – in summer or in warmer periods – water flowed down the valleys, removing the chalk rubble. Over the millennia, this cut back and steepened the warmer side of each valley, while the colder side remained shallower.

Before the last Ice Age the valleys were inhabited by giant mammals such as the mammoth, rhinoceros and reindeer. Then, one day after the ice had retreated for the last time, there came roaming a band of creatures that have left a new kind of record in the ground – Mesolithic axe-heads, metal artefacts, deep wells, lime pits, tunnels and railway cuttings, even bomb craters – *Homo sapiens* had arrived in Kenley.

SOURCES

ANDERTON, R, BRIDGES, P H, LEEDER, M R & SELWOOD, B W (1979) *A Dynamic Stratigraphy of the British Isles.* George Allen & Unwin

DAVIS, A G (1926) *Proc. Geol. Assoc.* Vol.37, pp 211, 213

DIBLEY, G E (1921) *Proc. Geol. Assoc.* Vol.32 p.35

DINES, H G & EDMUNDS, F H (1933) *The Geology of the Country around Reigate and Dorking* HMSO *(Mem. Geol. Surv. Eng. & Wales, explanation to sheet 286)*

FRENCH, H M (1976) *The Periglacial Environment.* Longman

MONKHOUSE, F H (1966) *Principles of Physical Geography* 6th edn.

OWEN, T R (1978) *The Geological Evolution of the British Isles.* Pergamon

PETTIJOHN, E J (1975) *Sedimentary Rocks* Harper-Row

SHEPHERD, W (1972) *Flint.* Faber

SMITH, A(1798) *Fossils of the Chalk.* Palaeonotological Association

TRUEMAN, A E, REVD WHITTOW, J B & HARDY, J R (1971) *Geoogy & Scenery in England & Wales.* Penguin Books

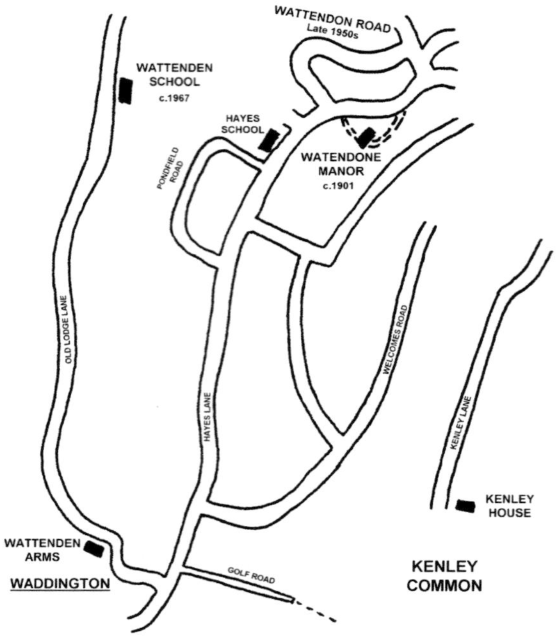

WADDINGTON Village and the WATENDONE place-names

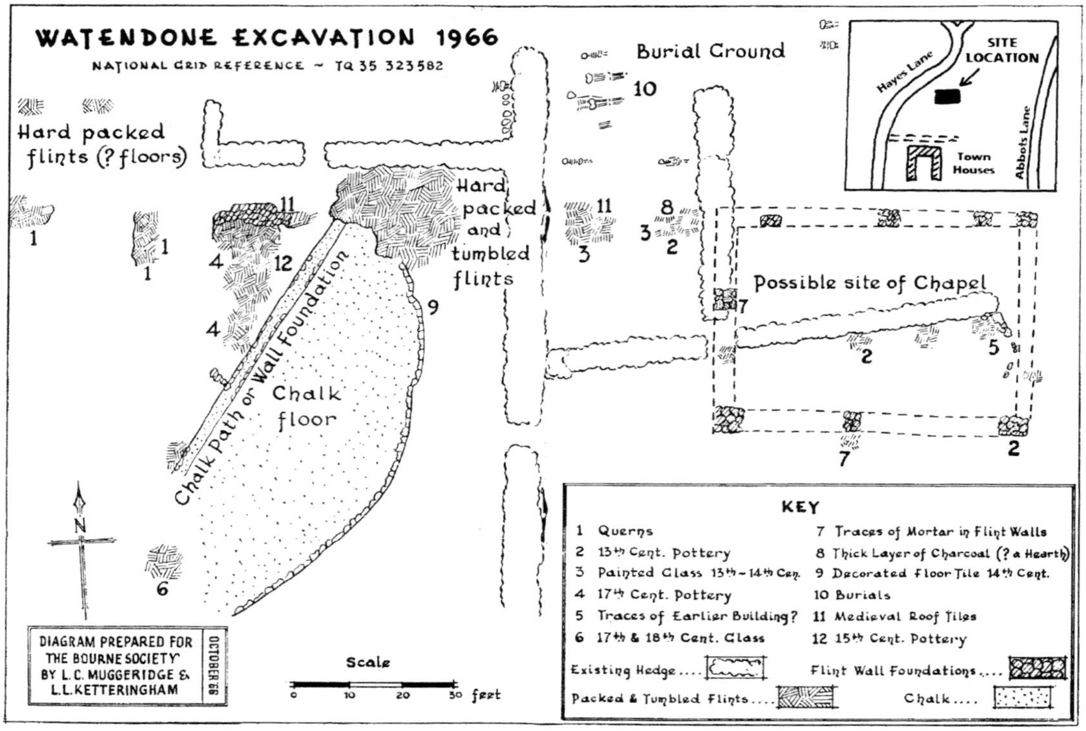

Chapter 3

The Wheaten Down

by Frances Perry

A Tale of Two Villages

Kenley is an ancient name, but it is not the name of a village. There never was a Kenley village. When the railway company ran a line up the Bourne valley in 1856 and named its stations after the nearby hilltop villages, 'Coulsdon' station at the bottom of Kenley Lane was quickly renamed 'Kenley' — at the census in 1851, Kenley House and its stables and lodge housed 20 people in four households, including a prosperous banker and his East Indian-born wife. The name that was never used was that of a village a quarter of a mile southwest of Kenley House on the flat hill-top, with just 60 inhabitants crammed into 10 cottages and an alehouse-cum-bakehouse. A century later, the identity of the village had almost, but not quite, vanished beneath that of its new suburban neighbour. In the 1950s, people moving into the new bungalows at the top of Old Lodge Lane were told that their address was:

Waddington, Kenley, Surrey.

If a hamlet is a cluster of cottages without a church, then Waddington was a hamlet. Today it is unrecognisable. Beside the mini-roundabout on Hayes Lane that attempts to calm the traffic, there is a grassy hollow that was the village pond. The neat flint-and-brick terraced houses opposite the top of Old Lodge Lane are 19th century estate cottages. Beyond it on Old Lodge Lane there stood until the 1980s a cedar tree, beside gate-posts marking where Garston Hall once kennelled the Old Surrey fox-hounds. The lane wriggles past *The Wattenden Arms* on the left and a 1930s terrace on the right, with Betts Mead Cottages behind. One thatched flint cottage (once the *Pig and Whistle)* and a few 20th century dwellings complete the picture.

Waddington is unrecognisable, but its older name Watendone is recalled in four different places along the hilltop. There is *The Wattenden Arms.* In 1967 Wattenden Primary School was built further down Old Lodge Lane on the hillside below Hayes Lane. Wattendon Road, dating from the 1950s, branches off Hayes Lane just north of The Hayes School. Within the curve on the other side of Hayes Lane, there stood until 1966 the grand Victorian house called 'Watendone Manor'.

For as Waddington village was absorbed into the new suburb of Kenley, interest in the original Watendone village had grown. The Domesday book of 1086 refers to 'Watendone' as a place of some substance, with a church, 17 villagers and two cottagers plus their families (twice as many households as in 1851!) and land for eight ploughs. By comparison, Coulsdon in 1086 had only 10 villagers and four cottagers. Somehow, over the course of eight centuries, Watendone had declined while Coulsdon had flourished. There were hints, too, that although Waddington and Watendone had versions of the same name their locations had been different. A field near the Old Forge was called 'Chapel Field' in memory of a stone barn, burnt in the 1780s, which was said to have been a chapel, while it was also rumoured that in the building of 'Watendone Manor' human skeletons had been uncovered. In 1966, with 'Watendone Manor' demolished and the site about to be built over, Mary Saaler of the Bourne Society conducted a dig which uncovered the remains of graves, a rectangular stone building, a much larger floor of beaten chalk and some sherds of mediaeval pottery. The lost village of Watendone had been found: Hwaete Dun, the Wheaten Down or, as it was commemorated in a road name when the site had been built over, Wheat Knoll.

So the history of the village before the railway came is not a history of 'Kenley' but of the Domesday manor of Watendone, which gave its name to the Victorian hamlet by the airfield and to the lost mediaeval village under Wheat Knoll.

The Earliest Settlements

In 1851, the area we now call Kenley between Old Lodge Lane and the Bourne valley included the hamlet of Waddington and the farms of Kenley, Welcomes, Hayes, Waterhouse, Little Roke, Great Roke and Garston, making a total population of 249 people. To piece together the history of this scattered community and its origins, we have to rely on old maps, Anglo-Saxon and mediaeval references in legal documents, the likely original meanings of old place-names, published descriptions of mediaeval buildings, the Domesday record and a few excavated artefacts.

On the ground, probably the oldest feature and one which formed the old boundary of Coulsdon is the road along the top of Riddlesdown, from the modern Riddlesdown Road to *The Rose and Crown.* Used by the Romans long before it became the coach road to Brighton, it may have followed a still more ancient track: the district had been inhabited since the Middle Stone Age, as indicated by occasional finds of Mesolithic, Neolithic and Bronze Age tools. By the time the Romans arrived there were Iron Age settlers in Sanderstead, below the Dobbin in Whyteleafe, on Farthing Downs in Coulsdon and at Cardinal's Cap in Caterham.

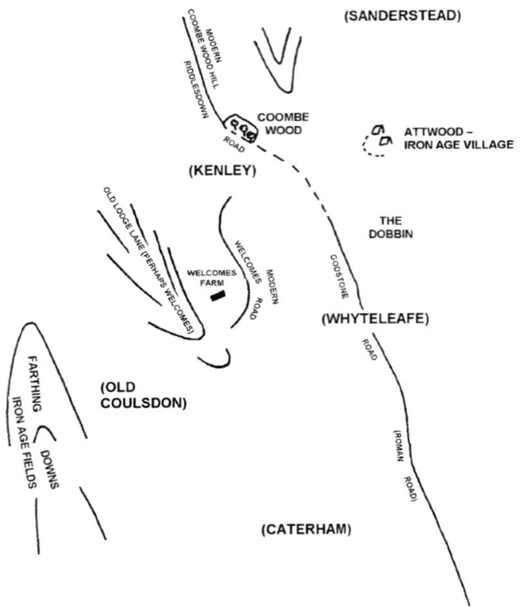

CELTIC/IRON AGE SITES and possible CELTIC place names 'coombe' and 'ca(s)ter'

In Kenley itself evidence of pre-Anglo-Saxon inhabitants is preserved in the British word 'coombe' (the Welsh 'cwm') which was retained in English as 'Welcomes' (coombe with a spring) and, on top of Riddlesdown (marking the boundary with Sanderstead), 'Coombes Wood'. The early Anglo-Saxon settlers seldom borrowed words from the older inhabitants, but 'coombe' was so like a word of their own meaning 'basin' or 'cup' that they were evidently able to recognise it as appropriate for the basin-shaped heads of the little, dry valleys. The name 'Coombes Wood' was perhaps adopted by the Saxons whose graves have been discovered in Mitchley Avenue, and 'Welcombes' probably referred originally to the head of the Old Lodge Lane valley, where the spring at Waterhouse was said never to run dry.

The first evidence of activity on 'the down where wheat is grown' (now the plateau along which Hayes Lane runs) is a written reference. *Hwaetedune* is named in a document dating from around 880, *Hyaetedune* in 1062 and *Watendone* in 1086. Copies made in the 13th century, supposedly of earlier charters, mention *Whatindone* as having existed in 675 and *Whetindune* in 967. This Hwaetedune or Whatindone was among the lands said to have been granted by Frithwald, the sub-king of Surrey, and Bishop Erkenwald to Chertsey Abbey, with the grant later confirmed by King Edgar. The date of the grant is given in the charter as 727, but as Frithwald and Erkenwald lived rather earlier it is thought that the lands must actually have been given to Chertsey in the late 7th century, around 675.

The first village

Watendone became a village at some stage during the centuries under Chertsey Abbey before the Norman Conquest. In 1086 King William's commissioners, collating the information supplied to them by the contingent (six villagers and the priest, if Watendone had one) sent over to Wallington in response to their summons, noted the following:

> *'In WALLINGTON hundred: The Abbey of St. Peter's of Chertsey holds WATENDONE. In the time of King Edward it answered for 20 hides, now for 5 hides. Land for 8 ploughs. In lordship 1 plough and 17 villagers and 2 cottagers with 5 ploughs. There is a church, woodland, 6 pigs from pasturage. Value before 1066 £6; now £7.'*

It is interesting that the villagers from neighbouring Coulsdon reported a settlement with more ploughland but fewer inhabitants.

The fall in taxable value at Watendone from 20 hides before 1066 to only five hides in 1086, has long been thought to illustrate the disastrous effects of the Conquest on the rural population. Nevertheless, there is a brief snapshot of a village of 19 households, probably living in wattle-and-daub houses made with hazel from Foxley or Pitlands Woods and clay from the fields. The church would almost certainly have been timber-built but could

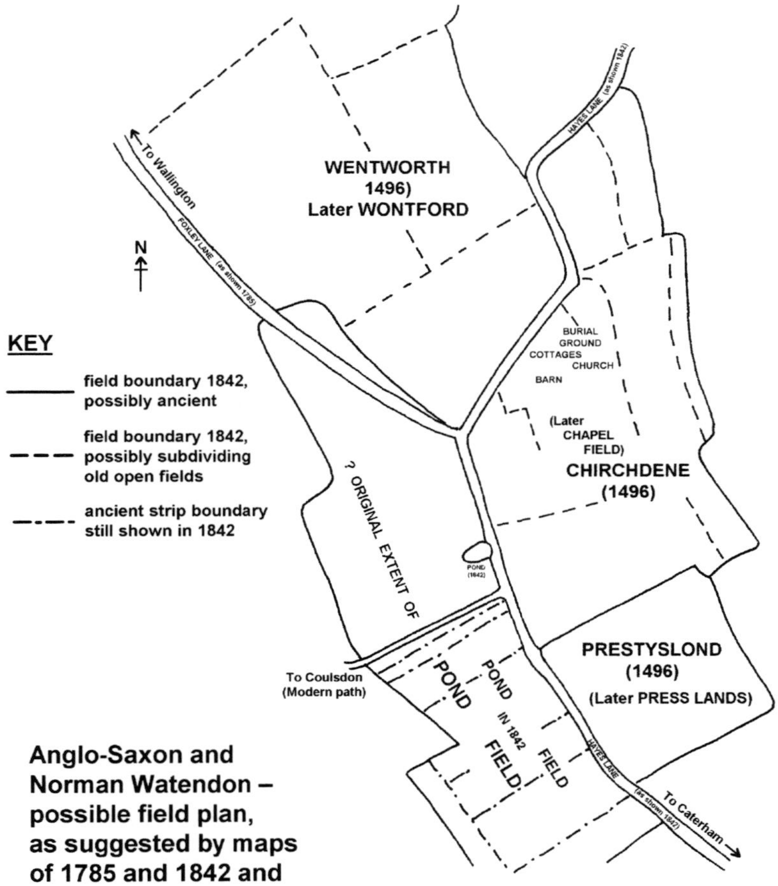

Anglo-Saxon and Norman Watendon – possible field plan, as suggested by maps of 1785 and 1842 and by field lists of 1496

just possibly have already been of stone – the 1966 excavation uncovered a fragment of what seems to have been the line of an older wall on the site of the 13th century stone church. Lime for plastering and whitewashing the interior was easily come by. The village was surrounded by ploughed fields on the fertile hill-top, managed on the strip system common among the Anglo-Saxons: one of these, Pond Field, was still in strips as late as 1842 and another, Wontford (now Cullesden Road), was probably divided in the 18th century. The old Churchdene, presumably Chertsey Abbey's demesne land, lay adjacent to the village itself and the field beyond was later called Priest's lands (Prestyslond).

Four tracks led from the village between the open fields—

- northwards through Foxley Wood to the administrative centre at Wallington – part of this lane has disappeared under Firs Road, but it ran roughly along the line of modern Higher Drive, Foxley Hill Road and Coldharbour Lane, Purley;
- north-eastwards, down the modern Hayes Lane and over Riddlesdown towards the minster at Croydon;
- southwards, along the modern Hayes Lane towards Caterham-on-the-Hill, Blechingley and the minster at Godstone;
- westwards across Pond Field towards Coulsdon.

Another likely Anglo-Saxon lane – from Riddlesdown towards Wallington via Downs Court Road

Photograph: Grahame Brooks

Early farms

The 19 households were probably not based only in the village but were already in outlying farmhouses. Portions of land had been granted to individuals long before the Norman conquest: in the time of King Alfred, 'two hides in Whatedune' had been given by Duke Ælfred to his son Æthelwald. In 1269, when the manors of Coulsdon and Watendone had been merged into 'the whole vill of Coulsdon', we hear of seven payments received from smaller 'vills', consisting of buildings as well as land, that had been detached from the combined manor and were assessed independently for a property tax of a tenth or a fifteenth. The smallest of these payments was the eightpence owed for his freehold by one Walter de Kenele.

Kenele is a name of Anglo-Saxon origin, probably derived from *Coena's leah* (Coena's clearing in the woods). The first mention of it dates from 1255 and it appears regularly in documents over the next century, until by 1403 it was spelt Kenle. Its location is most likely to have been that of the modern Kenley House.

SOME EARLY FARMS AND OTHER LANDMARKS OF THE 1330s, WITH THEIR POSSIBLE LOCATIONS

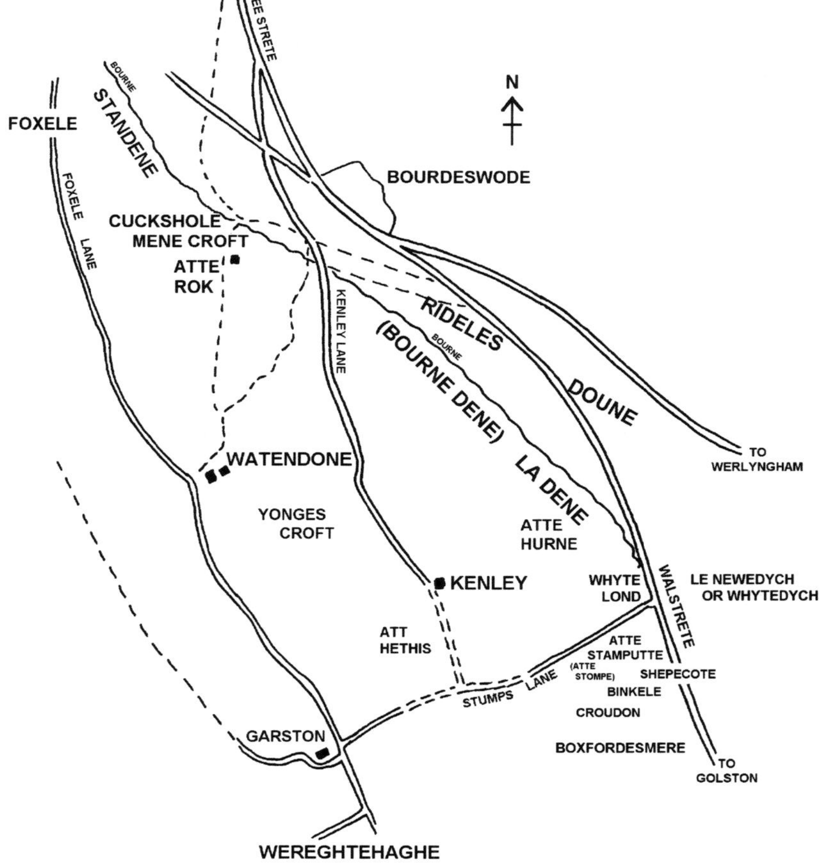

Another important farm was mentioned at around the same time: in 1269 Joel de Garston and his wife Philippa, who owned land in Coulsdon, also had a tenement in Whatingdon called *Garston*; the name associated with land near the modern common.

Further familiar names began to appear in the Chertsey Abbey records: *Fox(e)le* in 1279, 1294 and 1431; *Ridelesdoune* (from *leah, down* and the Middle English *ridde*) in 1331, shortened to *Redele* in 1338, *North Ridle* in 1422 and *Riddeleys* or *Northriddeley* in 1461; and mention of Thomas *atte Rok* in 1329, Adam *atte Roke* (*atter oke* or at the oak) in 1367 and Adam *atte Rock* in 1392. The Bourne valley is mentioned simply as *la Dene*: in 1332 the Abbot of Chertsey exchanged 'a tenement called Whetyndon next Hudelesdoune (Riddlesdown) in la Dene in various perches' for Thomas North's acre of woodland and 20 acres of arable called Eldelond, in Smitham Dene (the Brighton Road valley). By 1496 there is reference to 'Borneden' (Bourne Dene). In 1330 an entry records Thomas Sokelyng, a 'native' (Anglo-Saxon), producing the charter under which he held a house and curtilage 'in Whatedon next *le Wereghtehagh*': this looks very much like the first mention of Waterhouse Farm—

- Luke *atte Stompe or atte Stamputte*, recorded in 1329 and 1339, suggests Stumps Lane and
- Pitlands, now part of Kenley Common, where 'lands called Putland lying in Whatyndone' were later held by Thomas Hayward, John atte Heth and in 1496 John Attwood; there are small pits below Kenley House on Hawkhirst Road and a larger one down Stumps Lane above Marlings Close.
- The free-holding of the *atte Hethe* family ('lands and tenements lying in Whatyngton called Att Hethis formerly of John att Heth' held in 1496 by John Marshall at an annual rent of 14s 8d) may be identified with Heathfield on the edge of Kenley Common, between Golf Road and The Avenue.
- Where was the tenement 'Mayheu', mentioned with 'le Whyte' in 1339 as held by Robert Colgrym? Was it part of the later Colgrimes Farm, at the top of Old Lodge Lane? The 'native' Colgrym family, whose disputes and felonies earned them numerous entries in the records, held lands in Coulsdon as well as Watendone.
- Where 'in Whadyngton' – which stretched almost from Purley Oaks to Reedham and Whyteleafe – were 'Whytelonds', 'atte Hurne', 'Cuckshole near Meancroft', or in 1496 'Nokattes', 'Holles' and 'Bryggers, otherwise Wodwardysland'?

One holding listed in detail in 1496 confirms that many of the field names recorded on the 1842 Coulsdon tithe map were indeed those used in the 15th century, if not earlier—

Thomas Canceler held 'divers parcels of land formerly of Adam atte Rukde... namely'

one field 'Sewardsfield' (between Park Road and Hayes Lane),

one croft 'Purifeld' (later Lower Bury, between Hayes Lane and Abbots Lane),

'Middellfeld' (the field down which Roke Road runs),

'Benifeld' (Barnfield, between Welcomes Farm and Uplands Road),

'Lewellcroft' (Great Lew and Little Lew, on Welcomes Road between Zigzag Road and Uplands Road),

'le pyghtel' (the plot next to the Welcomes Farm buildings), 'le garden plott' (quite possibly the later Kitchen Field behind the farm),

'Yongescroft' (tenuously identified as Yellowleaves, another enclosed strip between Hayes Lane and Abbots Lane),

'Molthawe', with other land in the common fields of

'Wentworth' (later Wontford, on the Cullesden Road side of Hayes Lane),

'Chirchdene' (later Chapel Field),

'Prestyslond' (later Press Lands, opposite Pond Field)

and in 'Borneden' (Bourne Dean, the old communal grazing meadows in the Bourne Valley and later the name for a series of fields along Valley Road from Church Road to Hazeldene Court).

The holding of lands in the common fields and demesne land at Watendone village is coupled with holdings on the Roke hillside and the nucleus of the Welcomes Farm lands (which still included Bourne Dean in 1762) – these are the two properties in Watendone granted by Henry VIII to Sir John Gresham in 1545, called *Welcombes* and *Lawrences*. Welcomes had first been mentioned in 1395 and Lawrences was later to become Hayes Farm, which stood just beside where the old Watendone village had been.

New Church, New Barn, New Ditch

In 1269 when Walter de Kenele was farming his eightpenny freehold at the far end of the hilltop, the old village was still flourishing. The most significant building in the history of Watendone was erected at around this time: a new stone church. Traces of an earlier stone wall on its site suggest that it may have replaced a smaller or plainer stone building, perhaps built around 1100 and resembling the barn-like old St Agatha's at Woldingham. It was a plain rectangle in plan, 60 ft long and 40 ft wide. The walls were of flint and were 2-3 ft thick, while the corners were of dressed sandstone (Reigate stone) and the roof, perhaps at first thatched or shingled, was at some stage tiled; there was coloured glass in the windows and plaster on the walls. A document of 1339 mentions that Watendone church had its own parson, at that time John de Cattesfeld; this was quite a different situation from that of a century later, when in 1453 Henry Gerbregge was instituted as rector of Coulsdon '*cum capella* Whatingdon' – with the *chapel* at Watendone.

A second important building at Watendone was represented by the large flat area of chalk, 100 ft long and 50 ft wide, excavated to the south of the graveyard. It was probably the floor of a wooden tithe barn, more than twice the size (if it covered the whole chalk area) of the new stone church. The tradition that at some stage this old barn was deemed redundant by Chertsey Abbey and a new barn erected on the parish boundary, where the Roman road from Godstone began its climb up Riddlesdown, has been questioned by research suggesting that the supposed 14th century New Barn was in fact much more recent, perhaps *c.*1800. Well-built of black flints with firestone dressings and narrow loops of the same stone in the walls, it was 50 ft by 19 ft in size, with walls a foot thick, a roof of slates and huge double wooden doors. It was used by *The Rose and Crown* as stables for many years, by Balch's Dairy for storage and was finally burnt down accidentally by four small boys in 1938. Confusingly, 19th century maps show another

Dressed stone showing medieval tool marks: height 15 inches

From *Local History Records* VI

'New Barn' on what is now the airfield, comprising buildings around a yard with a pond; censuses record several families living there. Fields alongside this New Barn are named Little Size Tithes and Great Size Tithes, adding weight to the suggestion that the plateau New Barn was the ancient New Barn.

The 'New Barn' opposite *The Rose & Crown,* dating probably to the late 18th century.
Photographed *c.*1930, when occupied by Balch & Sons.
Courtesy of East Surrey Museum

The other 'new' feature of the parish is undated. A description of the boundaries of the combined Coulsdon and Watendone manors in 1347 mentions 'le Newedych or Whytedych' (by 1496 'le Newedich or Widedich'). In the late 18th century, Manning identified this New Ditch as the three parallel banks with two ditches between them, running straight up the slope of Riddlesdown above Roke to meet the Roman road and possibly a continuation of a similarly aligned ditch some miles away at Hooley Lane. One of these two ditches was eventually destroyed by the building of houses along the northwest edge of the common but the other survives.

However, a more careful reading of the boundary description shows that this ditch was not the 'Newedich or Widedich' described in the Chertsey Abbey records, which was clearly much further up the valley than Roke and was not on the Riddlesdown side. The boundaries are likely to have changed little and can easily be traced along the modern Brighton Road, Sanderstead parish boundary and Greater London boundary. Starting from the valley called Smetheden (Smitham Dene or Bottom, now the Brighton Road valley), the line followed *Purlestrete* to *Bourdeswode* (1347, called *Combeswode* in 1496), then crossed '*Sondayesfurghes in the heath*' towards

'The (incorrectly identifed) Wide Ditch' where it follows the north-west boundary of Riddlesdown, November 2001

Photograph: Gwyneth Fookes

Werlynhgam. This clearly implies climbing Riddlesdown Road from Purley Bury, passing Coombes Wood and following the bridleway that still runs along the top of Riddlesdown towards Warlingham. Where the modern boundary plunges down beside the far edge of the quarry, the ancient boundary made a '*descent by said heath into the valley towards the King's way to Golston called Walstrett*' (rejoining the Roman road just beyond *The Rose & Crown*) '*and so by the said King's way to the ditch called le Newedich or Widedich and so by that ditch to Shepecote*' (possibly on Hornchurch Hill), '*Binkele, Croudon, cepes et haias*' (hedges, climbing up the edge of the modern common on the Whyteleafe Hill side) '*to the pit called Boxfordesmere*'. The boundary reached Hayes Lane via '*a field called Bokyneheswort he*' and continued along the Caterham border via fields and commons to the Reigate road, thence to Smitham Cross and back along Smitham Dene to Purlestrete.

The 1966 excavation at Watendone uncovered a number of piles of flints which suggested the remains of flint cottages. Pottery was starting to be bought rather than made: quantities of pre-1250 shell-tempered pottery found in a thick layer of charcoal surrounded by stonework, outside the northwest corner of the church, presumably represented an earlier kiln or hearth, but later finds included sherds of a big cooking pot of around 1250, a decorated jug and a black cooking pot from about 1300 and green-and-white Cheam ware from around 1350. Beyond the chalk floor of the old tithe barn were the broken remains of mediaeval querns used for grinding the wheat, made of imported basalt (Niederemdig lava) from the Eifel in Germany.

Painted Glass – 13th-14th century,
Probably from the church at Watendone

From *Local History Records* VI (1967)

The fragments of painted glass, wall plaster and floor tiles of the 13th-14th centuries, found among piled flints near the church, are less likely to represent the interior decorations of cottages than debris from the church that was swept aside in later centuries, but still add to the picture of a flourishing, prosperous community at the time when John de Cattesfeld was parson in the 1340s. An outlying farmer, Luke atte Stumputte, received the following settlement when he passed on his land to his daughter and son-in-law in 1339: they were to 'harbour Luke in messuage for life and board him at their table, and to pay him a garment value 3s, 1 pair of *linee tele* value 12d, a pair of boots value 6d, 2 prs shoes value 10d and a small pig value 18d at Christmas, if he shall not remain at their table'.

Decline

Plague first swept England in 1347-9, but 15th or 16th century earthenware pottery from the old village shows that if Watendone was deserted because of plague the epidemic must have been one of the later ones or the process of abandonment gradual. The church, still referred to as 'the Church of Whatyngdon' in 1367, had been demoted to a chapel by 1453; by 1496 the Watendone area was referred to as 'Cullesdone and Whadyngtone' and by 1549/50 the old village church could be described as 'the *former* chapel of Whattingdon in Coulsdon with the burial-ground belonging to the chapel and all its appurtenances'. The abandonment of the chapel may have been a direct result of the Reformation, but it seems from the scarcity of post-14th century pottery that villagers may already have been living at the Garston end of the hill-top, in new Waddington, from which St John's church in Coulsdon was almost as easily reached as the chapel. Even St John's was in disarray – Henry Gerbregge, the combined rector, was non-resident in 1464/65 and because of dilapidations his rectory was confiscated.

In many villages where plague had left too few villagers to work the fields properly, the landowners razed the remaining cottages to the ground and turned the land over to sheep; both Watendone and Woodcote have been identified as classic examples of such 'sheep-farming depopulation'. In that case, the 15th century decline was only the prelude to a catastrophe signified by the change from Wheaten Down to 'Hayes' – hedged enclosures, perhaps of the blackthorn that still fringes the fields on what is now Kenley Common – converting the old ploughlands and commons into pastures. The abbey's records of land-holdings in 1496 indicate that sheep were not the only alternative source of revenue: there was a coney (rabbit) warren at Putland and another on the Roke lands, while later maps show Coney Bank Dean and Rabets below Waterhouse Farm.

The Kenley freehold, meanwhile, had been bought by Peter atte Wode of Wood Place in Coulsdon, passing via his daughter Elizabeth to Hugh Quecche and from his daughter Joan, who inherited in 1403, to her husband John Norton. In 1406 John Norton granted the tenement of Kenley to the chantry chapel of St Mary in Steyning church, Sussex. By 1496 it was held by the masters of the Hospital of St Thomas of Acre in London and '*rendered by the year 5s 1d*'. Passing to the Crown when the chantries were suppressed in 1547, it was granted first to Henry Polsted and then in 1553 to Sir Francis Carew, as part of Coulsdon manor.

The Chertsey Abbey estates in Watendone, passing to the king in 1538, had been annexed to Hampton Court and quickly broken up, the messuages of Welcombes and Lawrences being granted by Henry VIII to Sir John Gresham in 1545. With the sale of the old church and graveyard to Henry Polsted in 1549/50 and transfer to William Worde in 1550/51, the break-up of the manor of Watendone was complete.

The church was used as a barn until it burned down in 1780; most of the flint and dressed stone was carried away in the succeeding century and by 1900 there were only the skeletons in the graveyard left to be disturbed by the builders of the modern 'Watendone Manor'.

SOURCES

BOURNE SOCIETY, (1967) *Local History Records VI*

Census for Couldson 1851

Chertsey Abbey Cartularies

GADSBY, J (Ed) (1998) *Village Histories – 3. Sanderstead* Bourne Society

HOSKINS, W G (1955) *Making of the English Landscape* Hodder and Stoughton

MALDEN, H E (Ed) (1902-12) *Victoria County History of the County of Surrey*

MANNING & BRAY (1809) *History of Surrey*

MORRIS, J (Ed) (1975) *Domesday Book - 3. Surrey* Phillimore

RESKER, R R (1916) *History and Development of Purley* Cassell

SAALER, M *(oral communication and slides)*

SCALES, I (Ed) (2000) *Village Histories – 5. Coulsdon* Bourne Society

SKUSE, P R (1987) *History of Whyteleafe* Bourne Society

STENTON, F (1971) *Anglo-Saxon England* Clarendon Press

The Oxford English Dictionary

Tithe Apportionment for Coulsdon – 1842

TURNER, D (1988) *Ordnance Survey Historical Guides - Surrey* Ordnance Survey

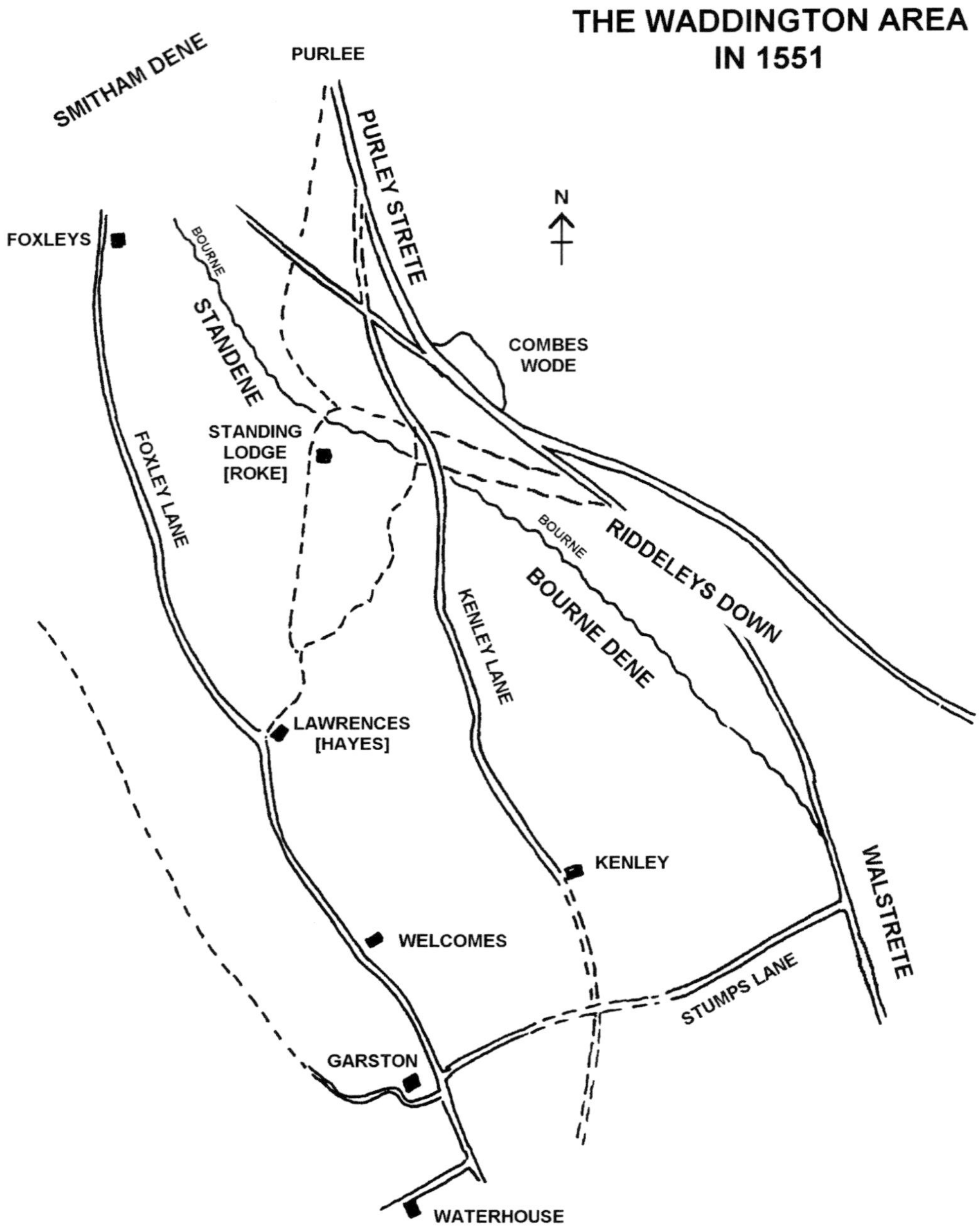
THE WADDINGTON AREA
IN 1551
SMITHAM DENE
PURLEE
PURLEY STRETE
N
FOXLEYS
BOURNE
STANDENE
COMBES
WODE
STANDING
LODGE
[ROKE]
FOXLEY LANE
BOURNE
RIDDELEYS DOWN
BOURNE DENE
KENLEY LANE
LAWRENCES
[HAYES]
KENLEY
WALSTRETE
WELCOMES
STUMPS LANE
GARSTON
WATERHOUSE

Chapter 4

The Rural Community

by Frances Perry

The Kenley area in 1551 would have been recognisably the same as in the census year of 1851.

The villagers of what was still called Waddington were scattered along the hilltop and hillsides. Spaced out along the plateau were Garston, Waterhouse, Kenley, Welcomes and Lawrences (later Hayes) Farms. Further on were the Foxley fields and woods. In the valley, there was Roke (at one point called Standing Lodge) in Standene to the north and Garston Down, newly separated from Garston, in Bourne Dene to the south. Stumps Lane led from the hilltop Garston down to Godstone road.

Running along the hilltop was Foxley Lane, later to be called Hayes Lane after the new *hayes* or hedges enclosing the old open fields around Hayes Farm. It ran southwards straight across what is now the aerodrome, towards Caterham. To the north it followed the hilltop, passed Welcomes and Lawrences Farms on the right and what remained of the original strip holdings on the left, and continued via Foxley Woods towards Wallington. No branch towards Riddlesdown is shown on Rocque's map of 1764, though a track probably still skirted the old village and cut down towards Roke across Middle Field, where the modern Roke Road runs.

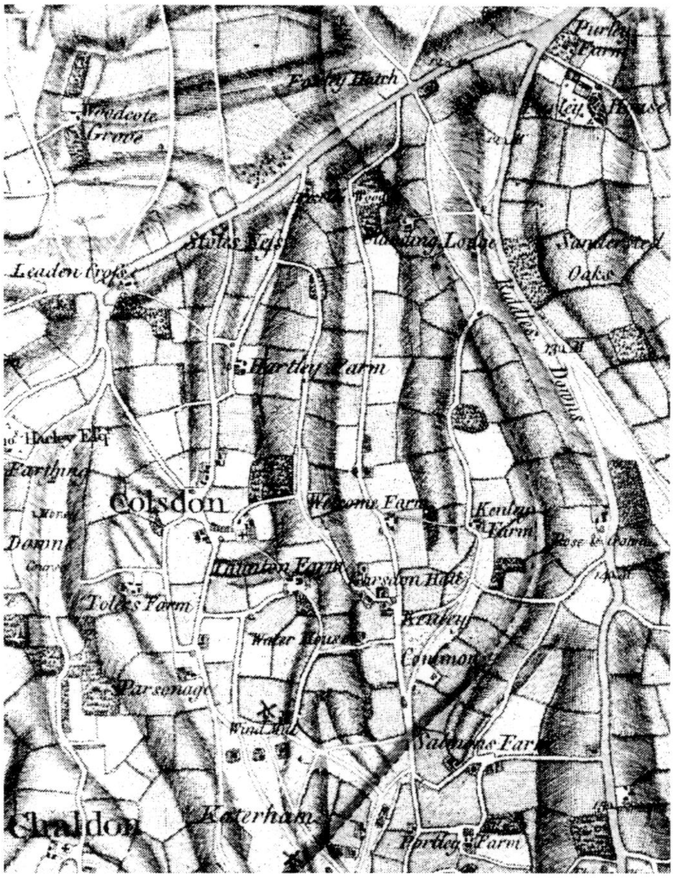

Extract from the Rocque Map (1764) showing the Kenley area

The lane that Rocque's map does show plunging down its familiar steep, narrow section towards the Bourne valley is Kenley Lane. It crossed the boggy valley bottom by the shortest route, at what is now the south end of Station Road, and branched northwards and southwards up the side of Riddlesdown to join the ridge-top London road; the northward branch heading for Croydon was a lane, not precisely where the old Hayes Lane runs today but a few yards higher up, where a lane-sized gully can still be seen crossing the Old Ditch (Manning's 'Newe Ditch'). The southward branch, in the direction of Warlingham and Godstone, was and is only a track.

Changes

So what did change between 1551 and 1851? Very slowly and almost imperceptibly, the traffic along the Roman road began to increase. Instead of the occasional pack-mule or slow team of oxen lugging iron from the bloomeries in the Weald, or the horse of an estate manager from a distant landlord, there began to be more riders, pack animals, beasts being driven to Croydon market and wheeled vehicles. In 1681 a carrier made the journey from London to 'Bredhempstone' (Brighton) once a week; the local children must have run down the hillside and waited to see him pass. By 1732 a coach set out from Borough High Street every Thursday and a van on Tuesday. In 1723 there was so much traffic that a wayside inn was built, so that the London-bound horses could rest or be changed before the long pull up Riddlesdown. Local drinkers at *The Rose* or, as it later became, *The Rose and Crown* were soon able to watch an even more dashing vehicle, the 'Flying Machine', which in 1745 used to leave Brighthelmstone at 5.30 a.m. and reach Southwark the same evening! By 1762, the road had been turnpiked to pay for its repair and upkeep. Then in 1784 the Prince Regent began his yearly visits to Brighton and the whole of high society followed him. The return climb over Riddlesdown must have been notorious, for in around 1790 it was decided to abandon the old road and to create instead one of the two major features of modern Kenley: the new Godstone Road.

The building of the new Godstone Road was at that time by far the largest civil engineering project ever undertaken in Kenley. Wide enough for two vehicles to pass, it was constructed on a level embankment partly cut into and partly banked out from the side of Riddlesdown, so as to avoid the treacherous valley bottom with its Bourne floods. On 1 May 1795, the Brighton mail-coach made its first journey, drawn by two horses and taking 12 hours.

Meanwhile, local residents had already developed a new lane of their own to take carriages and other wheeled traffic across the valley from Hayes Farm to the turnpiked London Road on Riddlesdown. The new Hayes Lane wound its way down into the valley and was carefully graded and ditched to follow a new, slightly less steep route up the side of the down towards Croydon.

Godstone Road, Kenley *c.*1905

The boy in the foreground is on the old stretch of Hayes Lane where it crossed Godstone Road. This part of Hayes Lane is now merely a footpath

From a postcard in the Roger Packham Collection

The Farms and their Owners and Tenants

One of these London-bound residents was Captain Coombes, who rented **Welcomes Farm** from its owner, a Fenchurch Street corn chandler, at Michaelmas 1779 and left his son in charge while he continued a lucrative career at sea. It was not until 1785 that he abandoned his cargoes of American rice, deerskins, pitch, indigo and furs and turned gentleman farmer on the proceeds. The last five years of his life were devoted to his sheep and enlivened only by the complaints of his neighbours when his flocks strayed from the extensive Welcomes Farm pastures.

Other prosperous inhabitants of the Hayes Lane hilltop are recorded by the monuments and records of donations in the parish church of St John's, Coulsdon, where Captain Coombes was buried under an ornate lead plaque. By 1826 the Pitters of **Kenley House** had a family vault in the church, presumably beneath the newly widened section of the north aisle. John Pitter was commemorated by his son with: *'A donation of £100 Stock 3 pr Cent Consols... for the benefit of the Poor residing in the Parish'.* Another marble tablet in the north aisle records the Hitchens family of **Garston Hall**, which stood at the corner of Hayes Lane and Old Lodge Lane.

Neither of these leading families of the 1820s is mentioned on a 1762 estate map of Kenley Farm, which includes the names of its neighbouring landowners, and neither of the surnames appears in the listings that accompany the 1842 tithe map.

- **Welcomes Farm**, long in the Gresham family after 1545, apparently belonged to Thomas Clements in 1762, was farmed by Captain Coombes in the 1780s and belonged to John Keen, who was farming it himself, in 1842.
- **Kenley Farm** was granted to Henry Polsted in around 1547 and Sir Francis Carew in 1553, but was bought by Joseph Hodgkins in 1750. It was inhabited by the Pitters in the 1820s and was owned and farmed by Thomas Marson in 1842; William Barllet or Bartlet, of Kenley, who died there in 1719 may have been yet another owner.
- **Garston Hall** was also purchased by Joseph Hodgkins in 1750. The John Hitchens Esq who died in 1824 was a newcomer. From 1815 onwards the parish registers record the baptisms of a succession of infants born to Sarah and Francis Hedger Esq of Garston Hall.
- The Lucas family, who in 1762 had owned land along Hayes Lane (including strips in the Pond Field and a copyholding at Foxley), were still resident at **Hayes** when Sarah and Robert Lucas, Gentleman, had their son baptised Arthur Bray in 1814 and later buried his little sister Jane in 1818, but by 1851 a Croydon attorney, Robert Rusell, was living at Hayes Farm.
- The most substantial tenant farmer in the district by 1842, one Henry Rowland of **Great Roke**, had come up from Wiltshire and brought a number of Wiltshire-born farm hands to lodge in the farms and cottages at both Little Roke and Hayes.

The land-holdings of the different farms had also changed over the centuries, with consolidation by sub-letting and transfers of land from one farm to another. The 1762 plan of the freehold estate of Kenley Farm shows a compact holding of fields and woods along Kenley Lane. Thomas Clements of Welcomes Farm owned most of the land to the east and west, while Bray Lucas of Hayes occupied fields east of Kenley Lane (where Church Road now runs) and Lord Folkestone owned much of what is now the common to the south. The Kenley Farm freehold also included three fields south of what is now Golf Road, just across Hayes Lane from Garston Hall. They are likely originally to have been part of the ancient 'tenement at Garston', to judge by their names: Great Garstons, Little Garstons and Pitt Garstons.

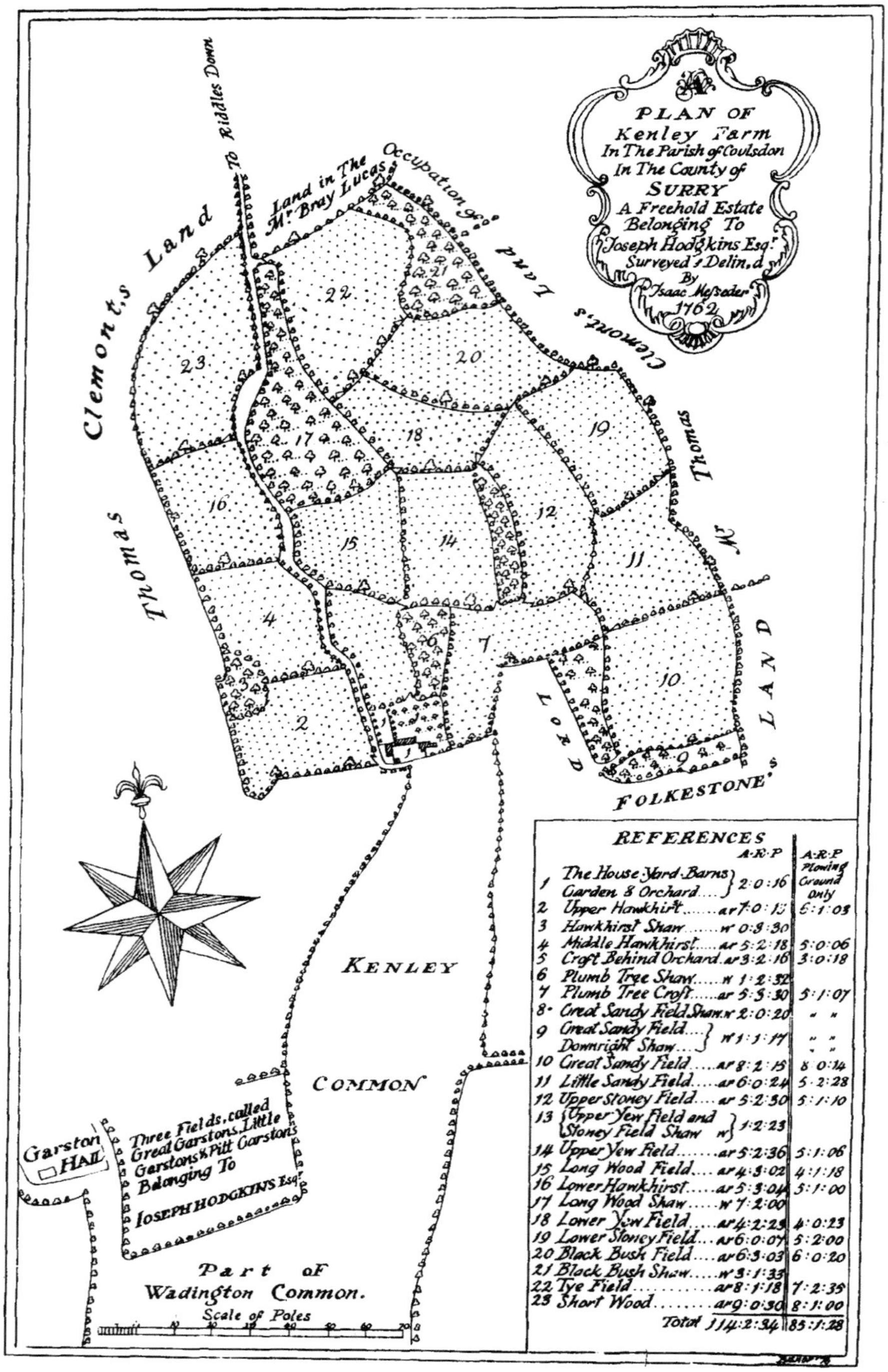

Isaac Messeder's Plan of Kenley Farm 1762

(Now Kenley House)

By the time of the **1842 tithe map**, these outlying Garston fields had been transferred to John Keen of Welcomes Farm. Thomas Marson, who now owned Kenley Farm, had expanded his freehold to include—

Garston Down farmhouse on Godstone Road (where Bourne View now is),

former Welcomes Farm lands in the lower part of Welcomes Road valley,

Little Roke Farm, and

Hayes Farm.

All the land at Roke and Hayes, as well as Welcomes Road fields, was sub-let to Henry Rowland. Thomas Marson was himself renting land eastward in the Bourne valley from the lord of the manor and from a small landowner, Sarah Selmes, who owned *The Rose and Crown*.

All that was left of the manor of Watendone in 1842 were—

the Garston tenements, with Garston Hall on the hill and some of Garston Down's land in the valley,

a few cottages in Waddington village,

some strips in the old village field and

76 acres of 'waste' on Kenley and Waddington commons.

They were held with Coulsdon manor by Thomas Byron, who rented—

Garston Hall, kennels, meadow and orchard to Sir Edmund Antrobus,

the Garston fields around Waddington village (including much of the modern common and airfield) to John Walker of Waterhouse Farm,

some of the Garston Down lands in the valley (where Kenley Primary School now stands) to Thomas Marson,

the village alehouse (near the modern *Wattenden Arms*) and adjacent house and stables to Edward Percival,

the three strips in Pond Field to Thomas Marson, and

the commons to 'Marson and others'.

Henry Rowland, the former Wiltshire farmer, was tenant of 600 acres and by 1851 employed nine farm hands. As well as the Roke and Hayes farm lands, he rented the farmhouse and land at Great Roke from Dalton Wigsell Attwood of Sanderstead manor.

Welcomes Farm's 300 acres stretched from the Caterham and Warlingham parish boundaries to Wise Wood in the Welcomes Road valley (just above Zigzag Road).

Pasture, ploughland, ponds, pits and kilns

The spread of the sheep enclosures can be guessed from the patterns of the field names. In the 14th century a 'sheepcote' or shepherd's cottage, far down the hillside on what is now the Whyteleafe boundary, was unusual enough to constitute a landmark. At that time, few of the 'fields' along the hill-top and upper hillsides may have been enclosed: the Old English (Anglo-Saxon) word 'field' signifies simply an open piece of land. 'Croft', on the other hand, indicates enclosure and 'hayes' or 'hawe', both from the same root, suggest hedges (as in 'hawthorn'). The old names along the hill-top were recorded on a succession of maps from 1762 onwards, but some were mentioned in 1496 and most probably date from much earlier. Some are descriptive but others are of forgotten origin and do not even mention the word 'field'. Starting from the aerodrome they include—

FIELD NAMES 1842

Some 1762/1785 names in brackets

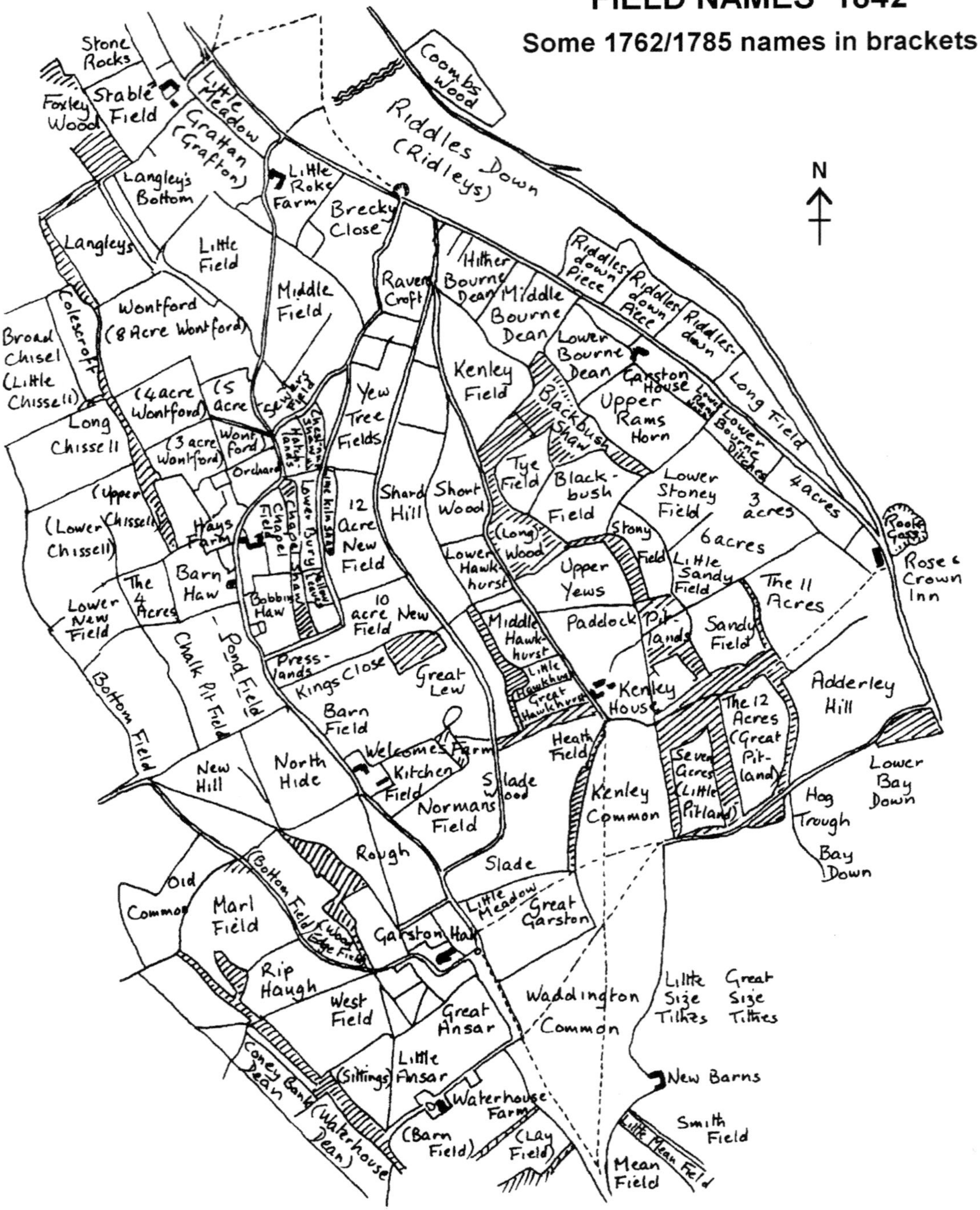

> Mean Field, Lay (or Ley) Field, Barn Field, Settings (or Sittings), Lower and Upper Amwers (or Little and Great Ansar), Long Haugh, West Field, Rabets, Rip Haugh, Greenaways (or Gunaway, Grinaway), Scogging (or Scaggin) Acres, The Pond Field, King's Close, Press Lands, Yellow Leaves, Hatchlands, Barn Haw, Bobbins Haw, Wontford (or Watford), Little Foxley Hill, Great Foxley Wood Shaw and Upper Langley Bank (now Higher Drive recreation ground).

The early hedging of some of these is indicated by the word 'hawe': Long Haugh and Rip Haugh on the Old Lodge Lane side, Barn Haw and Bobbins Haw close to the village in the midst of the open fields, and perhaps the Hawkhurst fields along the top of Kenley Lane.

The mediaeval 'crofts' or enclosures were scattered over the hillsides, some along the lower edges of the open fields - Colescroft and Peasecroft on Wontford, Scogging Acres on Pondfield, Lower Bury and a possible former Yongescroft (Yellowleaves) on Churchdene - but others, such as Lewellcroft (Lew) and Ravens Croft, further away from the old village. Many of the hillside field and wood names, however, included elements such as 'Upper', 'Middle', 'Lower', 'Long', 'Great' and 'Little', which suggest the dividing of a slope into a number of smaller pastures, or recognisable descriptions such as 'Yews', 'Bay', 'Chestnut', 'Black Bush', 'Sandy', 'Stoney' and 'Marl'. Above the Bourne valley there were also New Purchase, Sewers Field, Bone (Bourne) Dean Bottom, Tye Acre, Shard Hill, Rams Horn, Little and Great Pittland, Adderley Hill, Hog Trough (the gulley on the Whyteleafe side of the modern common) and Bay Down. In the upper Welcomes Road valley were Slade, Norman's Field, Great Lew, Little Lew and Wise Wood, while on the slopes of the Old Lodge Lane valley were Upper New Field, Chissel, Great Woodage (Wood Edge) Field, Water-House Dean and Coney-Bank Dean.

Especially in the valley bottoms, many names had an even more recent sound: some were called 'Close' (enclosure) and some were 'New' or even nameless, just numbered with their acreage. They included Grafton (Grattan), Rook-Roffet Close, Brake (Brecky) Close, House Close, Little Bone Dean Bottom (Hither Bourne Dean), Garston Dean, Rook Goss (gorse, at *The Rose and Crown* quarry), Meadow, Lower Bourne Ditches and Long Field. The lower part of the Welcomes Road valley had 10 Acre New Field, 12 Acre New Field and Yew Tree Fields, while there were two Bottom Fields on Old Lodge Lane.

At some stage, new enclosures had ceased to be for sheep: perhaps it was as late as the Napoleonic wars, when grain prices soared, that the land under plough had begun to spread again. In 1842 almost the whole of the Kenley area was arable: the only recorded pastures left were valley bottoms or paddocks adjacent to dwellings and the only unenclosed land was on Riddlesdown, Kenley and Waddington commons.

The transition of the boggy valley bottoms to ploughland was certainly late. The field where Roke School now stands, at the foot of Hayes Lane in what must for a long time have been a summer pasture and winter quagmire, was by 1762 called 'Brake Close' and by 1842 'Brecky Close'. *The Oxford English Dictionary* defines a *brecky* as a piece of ground newly converted to arable and dates the word to the 18th century. Farming economics fluctuated as wildly in earlier centuries as they do now, so the transition from pasture to arable is unlikely to have been a steady one-way process.

As well as fields, the tithe maps meticulously recorded every scrap of wood, hedgerow or 'rough' ground, valuable as sources of game and of small wood or timber. The grazing of stock also required supplies of water additional to the farmhouse wells, traditionally in hilltop ponds made of puddled clay. The 'Pond Field' pond was shown in 1842 as at the entrance to the modern Hayes School, but in 1785 had apparently been on the opposite side of Hayes Lane. The 1842 maps record a 'New pond' opposite Welcomes Farm, while on the corner of Old Lodge Lane was a pond for the Waddington villagers and the stock from the commons. Along the top of Riddlesdown and in Coombes Wood are a whole series of smaller hollows, some surely ponds to water drovers' stock after the long pull up the hill.

Not all hollows were ponds, however. Many of the pits on Riddlesdown are thought to have been the source of flints for resurfacing the rutted roadways across the top of the common. The series of 'Pittlands' field names may refer to pits on Hawkhurst Road or a large one down Stumps Lane, while the slope beyond Old Lodge Lane below Waddington village bore the names 'Marl Hill, Marl Wood, Marl Field'. The chalk pits along the foot of Riddlesdown are familiar to this day: the huge modern pit opposite *The Rose and Crown*, the smaller one opposite *The Kenley Hotel* and a tiny, overgrown one opposite Little Roke Road evidently originated on sites convenient for transporting lime to marl the heavy clay soils of Roke, Hayes, Kenley and Garston. There were two lime kilns in *The Rose and Crown* quarry into the 20th century, but lime was certainly burnt in the vicinity of the old Watendone village at one time as, amongst other narrow stretches of woodland, a Lime Kiln Shaw near what is now Abbots Lane was labelled on the 1842 tithe map.

The forgotten people of Waddington

The Coulsdon parish registers seldom specified that people lived in the Waddington area, except to distinguish between those with the ubiquitous surname of 'Wood'. Thus in 1688 the clerk identified Thomas Wood buried on 28 June as the 'son of Thomas Wood *of Waddington*' and in 1735 it was again specified that it was 'Robert Wood *of Waddington*' who was buried on 13 March. John Brown *of Waddington* was buried in 1759 and William Barllet *of Kenley* in 1719, while Richard and Martha Chandler *of Kenley* had a son Thomas baptised in 1761. In 1782 it was mentioned that the baptism of James and Sarah Lord's infant son took place not at the parish church but at *The Rose and Crown*.

Except to confirm that Waddington was still used as a place-name in 1688, 1735 and 1759, these references tell us nothing of the community of the time. The occasional scandals or violent tragedies of the 18th century cannot always be identified with a particular part of the parish: in 1765 it was noted that a woman who 'forbade her own banns at the third time of asking' was a servant from Garston Hall, but 30 years earlier there is no indication where Dame Kerrill lived when on 14 February 1734, 'in a fit of insanity', she took a razor and cut little George Cooper's throat. We know from a Bishop of Winchester's survey that in 1781 there were no Papists among the farm households and cottagers of the Waddington area and that no meetings of Protestant dissenters were held, but the formal response gives us no indication of whether family prayers or Bible reading had survived in any of the farmhouses in the 130 years since Puritan rector Anthony Hoare.

Only in the 1820s and 1830s do the registers begin to show who lived on Godstone Road, on Hayes Lane, at the New Barns on 'Kenly Common' or in Waddington village.

SOURCES

BAINBRIDGE, T (1785) *A Plan of an Estate within the Manor and Parish of Coulsdon in the County of Surrey together with the Boundary of the said Manor belonging to Thomas Byron Esq*

Census for Coulsdon (1851)

Coulsdon Parish Registers

Inscriptions in St John's Church, Coulsdon

MALDEN, H E (Ed) (1902-12) *Victoria County History of the County of Surrey*

MESSEDER, I (1762) *Plan of Kenley Farm in the Parish of Coulsdon in the County of Surrey, a Freehold Estate belonging to Joseph Hodgkins Esqr*

ORDNANCE SURVEY Maps (1870, 1914)

RESKER, R R (1916) *History and Development of Purley* Cassell

ROCQUE Map (1764)

SAALER, M *(oral communication)*

Tithe Apportionment for Coulsdon (1842)

The Oxford English Dictionary

Chapter 5

The Victorians

by Roger Packham

At the beginning of the Victorian age, Kenley was still a remote part of Coulsdon parish but by the end of that era it had assumed its own identity. Despite some later development and demolition, it became the Kenley which we would easily recognise today.

Kenley 1837-51

Kenley in 1837 consisted of a collection of hilltop farms (Waterhouse, Kenley, Welcomes and Hayes); the splendid Garston Hall with some neighbouring cottages in Old Lodge Lane including the delightful thatched house; Old Forge Cottage; the isolated buildings along Godstone Road; *The Rose & Crown;* Garston Farm and Little and Great Roke. By the time of the 1851 census there are also seven dwellings recorded along the foot of Riddlesdown and farm cottages at New Barn and Garston Down.

The Forge, Hayes Lane, 1905

From a postcard ***Courtesy of Roger Packham***

The Coulsdon parish registers provide a glimpse of people's lives at this time. In 1837, Gabriel Lovelock was the bailiff at Welcomes Farm; James Freeman was feeder of hounds at Garston Hall; William Bentley was a groom there; Thomas Mead was an ostler at *The Rose & Crown* and his brother John was a farm labourer who lived at Hayes Lane.

The registers also record that the huntsman at Garston Hall in 1839 was the celebrated Thomas Hills, whose wife Caroline had a daughter in July of that year and twins the following June. Elizabeth Payne of Hayes Lane and

No.1 Welcomes Cottages, Hayes Lane

***c*.1900**

Photograph courtesy of Purley Library

Rebecca Standen of Godstone Road were apparently unmarried when they bore their daughters in 1834 and 1839. The spring of 1840 was a sad one for the Freemans of Waddington, the Lovelocks of Welcomes Farm and labourer John Allee and his wife Jane of Godstone Road because Rebecca Freeman (aged two), Susan Lovelock (aged 14) and John Allee (aged 18 months) were buried. In 1842 there was an unusual entry in the register for a Hayes resident: John Dalton's wife, Hannah, the daughter of John and Elizabeth Tugwell, was baptised aged 41.

The evidence from maps, such as the Coulsdon Tithe Apportionment (1842) and that of the Byron sale (1867), confirms the sparse habitation as well as ownership and land use but it is the 1851 Coulsdon census (total population 713) that conveys details of Kenley before its imminent suburbanisation. Frances Perry has calculated that this census includes 138 male and 111 female residents of the Waddington and Kenley area, including Old Lodge Farm, of whom 63 were agricultural labourers, five were shepherds and seven were farmers and bailiffs. Thomas Johnson was a 32 year old shepherd able to employ a nurse to look after his four small children and the agricultural labourers ranged from 13 year old Thomas Alchin of Waddington to 70 year old Richard Clark at Hayes. James Doulton, of Hayes, a former agricultural labourer, aged 84, was on parish relief as were two widows of agricultural labourers. The same census provides details of the farms' occupants – Edward Tidy at Garston Down, Godstone Road; William Hay at Old Lodge; Henry Rowland at Great Roke (including Hayes and Kenley); Gabriel Lovelock, the bailiff at Welcomes and John Walker at Waterhouse.

The publication of *The Post Office Directory* for 1855 identifies a few more important Kenley residents for in addition to Hay, Tidy, Rowland and Walker (above), the following also appear—

George Drew Esq	Kenley House
Robert Russell Esq	Hayes
Furness	*The Rose and Crown*

The name of George Drew is significant because he had undoubtedly acquired 'Kenley House' with a view to developing the area. He was a solicitor and a director of the Caterham Railway Company, having subscribed £3,000 towards the cost of the line's construction. He had succeeded Charles Burnett at 'Kenley House' who had lived there with his East Indian-born wife, Mariana, a young family and nurse, nurserymaid, footman, cook/housekeeper, housemaid and kitchen maid. Robert Russell was a Croydon-born attorney and solicitor who had moved to Hayes Farm from Croydon with his wife, a young family, an annuitant aunt, three domestic servants and a groom. Furness at *The Rose & Crown* may also have been involved with the railway's construction because the main contractor was Furness & Fernandez.

Descriptions of Kenley

Thomas Wright described the valley immediately prior to the appearance of the railway in 1856 and noted the fine sweep of Riddlesdown with its carpet of green sward speckled with innumerable little groups of dark shrubs. In the first few months of the railway's existence, an advertisement for *The Rose & Crown* claimed that it was in the centre of one of the most lovely valleys in England and that parties appreciating a rustic ramble would find every requisite for a happy and inexpensive day's enjoyment.

In 1867 T H Bentley was the new proprietor of *The Rose & Crown* and advertised the delights of the area – 'Riddlesdown is now in its splendour, most charming Walks, delightful Scenery, salubrious Atmosphere, pretty Gardens, superior Accommodation ...' Nearly 20 years after the opening of the railway, *The Post Office Directory* for 1874 was still able to describe a picturesque Kenley –

> 'It is delightfully situated on a part of the Surrey Downs. The several roads in which the residences are built wind up the hills, which are of considerable altitude and finely wooded: it contains some fine mansions, with extensive grounds attached, some of which are built on spots in the ascent of the hills, commanding very extensive views: there is a good supply of excellent water, also gas.'

Ernest Straker came to live in Kenley in 1877 and at that time he knew every field by searching them for wild flowers and later on took many of the photographs for a survey. He remembered Kenley as being almost entirely agricultural, there being, other than farmhouses and labourers' cottages, only a few houses of the villa type—

> 'It was a curious survival of a less sophisticated era, kept intact by the power of the Lord of the Manor, Mr Edmund Byron, a typical country squire...He was seen in his glory as Master of the Old Surrey Fox Hounds at that great annual event, the Boxing Day meet at the Kennels, Garston Hall ... At the General Election of 1885 he sent down the newly enfranchised farm labourers to vote for the Conservative candidate for East Surrey, at the Junction, in a great farm waggon... I was told by a man of middle age that an old lady of Kenley had informed him that she could remember the coaches going along the top of Riddlesdown.'

There is another description of Kenley in 1883 when about 10 members of the City of London, including the Lord Mayor, visited Kenley following the purchase of the local commons after William Hall, the owner of Roke Farm, had defeated Edmund Byron in a famous legal case. The procession, headed by the Surrey Volunteers' band, passed over the Hayes Lane railway bridge and the report states—

> The way from the bridge to the Common of Kenley is up a steep hill lined on either side with thick fir trees, the ground being coloured by a profusion of primroses and wild hyacinths. This is certainly one of the prettiest glades in the neighbourhood of Coulsdon. At the top of the hill is Mr Young's mansion and beside the house are a number of iron fences which had been used for enclosing a part of the common and which had evidently been only recently removed.

F T Hainge, who was born in 1892, recalled blackberrying along a footpath that became Valley Road and bird-nesting on the Kenley House Estate.

Housing Development

The development of Kenley for residential housing can be summarised into three main phases. Firstly, there was the gradual construction of superior gentlemen's houses in the 1860s; secondly there was the more modest housing and shops along the line of Godstone Road in the 1880s and, finally, the compact housing of the Roke area at the end of the century.

The gentlemen's houses that began to appear shortly after the arrival of the railway were, without exception, magnificent houses in substantial grounds and they have given Kenley a distinctive appearance on its western hillside. The Ordnance Survey map of 1868 shows few new houses apart from 'Oaklands', 'Little Roke House' and 'Elmwood', all in Hayes Lane. There is, however, evidence that several other large houses had arrived by this date, including 'Cumberlands', 'Hillside', 'Copenhagen House' (later 'The White House') and 'The Towers'. The Coulsdon Estate sale of 1867 also notes a capital newly erected farm residence at Waterhouse Farm with 'The Old Farm House, now converted into tenements and outbuildings'.

An advertisement in *The Builder* for 6 May 1865 for an auction for the second portion of the Kenley Park Estate, adjoining Kenley Station, offered about 100 acres for building—

> 'the situation being one of the most healthy on the range of the Surrey Hills, the soil and climate remarkably dry, the air pure and bracing and the surrounding scenery exceedingly picturesque'

In 1876, *Ward's Directory* recorded that many additional large houses had arrived. In Hayes Lane there were 'Edlington House', 'Willesborough', 'Sunnyside', 'Hazelshaw' and 'Yateley House'; in Kenley Lane 'The Mount' had appeared with 'The Yews', 'Riddlesdown House' and 'Chinaurah Lodge'; and in Park Road there was 'Oak Villa' and 'Woodlands'. Other houses had arrived in Valley Road and Godstone Road.

Yateley House (lower centre) at the junction of Godstone Road and Hayes Lane. *c.*1890

Photograph by E Straker, courtesy of Purley Library

There were some later large houses, including 'Shord Hill', 'Sherwood Oaks', 'Viewfield' and 'Watendone Manor', but the next phase of intensive building activity appears to have been the ribbon development along Godstone Road at the foot of Riddlesdown. There are several neat cottages towards *The Rose & Crown* that still bear the date of 1883: 'Laurel Cottages', 'Hillside Cottages', 'Sunnyside Cottages', 'Shelley Cottages' and 'Elm Cottages'. A Victorian letter box, by 'Fair View' (Nos.77-79 Godstone Road), is still in use.

James Monger appears to have been active in the building of local houses. He is first noticed in 1882 as a bricklayer from Little Roke and is later shown as a builder from 1887 until the end of the century. The compact area of Little Roke Road, Little Roke Avenue and Lower Road no doubt owes much to the industrious Monger and provides a complete contrast to the opulence on the other side of the railway.

The population of Kenley in 1901 was only 1299 but it was now a prosperous, industrious village, undoubtedly socially divided but possessing its own parish church, railway station, waterworks, gasworks, police station, library, post office, fire brigade, schools, cricket club and golf club. Dr Diver had even run a cottage hospital on Godstone Road, Riddlesdown from 1872-75 before it moved to Caterham. In 1897, Sir Joseph Lawrence provided the community with a handsome hall, The Commemoration Hall, at the foot of St James' Road, now embraced by the school buildings, and by the end of the century Kenley's great popular attraction, Gardner's Pleasure Grounds, had brought countless children to the area and afforded considerable local employment.

This Victorian postbox, standing nearly opposite the milestone in Godstone Road, is still in use.

Photograph: Grahame Brooks

Some Memorable Events

Kenley was a quiet, remote area for much of the Victorian period but it experienced certain events likely to have been remembered for a generation. In 1854, the neighbourhood was scandalised by the deaths of William and Harriett Attlee and their three children from Waddington. Following some lively inquests, accusations and exhumations, it was found that the family had contracted typhoid from using impure water. The death of Harold Frederic, of 'Homefield', Valley Road, in 1898 aged 42, also caused a stir. Mr Frederic was a prolific American novelist and the dramatic inquest at *The Kenley Hotel* revealed stories of Frederic's mistress and the part played in his death by 'an exponent of an alien and fraudulent creed' (a Christian Science practitioner).

The official opening of the single track railway on 4 August, 1856 was celebrated by a special train with directors and friends and there were other important visitors in 1871 when All Saints' Church was opened by the Bishop of Winchester. When ecclesiastical parish status was granted in 1888, Kenley's independence from Coulsdon was confirmed.

Kenley from Riddlesdown.

Above—

Kenley from Riddlesdown in the early 1900s, showing the Kenley Hotel and the two shops that had been built at that date, and Kenley Police Station to the left of the picture

From a postcard, courtesy of Roger Packham

Right—

Roke level crossing, looking towards Roke Road. *c.*1890

Photograph by E Straker, courtesy of Purley Library

The dedication of Riddlesdown and Kenley Common to the public took place with much civic ceremony on Saturday, 19 May 1883. It has already been referred to and the occasion is of the greatest significance in the history of Kenley and the fight against the urban sprawl.

A Memorable Year – 1871

In the same year that All Saints' Church was opened, Kenley's progress was further marked with the opening of the Riddlesdown National School, at the foot of Downs Court Road for the children of Purley and Kenley. The present Riddlesdown School has a sampler by Lillie Markham, inscribed 'Riddlesdown School, Kenley, 1883'

Kenley's agricultural past was acknowledged when Roke Farm was chosen as the 1871 venue for the Annual Ploughing Match of the East Surrey Agricultural Association. The event was a prestigious one and Albert J Brown of Roke was doubtless kept busy by the many competitors and visitors. The Association later had the benefit of the judging skills of William Cutt (Welcomes Farm) at its Annual Stock Show at Croydon Cattle Market in 1874 and of Thomas King (Waterhouse Farm) at its event at New Barn Farm, Beddington, in 1875.

The Saxon graves on Farthing Down, Coulsdon, were excavated in 1871 by J Wickham Flower and a skeleton was also found at Kenley that year. It was discovered by a workman on the estate of William Hall whilst levelling the ground in front of a new building and was examined next day by Dr Hooper, surgeon of Caterham, who identified it as a female, probably killed by a sword hundreds of years previously and buried close to the old road from Kenley Station to the little hamlet of Waddington.

Other Kenley residents would have remembered the Shepherds' Feast that year which took place at the Old Surrey Kennels, Kenley Common, in a large room set apart for the purpose. About 160 men and boys sat down to a substantial repast provided by Samuel Hills. Alfred 'Tupwood' Smith officiated with the carving knife, congratulated all present including Mr Hills and his father and then sang some of his good old songs in his usual style. The proceedings were marked with the greatest good feeling and conviviality.

Disasters

In 1869 Hayes Farm was destroyed by fire. The alarm had been given from Kenley Station, the only place with telegraphic facilities, to the Purley and Caterham fire brigades but neither would turn out as Kenley was outside their jurisdiction!

In October 1878, *The Croydon Advertiser* reported a fire at Mr Stubbington's Great Roke Farm and the same gentleman was burgled the following month. In 1883, in a strange example of history repeating itself, there was another serious fire at the farm and, whilst it was blazing, seven young live ducks were stolen! The report of the latter fire includes the following—

> The farm lies in a deep hollow to the right of the road leading to Caterham Valley, but happily a hydrant of the Kenley Water Company is in the main road near the farm and an abundant supply of water was obtained. News of the outbreak was sent to Croydon by telegraph and mounted messenger and in 20 minutes the Croydon retained steamer reached the spot. At that time there was a terrific blaze: one of the straw stacks had already burnt to the ground and there seemed little probability of saving any of the others or the farm buildings, one of which – a cart and store shed – was also on fire.

Fortunately by carrying the necessary lengths of hose across the fields from the hydrant and with a good supply of water, the efforts of the firemen were rewarded. Other fire brigades helped and Mr Stubbington's lovely old farmhouse was saved. The engineer from the Kenley Water Works advised that nearly the whole of the water in the company's reservoir had been consumed.

A far more serious disaster had occurred in the previous year, 1882, in a tunnel on the new line of railway being constructed under Riddlesdown. Two engines collided and were completely smashed, injuring 10 men who were attended to by Dr Diver of Kenley before being sent to Caterham Cottage Hospital and Croydon Hospital.

Early 20th Century

Kenley entered the 1900s as a distinctive parish, having largely forsaken its agricultural heritage but aware of the need to preserve its admired open spaces. Some of the benevolent gentlemen in the large houses made contributions to public life, notably Sir Joseph Lawrence, Carleton Tufnell, Revd Squire and Revd Dickson. It was Sir Joseph who built the Commemoration Hall in 1897 and this became a focal point for entertainment, lectures, a library and Coulsdon Parish Council meetings until it was re-built in 1914 as a secondary school.

Other public buildings to appear were the Methodist Church (1906), Roke School in Purley Vale (1908) and the first sod for the building of St James's Church was cut in 1914. The years leading up to the Great War were perhaps a golden age despite obvious social divisions: thousands of people came to know Kenley by holiday visits to Gardner's and by exploring the commons.

Sir Joseph Lawrence presided over much of the activity and he is recorded as attending a fête with the Ranee of Sarawak at Purley in July 1914 shortly before hosting his own garden party at 'Oaklands' when Henry Chaplin MP made a speech. All this was to change. In August, Sir Joseph, accompanied by Revd Squire and C L Morgan attended a Patriotic Fund meeting at Purley and Percy Woodland from Welcomes 'a household name in Coulsdon' had volunteered for the front. Tragedy awaited Kenley and Carleton Tufnell junior was killed in Belgium before the end of the year. Mr Morgan and Revd Shilcock (of St Winifred's School) also lost sons and the horrors of the Great War were apparent. There were many others and some of the older generation also passed away at this time: Walter Smith, headmaster of the National School in 1915, Thomas Stuchberry of Roke (a local councillor) died in 1917, Revd Squire in 1918 and, in October 1919, Sir Joseph Lawrence was seized with an illness on the train bringing him home to Kenley and he died. It was the end of an era.

SOURCES

BROADBENT, U & LATHAM, R(Eds) (1976) *Coulsdon Downland Village*, Bourne Society

Coulsdon Census 1851

Coulsdon Parish Registers

Coulsdon Estate Sale 1867

Coulsdon Tithe Apportionment 1837

Croydon Advertiser 1871, 1878, 1882

Croydon Chronicle 1867

Coulsdon & Purley Weekly Record 1914

DAWE, Donovan (1968) The Lord Mayor Opens Coulsdon Common Bourne Society *Local History Records* **VII**

HAINGE, F T (1962) 'Living Memory – Kenley' Bourne Society *Local History Records* **I**

Ordnance Survey Map 1867

PACKHAM, R (1981) 'The Prettiest Spot in Surrey' Bourne Society *Local History Records* **XX**

Post Office Directories 1855, 1874

Village Histories – Purley (Ed A Higham) Bourne Society 1996

STRAKER, E – Typescript in Purley Library

The Builder 6.5.1865

Ward's Croydon Directory

WRIGHT, Thomas (1856) *Guide to the Caterham Railway near Croydon in Surrey*

Garston Hall, Old Lodge Lane
3 May 1939

The brick pillar on the left is all that remains today

Garston Hall was the home of the Surrey Hounds in the 19th century

Photograph courtesy of Purley Library

KENLEY PARISH MAGAZINE.

JANUARY, 1918.

His Majesty the King has issued the following Proclamation with regard to the observance of the First Sunday in 1918 by all his people as a special day of prayer and thanksgiving in connection with the War.

" TO MY PEOPLE,

" The world-wide struggle for the triumph of right and liberty is entering upon its last and most difficult phase. The enemy is striving by desperate assault and subtle intrigue to perpetuate the wrongs already committed and stem the tide of a free civilisation. We have yet to complete the great task to which, more than three years ago, we dedicated ourselves.

" At such a time I would call upon you to devote a special day to prayer, that we may have the clear-sightedness and strength necessary to the victory of our cause.

" This victory will be gained only if we steadfastly remember the responsibility which rests upon us, and in a spirit of reverent obedience ask the blessing of Almighty God upon our endeavours.

" With hearts grateful for the Divine guidance which has led us so far towards our goal, let us seek to be enlightened in our understanding and fortified in our courage in facing the sacrifices we may yet have to make before our work is done.

" I therefore appoint January 6 the first Sunday of the year—to be set aside as a special day of prayer and thanksgiving in all the Churches throughout my Dominions, and require that this Proclamation be read at the services held on that day.

" GEORGE R.I."

" November 7, 1917."

The above date, being also the Feast of the Epiphany, will render it still more appropriate for the sacred object to which our King is thus dedicating it.

Monday, the 31st December, being the last night of the year, will be used for a Special Service at 8.0 p.m., which it is hoped will be attended by all those who are able to be present.

And on the following morning—New Year's Day—there will also be a Special Service with address and Holy Communion at 11.0 o'clock.

Chapter 6

The Great War 1914 – 1918

by Gordon Newall

War and Peace

Grand Admiral von Tirpitz, father of the pre-war German Navy and a powerful political voice in the Fatherland, attributed his rapid promotion to personal involvement in the development of the torpedo. This activity reached its peak in 1878.

That same year the Corporation of the City of London was authorised by Act of Parliament 'to acquire lands within 25 miles of the City as open spaces for the recreation and enjoyment of the public and to preserve the natural features'. Kenley Common was one of the four Coulsdon Commons acquired by the Coal and Corn and Finance Committee (CCFC) of the Corporation in 1883 – the very same year that von Tirpitz purchased torpedo boats..... from Britain.

Count Ferdinand von Zeppelin headed the newly formed Joint Stock Company for the promotion of Airship Flight from May 1894. His rigid airships became world leaders in air transport.

Just 20 years later Tirpitz, Zeppelin and Kenley – amongst others! – were to be locked into a world war. On 4 August 1914 Great Britain declared war on Germany. The same day German troops invaded Belgium and within a month most of that country had been overrun. Belgian forces retreated along with the French Army and British Expeditionary Force (BEF).

Belgian Refugees

By contrast, Belgian civilians put up considerable resistance and many were severely wounded. Evacuation to hospitals in Britain was organised. Other Belgians joined in an exodus from their homeland. These refugees began to arrive at English ports as early as August and were sent, temporarily, to Alexandra Palace for accommodation, medical examination and classification under one of three categories – those having the means to support themselves financially; the well educated and students; or tradesmen, agricultural workers and labourers.

First priorities were dispersal, accommodation and food. Care and subsistence were provided by The War Refugees Committee, The Catholic Women's League and The Belgium Committee. Initially some 37 local committees were set up including Croydon and each town or borough had a number of sub-committees.

Under Surrey of local interest were—

Croydon:
1. Central Committee – Miss Scarf, 3 Park Street, Croydon
2. Croydon Belgium Relief Comm.– D Scanlan, 10 Station Road, West Croydon

Purley:
1. Miss A E Richardson, Eversleigh, Brighton Rd
2. C J Barker, Men's Club, Purley

Caterham: Miss Burgess, Bethany Home, Whyteleafe

Kenley: No entries, but early in October 1914 *The Coulsdon & Purley Weekly Record* had reported 'a home has been opened at Kenley, and another at Purley. Edgar H Tomlin offered his former residence, then vacant, named 'Leenane', Brighton Road, (subsequently renamed 'Newlands', now No 155). This house opened to receive refugees during the first week of January 1915.

The refugees were at first treated as guests, not being permitted to take employment in case jobs were taken away from local people. Due in part to the heavy losses on the western front, the Government changed its views, and many Belgians were thus able to support their families. However, this did have repercussions. Questions were asked as to why our men were in Europe fighting for the liberation of Belgium whilst Belgians were living and working here in comparative safety.

The resulting enlistment of men into the Belgian Army, in fact, caused the alternative problem of their families then having no financial support – which had to be found by the committees. Fund-raising events such as concerts were arranged. Mayors donated part of their annual Fund to this cause. In 1915 and 1916 miniature Belgian flags were sold on the streets following the already established Alexandra Rose Day collections. Today's 'flag days' take their name from these flags irrespective of what cause is being represented: Poppies, Lifeboat lapel stickers or Wings. Mrs Grieve of All Saints', Kenley collected nearly £10 for the Belgian Soldiers' Fund at the end of 1915.

The Home Front

Within 10 days of the outbreak of war Special Constabularies had been formed based largely at local police stations. Volunteers included former police officers and constables who came out of retirement to serve their country and local community. One such was Constable Sidney Wheeler who served 25 years in the Metropolitan Police from 1883 to 1908 and enlisted in August 1914 as Z 200. PC Wheeler lived at 188 Hayes Lane, having been steward of the Golf Club before Kenley Common was taken over by the Army.

The East Surrey Water Company was responsible for guarding various pumping stations and for keeping the railway open. In February and March there was an appeal for further volunteers to serve in the Company and lessen the strain on those already serving. It appears that, since East Surrey Water was a private business, there was some public criticism that the Company was only protecting its own financial interests.

Women's patrols were formed, which were wholly voluntary. Women were also urged to form brigades to render first aid and fight fires in churches, schools, hospitals and other public buildings. Training was offered by Merryweather, the fire appliance manufacturers of Greenwich.

Croydon along with other towns had introduced a strict blackout which included the dimming of street lighting. Under the Defence of the Realm Act, All Saints' Church lit only the eastern half of the nave, raising a problem when pews were rented, or habitually used, by certain families. This was overcome by releasing all empty pews five minutes before the commencement of the service to those from across the aisle. The duties of the Specials were to enforce the blackout regulations, arrest aliens, guard vulnerable locations and facilities, perform air-raid duties and control food queues in the winter of 1917/18 when food and fuel were in short supply.

The authors of *Croydon and the Great War* claimed that the effectiveness of Croydon's blackout on the occasion when 'bombs fell on Kenley and Streatham' (p.158) had been proven, their town having been 'passed over..... sheltered in its darkness.'

Rural to Urban

When Kenley entered the war in 1914 it was one of the villages in Croydon Rural District. A local election was held on 15 March 1915 preparatory to the formation of Coulsdon & Purley Urban District Council, having a total of 25 councillors. Of these three were to represent Kenley. There were four candidates and the result was:

Powell, E H	157 votes
Shilcock, Revd S I	153
Harper, A C	131
Skeats, Mrs G E	92

A Kenley parishioner, Mrs Arkwright, stood in Woodcote Ward and was duly elected.

The subjects on the Council's early agendas make interesting reading and, not surprisingly, reflect the progress of the war as it affected the Home Front, running through from air raid precautions and updating the Fire Brigade's communications to food rationing and control by early 1918.

At the second UDC meeting on 22 April 1915 the Clerk reported on the Recreation Grounds, Fire Brigade and Public Lighting Committee:

The Fire Brigade comprised—

3 Chief Officers Retaining fee £3.0s.0d p.a. each

13 Ordinary Firemen, 1 Supernumerary £2.10s.0d p.a. each plus for first hour 2s.6d , and Firemen 1s. 0d per hour subsequently.

Horsing Brigade

Skeel, W – Kenley Hose Cart Retaining fee £3.0s. 0d p.a.

2s. 6d per hour, minimum 10s. 0d, for all calls attended.

To City Corporation Rent of land for Kenley Hose Cart 1s.0d p.a.

The horse, as confirmed by Ron Monger, grazed on the Cricket Club's field whilst the cart was kept between Godstone Road and the former chalk quarry, by that time within the curtilage of Riddlesdown Common owned by the City of London, and now occupied by Optical Surfaces Ltd under licence.

The Recreation Grounds, Fire Brigade and Public Lighting Committee, held on 7 June 1915 reported on the following—

Fire Alarms – Recommended alarms be 'fixed in each house of members of the Coulsdon, Kenley and Purley sections of the Coulsdon Brigade'; such alarms 'to be connected with the residences of the three Chief Officers.'

T G Dyson stated that the Fire Escape of the Sanderstead Brigade required painting.

Chairman's and Surveyor's interview with the Chief Commissioner of Police regarding 'protection .... against fire caused by the dropping of bombs .... Advised that all householders should be informed that sand and earth were the principal factors for the extinction of flames caused by bombs.' Clerk to prepare and arrange distribution of a suitable circular, approved.

A public meeting had been held at the Kenley Institute on 26 April 1915, organised by the Kenley Platoon of the Croydon, Surrey, Volunteer Training Corps accompanied by the Band of the Black Watch which marched from Upper Warlingham via Roke to Purley. A small number of men was recruited.

Zeppelin Raiders

Although the Grand Admiral on 18 November 1914 (Charville) advocated the 'setting fire to London in 30 places (simultaneously) in order to swamp the emergency services and destroy morale'; and from Bruges 22 January 1915 'All that flies or creeps should be concentrated against that City', London did not receive its first raid until 31 May 1915 when a military Zeppelin made a night sortie.

The second raid on 17/18 August was by a naval Zeppelin. Tirpitz, Danzig 18: 'Today news came of an air raid on London.' It was not until 13 months later that Kenley felt the blast of four 128 lb bombs.

On the night of 23/24 September 1916 naval Zeppelin L31 captained by Kapt-lt Heinrich Mathy set out with L32 and L33. Mathy headed for the Straits of Dover and crossed the coast near Rye at 11.00 pm proceeding towards London. His route took him over Hawkhurst, Horsmonden, Tunbridge Wells, Brasted, Oxted and Caterham. 'At Kenley he dropped four high explosive (bombs) at twenty-five past twelve, which wrecked two houses and injured two people.' (*Zeppelins over England* Poolman).

On duty that night was Constable Sidney Wheeler who was patrolling near Hall Way during the raid. PC Wheeler was blown off his feet by the blast. Purley's searchlight had a defective mirror but in any case Mathy had his own method of negating the usefulness of probing searchlights, namely, the dropping of flares.

On 28 November aeroplanes replaced airships at first in daylight but soon reverting to night raids. Raids continued until May 1918 and incited the populace to complain that enemy aircraft roved the skies virtually unchallenged.

War Work and Casualties

As the war wore on a number of new routines had been established interspersed with the old. Kenley Workmen's Benefit Society, otherwise known as 'The Slate Club', continued to hold its annual meeting just prior to Christmas. King George V had called for a Day of National Intercession on 3 January 1915, and the first Sunday in successive New Years. All denominations in Britain, the Empire, the United States of America and in Russia, the Orthodox Church, agreed to participate. Kenley's turnout was reported 'not as it should have been' (*Parish Magazine*, February 1915).

In June 1915 a list of those serving in the Armed Services was published: 'Land Forces 22; in the Fleet – 12; injured 2.' Updates were published in July and from time to time in subsequent months. Eventually well over 100 men joined either the Army or Navy from Kenley out of a population of 1,317 (19/4/1915).

An innovation in October 1915 was *Sandbags for the Front* alias the Sandbag Guild. Mrs Wildy of 'Shord Hill' purchased the prepared materials from Mrs Scrace of Purley. Production soon reached 50 per week and by the end of four months in excess of 1,000 had been made at a cost of £27. These along with a similar quantity from Purley had been sent to 'the front'. Feedback from a member of the Mediterranean Expeditionary Force complimented the design with its drawstring for retaining the contents during stacking, stating also that the bags had been used as additional clothing and for keeping feet warm.

At home, the death of Walter Smith, headmaster of the National School occurred on 6 December 1915. Local residents contributed to the cost of a memorial in the Parish Church. Mr Smith had been Head of the School for 30 years; and honorary secretary of the Kenley and Coulsdon Horticultural and Cottage Gardeners' Society for only one year less.

Under a daylight saving scheme designed to conserve coal, clocks were advanced one hour on 21 May 1916, reverting to GMT in October.

Compulsory service was voted in on 6 June, which led to the well known poster, Kitchener's pointing finger and the slogan: 'Your King and Country Need You!'

Towards year end the All Saints' congregation annually contributed to the cost of sending a Christmas card and small gift to all NCOs and privates serving abroad and in training in the United Kingdom.

In 1915 £5.10s. 0d	to 42 men overseas; 22 in UK
1916 £6.10s. 0d	to 53 men overseas; 26 in UK
1917 £29.7s. 6d	a total of 114

In that July Platoon Sgt Victor Hugh Knight was reported 'killed in action on 30 April'. Not yet 19 years old he died as a result of a gas attack whilst in the trenches on the Western Front. His mother received not only letters from the Major of his regiment, the 8th Queen's (Royal West Surrey), and his Second Lieutenant, but also from the Assistant Military Secretary.

Frederick Sell went down aboard the *Queen Mary* in the Battle of Jutland, 1 June 1916, the 'greatest sea battle in history'. The guns of HMS *Queen Mary* and *Invincible* were still firing with 'commendable accuracy' when the ships blew up. Poor design and lack of magazine protection were blamed for the British losses. Britain lost 6,907 men and seven warships; Germany far fewer men, and fewer ships.

Invasion

On 6 June 1917 under the headings 'Coulsdon Aerodrome' and 'Kenley Common Commandeered' *The Coulsdon & Purley Weekly Record* published two brief items of great significance to Kenley. These set out to give the 'reason why Kenley Common had been occupied', (not by the enemy but) by elements of our own Forces.

Perhaps to deflate the growing concern about enemy aircraft sorties, the newspaper reported that the Common 'is to be used as an aerodrome against hostile air raids, and as an Acceptance Park for the Royal Flying Corps' (RFC).

Motor Transport Section, Kenley Air Acceptance Park, October 1917
Postcard courtesy of Roger Packham

Both aspects were true but the Army would probably have reversed the order. Its priority was to cope with the greatly increased numbers of aeroplanes which the industry was producing at this stage of the war, along with machine-guns, compasses etc, all needing testing before being flown to France. In parallel with this it needed a flying field adjacent to aeroplane sheds where the parts supplied by a plethora of factories could be brought together in the construction of further aeroplanes. To this end, hangars were constructed west of Hayes Lane and occupied by Handley Page, a site chosen no doubt in order not to undermine the statement made by Mr Macpherson, Under Secretary for War, that: 'There is no intention of erecting any building on the common'.

Earlier in his reply to a question by Sir Frederick Banbury, Mr Macpherson had explained why Kenley Common had been chosen:

> 'The Common has been examined by many skilled pilots who all came to the conclusion that there was no place near at hand or near London so eminently fitted for their purposes. Farthing Down was also examined... but the conclusion was come to that it was entirely unsuitable...'.

The other report on the invasion of the Common describes the occupation by the Military and the felling of 'magnificent Beech trees and Fir Spinneys', bad enough in itself but made worse by there having been no prior notice given to the owners – the City Corporation. Nor had there been any consultation involving Coulsdon & Purley UDC.

Whether out of extreme patriotism or acting upon the adage: 'If you cannot beat them, join them', the minutes of the Coal & Corn & Finance Committee of the Corporation Vol. 85, p 109 (26 June 1917) record—

> 'Notice as to the taking over of Kenley Common, which was read. Resolved that the Town Clerk do communicate with the Military Authorities and suggest that the whole of Kenley Common should be taken over by them'.

CCFC minutes of 18 September, state—

> 'A letter, by Colonel Newenham giving notice that the competent Military Authority have now taken possession of the entire area of Kenley Common and have closed Stumps Lane and Golf Road leading thereto, was read.'

Year by year in July (see Vol 84 CCFC minutes) it was recorded that the Kenley Golf Club had made application 'for the usual permission to play golf on Kenley Common (page 33: 20 July 1915; page 176: 18 July 1916)'. The Resolution—

> 'that the application be complied with subject to the usual intimation sent by the Club Committee relieving the Corporation from all liability in respect of any accident that may occur to man or beast through operations of the Club; and no play taking place on Sundays. Ordered that Mr Solicitor do take the necessary steps accordingly'.

Each September Mr Solicitor duly reported back to the CCFC that this had been done. This annual ritual was brought to an abrupt end by the overrunning of the Golf Course. PC Wheeler lost the stewardship and was fortunate not to lose his accommodation as well. The Club House, 190 Hayes Lane adjoining, later reverted to residential use.

Volume 85 of the CCFC Minutes contains but two more entries in 1917 relating to Kenley at war. On 16 October under the heading 'Coulsdon Common: Chalk from pit', the chairman reported that he had granted permission to the War Office Authorities to take chalk from the pit in Hayes Lane by Kenley common. And on 11 December, 'the Town Clerk was heard as to Chalk taken by the War Department from said pit...',

The Royal Flying Corps wanted Hayes Lane closed since the aeroplanes built by Handley Page had to taxi across the road to reach the airfield for the purpose of flight testing. A compromise was reached, probably satisfying neither the military nor the general public. Persons whose work necessitated, or who for other approved reasons needed to use Hayes Lane, were issued with passes.

Kenley became No 7 Aircraft Acceptance Park. A set of by-laws was compiled under 'Military Lands Acts as amended by the Defence of the Realm Regulations made under the Defence of the Realm Consolidation Act, 1914.' These were placed on notice boards at all points where footpaths entered the defined area.

Mr Harding of Selsdon said that his father, who was in the police at Kenley, often spoke of the Canadian lumberjacks who worked at the airfield. They had officers directing them and his father told of the times they were called to disputes between the lumberjacks and officers. It was often difficult as the officers were from colleges and the lumberjacks were big and strong – and also there were more lumberjacks than officers.

By September there were 300 men stationed at the airfield and a meeting was called at 'Oaklands' by Sir Joseph and Lady Lawrence for the purpose of raising £800 for the provision of a YMCA recreational hut. At the meeting £200 was promised. Within a month this figure rose to £600, and by 21 November had reached £978.14s.0d, enough to erect and furnish a suitable hut in time for Christmas (1917).

After the Armistice Sir Hugh Trenchard caused the aerodrome to be established as a permanent Royal Air Force station. Its development between the world wars and its contribution to the Battle of Britain and beyond are dealt with in a separate chapter.

Food, Fuel and Clogs

Due to the heavy losses of merchant shipping, particularly in 1917, food rationing was introduced in London and the Home Counties during that autumn; and became compulsory throughout the country in the new year. The reverse side of ration cards was used for propaganda purposes.

Sugar was first to be rationed, at 8 ounces for each adult and child. Meat and fats followed. Cards were issued for these. Beef, lamb, pork, bacon – 15 ounces per week per person. Butter, margarine, lard – 5 ounces per week. The rationing of bread was somewhat sexist: Men on industrial or other manual work, 7 lbs weekly per head. Women on industrial work or domestic service, 4 lbs weekly per head.

Where there is a law there are always law-breakers. To cope with this additional dimension of public life the Urban District set up a Food Control Committee (FCC) and appointed an Inspector to report back to the periodic meetings of this Committee.

Minutes of the FCC Meeting held on 22 October 1918, include the following Inspector's reports—

> 'Kenley Aerodrome, Workmen's Canteen – Meat meals were being supplied without coupons .... Also other rationed articles of food .... were being obtained without the necessary permits. Proceedings to be taken against W H Geary.'
>
> Minuted on 26 November 1918, W H Geary had been fined £25.

Also on 22 October, in respect of the Apples and Perry Pears Order (1918), breaches of the law by the following traders—

> Mrs P of Coulsdon
>
> W Skeel and Mrs A K Clarke of Kenley, and
>
> Mrs G of Purley
>
> Minuted on 26 November, convictions with fines of 40 shillings each.

New Ration Books were issued during October 1918.

Fuel too was rationed before the end of the year as well as being the subject of price increases. To meet the demands of the miners the Government had raised the price bringing it to 2s.6d above the amount contracted by the Church's Provident Coal Fund with Hall & Co (Croydon) Ltd.

Actual amount to be paid:		Members price, reduced by Fund's bonus:
Best Derby Brights	38s.6d per ton	34s.8d per ton.

Best Kitchen	37s.6d per ton	33s. 9d per ton.
Kitchen-Nuts	36s.6d per ton	32s.10d per ton.

In addition the Government permitted only a limited supply to each householder:

Up to 4 rooms	2 cwt per week
Up to 6 rooms	3 cwt per week
Up to 7 rooms	1 ton per month.

Sculleries counted as a room only if containing a copper or fireplace. Excluded in the count were bathroom, cellar, pantry and outbuildings.

During 1917, apart from family losses which were bad all through the war, the situation at home worsened. Food and fuel were not only rationed but prices rose. By March the quality of boots and shoes had deteriorated due to excessive demands of not only our own armed forces but also those of some of our allies. It was suggested that southerners should follow the example of those in our northern cities and wear clogs. Samples were made available at All Saints' Vicarage for inspection. Due to shortage of leather women's boots were not to exceed sseven inches in height.

The Final Months

In the 1918 New Year's Honours List the Churchwarden, Lt Col Charles L Morgan RE was honoured with the award of CBE 'in recognition of his services to his country.'

The Vicar died on 11 February at the age of 64 years. Revd L Harding Squire had been appointed first vicar of Kenley parish after its separation from Coulsdon in 1889 and was succeeded by Revd Oliver Quick, recently returned from France where he had spent a year as chaplain to the British Forces. Almost incredibly, within about two months of his appointment, Revd Quick offered to return overseas. The churchwardens and sidesmen resolved to approach the bishop to ask for a postponement. Revd Quick was succeeded by Revd Francis Read in 1921.

On 8 April 1918 a meeting of the Recreation Ground Committee had minuted: 'Item 7 The use of Kenley Cricket Ground as a recreation ground for the children of Kenley was recommended. The Kenley Sports Company to be paid £10 per annum for out-of-pocket expenses.' Was this intended, at least in part, as being in compensation for the loss of Kenley Common? A Fire Brigade horse, and children playing there must have worked wonders on the pitch!

Amongst the prisoners of war who returned to the district following the end of hostilities were—

Pte A Riches and Pte C Riches both of 177 St James' Road.

Pte H Nevin of 159 St James' Road.

Pte J Anderton of 1 Waterworks Yard.

It is appropriate to conclude with a paragraph from the Vicar's Letter published in All Saints' Kenley Monthly Magazine for December 1918—

'My dear Parishioners,

> The end of the War has come; we hope and believe and pray that true peace is coming. That depends on ourselves, it depends on our willingness to bring the spirit of the Prince of Peace into a world tortured and distracted by the evil spirits of greed, envy, malice and mutual distrust, which, arming themselves in .... military power......... have so nearly wrought the ruin of us all.

In March 1919 a committee was formed to raise funds to erect a memorial hall (Chapter 12).

Above:

The memorial at St James' Church, Riddlesdown records local men who gave their lives during the 1914-1918 war.

This photograph, taken in the 1950s, shows parishioners repairing the paving.

Photograph courtesy of Purley Library

Right:

The memorial at All Saints' Church, Kenley lists all those Kenley men who responded to the call of King and Country, and those that sadly did not return.

At the foot of the plaque an inscription remembers all those who served in the Second World War.

Photograph: Grahame Brooks

In Memoriam

The memorial plaque in Kenley Memorial Hall contains the names of 21 young men who lost their lives in the service of their country. There are also war memorials at St James' Church, where of the 58 listed about half were Kenley boys; Kenley Methodist Church, and All Saints' Church has a memorial in the porch with a record of 24. Two young men associated with Kenley are also listed on the Whyteleafe War Memorial.

SOURCES

A Brief History of All Saints' Church, Kenley (1992)

All Saints' Kenley Parish Magazine 1914, 1918

BEAUBOIS, Henry. *Airships - an Illustrated History*

BISHOP, James. *Illustrated London News* Book of World War I

BROWN, Malcolm. *Book of 1918 - Year of Victory*, Imperial War Museum

FLINT, Peter (1985) *RAF Kenley* Terence Dalton

KELLY'S Surrey Directories

LUCAS, Sydney, grandson of PC Wheeler.

National Women's Suffrage Societies, Purley Br. Meeting Oct. 1914 (Report)

PEEL, C S *How we lived then*

VON TIRPITZ, Grand Admiral *My Memoirs* Vols 1 & 2

WARD'S Street Directories

Carleton Wyndham Tufnell (1892-1914), son of Carleton Fowell Tufnell of Watendone Manor, who was killed in action 6 November 1914. He was cricket captain at Eton in 1910, when he won the match at Lords against Harrow ***(see page 190)***

Chapter 7

Between the Wars Reminiscences

by Colin Burgess and John Bishop

An important aspect of local history is tapping into the memories of older residents. Their contribution gives colour to the black and white facts gathered from libraries and record offices.

Gladys Pygram recalls her memories of Kenley, assisted by her brother Ron Barnes, in conversation with John Bishop—

My parents Albert Barnes and Ethel Jewiss were married on 25 December 1912 in the small church of St James in Little Roke Avenue. The new St James' church in Commemoration Road, later St James' Road was still being built. My father came from the New Forest area and mum came from Gravesend. Dad served in the RASC in France during World War I. Dad came to Purley and worked for Raley & Co, a domestic & hardware shop selling a variety of goods ranging from paraffin, paint, pots and pans to raspberry jam. Raley's shop was on the site opposite to where Purley fountain stood and now where the old Sainsbury's stands. It was a shop typical of its time catering for a rural community. It was there that a colleague of dad's who knew he was intending to marry, told him of the empty house to rent in Little Roke Avenue, so dad promptly rented the house and moved in after getting married.

I was born in 1916 in 77 Little Roke Avenue. My brother Ron was born in 1921 and sister Joyce was born in 1923. We grew up in Little Roke and we all went to school at Roke School. The headmistress of the infants' was Miss Trafford and the headmaster of the seniors' was Mr Farr and later Mr Holland.

Gladys Barnes (later Pygram) (front left) at Roke School *c.*1926

In the 1920s and 1930s we had plenty of small shops in the neighbourhood and could buy everything we wanted. Mr Grimes ran the baker's shop with his bakehouse at the corner of Little Roke Avenue. On the opposite corner was a greengrocer's run by Mr Skeel. He used to break his horses in by running them down our road. He kept them in stables at the side of his house and you can still see the stables today from the road. On the opposite side of the road in Little Roke Road near the pillar-box was a boot and shoe mender and the other shop was a newsagent. Further down Little Roke Road towards Godstone Road was a shop that sold groceries and pots and pans run by Mrs Buckland. Later this shop became A J Pitman's. Further up on the right hand side was a fish and chip shop run by Mr King who also sold wet fish. I remember Harry Moss with his horse and cart. He was a tree feller and could always supply us with bean sticks. He kept his horse behind his house in Little Roke Road. A very important resident in our road was Mr Monger the builder, who built some of the houses on the estate. It was Mr Monger who donated the land for the first St James' church. We also had another general store in Lower Road and later an electrical store.

St James' Road (Commemoration Road) was only chalk surfaced in those early days and when it rained hard the water, all white with the chalk, gushed down the hill into Godstone Road.

A man with his horse and flat wagon stood outside Kenley railway station and took parcels, cases and trunks to various houses. I don't remember there being a carriage for people.

We were able to cross the Caterham railway by going through a gate and along a footpath across the lines to get to Roke Road but this was closed and a footbridge built when the line was electrified. The field just over the railway was used as a fairground once or twice a year.

When the weekend came we knew that there would be a lot of people coming down from London on the train to Purley. They would stream along the road going to visit Gardner's or take the road up to Riddlesdown and if we were walking into Purley we had to dodge the crowd by walking in the middle the road.

Mr Eden, a sergeant at Kenley police station ran a boys' club in St James' Hall in Little Roke Avenue.

On 11 May 1941 a bomb fell at the end of our road and demolished the houses there. Our house was damaged and every window was blown out. You could see daylight through the bedroom ceiling. Fortunately we were not injured and the lady of the house that was bombed was away when the bomb fell.

Barbara Cooper of John Kirk House, in conversation with Colin Burgess on 21 April 1994—

I was born in 1917 in Hayes Lane and lived in a house called 'Dawn House' opposite St Peter's Hall and lived there until just before World War II when the family moved to 48 Higher Drive.

There was no school in Hayes Lane before the present one was built. The posh children used to go to 'Colescroft' in Firs Road and used a room at the top of the house as a classroom. There were about six children in a class and we all sat around a large round table and worked at the basics, English, maths, reading and sums. I have no idea of the qualifications of the teacher but I had no problems with the entrance examination to Eothen School in Caterham, when I was 11 years old.

Whilst I was attending the classes in Firs Road, on one Saturday morning I was out shopping with my mother and we were walking along the narrow part of Hayes Lane on the way home. When we were near the top of Hayes Lane, we could hear an aeroplane that sounded low and the engines were making a funny sound, like coughing and racing. My mother said the pilot would not reach the top of the hill when suddenly there was a large bang and when we reached the top of Hayes Lane, the house where I went to classes was all aflame with very thick black smoke and very big high flames. The two airmen were killed and luckily no one else was hurt as the owners were visiting another house.

Barbara Cooper in the 1930s

They soon repaired the house and we were soon back to classes but the fire and smoke always terrified me.

I was very keen on the Girl Guides and we used to meet in the old St Peter's Hall. I was very interested in natural history and spent many hours in the woods studying plants. We used to go to Old Coulsdon to a large house by the church. Admiral Goodenough lived there; he was a lovely fellow and Lady Goodenough used to test us for our badges. The Admiral had a wonderful library and when he saw me looking at his books one day, he told me I could borrow one if I was interested, which I did. He had some wonderful books on plants, trees and bushes. His wife's interest was embroidery, which she tested us on.

A gimlet to some was a cocktail of gin and lime juice – it is also a small tool with a screwtip for boring holes. It was this tool that 'Gimlet Jim' used to break into people's houses. He worked on his own and the police had a very hard job catching him. He broke into houses in the Kenley area because they were big and were full of temptations for a thief. There was no doubt he had a way with dogs as they never bothered him or gave an alarm. The police, or should I say one policeman, studied the pattern of his break-ins and suspected he would enter a house in Golf Road at the end near the golf course. The police arrived early, hid in the bushes and true to form, a man walked up to the house and studied the outside. The police arrested him and in his hand was the gimlet ready for use. We all had a soft spot for him as he did not cause much damage and the items he stole could all be replaced. That was about 1937.

'Dalwhinnie House' was a lovely house, renamed 'Acorn House', but the grounds were very much bigger than they are today. Before the war, the house was owned by Mr Shepheard-Walwyn who was a bit strange, but he loved plants and his wife, we were told, was ill and spent most of her time in her bedroom. The husband had an assistant, a Miss Moffett, and they used to go into the woods to 'discover things'. His son was never allowed indoors and lived in a hut in the garden all the year round. They also had a daughter called Irene, but very little is known of her. There was a thick wood in the garden with many different trees and in the centre was a clearing where a stag and several deer lived.

Three days after the beginning of World War II the husband blew his brains out and the family broke up. It was a shame as he was an excellent naturalist and found many rare plants in the Kenley area.

On several occasions we went up to the airfield to see what was going on and on at least two occasions we saw the old Prince of Wales fly in and leave the plane and climb into a car to start an official visit. It was always a secret but the police would be called up to the end of Hayes Lane – they would not tell the residents why they were there but it was all very friendly and on many occasions Prince Edward was within touching distance.

Before World War II, the planes were flown by pilots who sat in the open, like the old Tiger Moths and often the pilots would fly low and wave to any groups of young ladies, often shouting something. With the sound of the engine and the wind, it was almost impossible to understand what they said but we would wave back and shout something back. It was all in good fun and we never met any of the pilots.

Mrs Martin of Whyteleafe talked to Colin Burgess in 1994—

I was born in 1927 and as a child, before World War II, I would often go to Hayes Lane to watch the gliders. There used to be a row of flint cottages in Hayes Lane, near the airfield and one used to sell sweets and ice cream. A cornet or a big piece of ice would have cost me a ½d. The lady also made her own toffee and made marvellous toffee apples. The lady in the shop also sold sweets and had them in glass jars with stoppers. Every now and then she would empty all the bits of broken sweets and put them in another jar and sell those bits for 1d for four ounces.

We often went to the side of the airfield and sat under a tree. We tried to be as quiet as dormice watching the gliders and were so excited seeing them go into the air. They used to be pulled along by a jeep type vehicle that went as fast as it could go, then had to brake hard and sometimes either the brakes were not good or else the driver braked too late. The driver usually had a mate and when they steadied the vehicle they would roar with laughter. It was always good fun watching them.

The military built a square block near the runway in Hayes Lane which the boys found very useful when watching the planes and gliders. The boys in devilment would climb up to have a better view and used to watch the RAF Military Police coming round and tell them to *'op it*, which they did before they arrived, only to return as soon as the RAF Police left. Near the airfield used to be a big house with very large gates. We used to walk past the property and have conversations on what it would be like to live in such a house.

Mr Carey used to live at 46 Downs Way and when the Bourne used to flood near the gas works, he used to take his boat over the fence and give kids a row. That was mostly on Sundays and as kids we always hoped it would rain hard enough to provide a flood. The water never had a smell nor did it leave rubbish, unlike the stream today.

One of my jobs before the war was to work in a shop opposite *The Rose & Crown* pub and make cakes all day. I used to receive 1s.6d a week and even if I say it myself, I made some lovely cakes. If they were not that nice, why did we always sell out by the end of the day?

During the war I worked in London in an office full of old men who hardly spoke. I used to travel to London by train and it used to cost me 1s.1½d each day. One day I was late because of heavy bombing. No trains were running and buses were very few. I thumbed a lift on the back of a coal truck to Brixton, then had a short bus ride and finished by thumbing a hearse that took me into the City of London. The route from just outside Purley to London was full of bricks and rubble from bombed buildings and there were several diversions as they feared a bomb was still alive and might go off. Several bridges were broken or damaged and that caused big diversions but I was late arriving at work and was fined 1s. 6d for being late and there was not one word of sympathy – the money was taken from my wages the following week.

John Easton of Caterham, talked to Colin Burgess on 22 April 1994—

My father was the head gardener at 'Old Place' in Uplands Road. Because I was a noisy lad and kept crying, the owner had a bungalow built in the grounds and as a child I learnt to be a gardener by watching and listening to my father.

At 'Old Place', they held some very big parties and Harrods used to come out and make all the food and put up decorations and we used to help them. Uplands Road would often be lined with Rolls Royces and it was the gardeners' job to look after the drivers. They were lovely cars with shiny leather inside and they were highly polished outside. As a kid I used to talk to the drivers and if my shoes were clean they might let me sit inside.

Before World War II they used to hold big flower shows at the Imperial Ice Rink in Purley. It was my job, when we took the plants down for the show in a lorry, to sit in the back and hold up a big pot off the floor of the vehicle as the road was very bumpy, so that the flowers did not drop off before we arrived. Dad would often win prizes for a nice display.

'The Willows', Bourne View, during the Bourne flood in February 1928
Photograph courtesy of Purley Library

From a postcard *c.*1938, The *Rose & Crown* is in the centre foreground, the 'Old Barn' to its left, and the Council's incinerator chimney to the far left
Courtesy of Roger Packham

Before the war there used to be a story about a ghost who appeared as a lady wearing white clothes and carrying something, seen at the end of Hayes Lane and Old Lodge Lane area. One night on my way home I stopped to watch a family of badgers moving house, walking across Hayes Lane, with mother in the front, then a line of young followed by the father, just in front of my boots. At that moment I suddenly saw a lady in white drifting down Hayes Lane and suddenly turned left into the woods. When the badgers had passed I walked up to the spot where the lady vanished and looked into the woods to see the reason why, when a lady suddenly said, 'Can't a person go to the toilet without a person being nosy?' I don't know who was more shocked but my heart was pounding on my way home.

When the war came many gardeners joined up in the military and the gardeners that were left helped each other when they were required. I went into the King's Own Royal Artillery and when I came home after the war, Kenley soon changed.

Maureen Bunn told John Bishop of her memories of Kenley—

I was born in 1937 at 1 Godstone Road, Kenley in the house called 'Purley Pines'. It was known as the first house in Kenley because, as you came along Godstone Road from Purley, the house was the first on the left after St James' Road, which is in Purley.

My grandmother had purchased the house in 1927. It was a large house with over one acre of terraced garden at the rear going up the hill next to St James' Road. We had a tennis lawn, a kitchen garden where we grew tomatoes, beans etc. and garages at the rear with entrances from St James' Road. I was told that the house was used as a nursing home for soldiers during World War I.

Widening of Godstone Road, with *The Rose & Crown* in the background, *c.*1930

Photograph courtesy of Croydon Local Studies Library

On the opposite side of Godstone Road was a small parade of shops. Mr Andrews ran the post office. There was Baker's sweet shop and Mrs Tattenhall ran the chemist's.

During World War II the tennis lawn was dug up (*Dig for Victory*). We did have quite a bit of bomb damage. The bomb that fell in Dale Road shattered all the glass at the front of the house. Then a VI demolished the kitchen and caused a lot of damage. We used to walk to the underground shelters opposite *The Kenley Hotel* when the bombing got really bad and along with many other people spent the nights there.

My father had his own firm of electrical engineers. He had a work bench set up in the house so that armature winders could continue their military work.

After the war the side of the garden bordering St James' Road was sold and two bungalows were built there. In 1964 my parents sold 'Purley Pines' to a developer and a block of flats was built called 'The Pines'. The pine trees are still visible today.

Katherine Abbott née Snow living in Hayes Lane talked to Colin Burgess on 27 April 1994—

I have lived all my life in Kenley and moved into my present house when it was numbered 51.

My first school was an annex to Croydon High at Downs Court Road at the corner of Godstone Road, which was a small building and when it became difficult for the teacher, because of the number of children present, some of us stayed at home and the teacher would visit us.

I particularly recall the very close knit society in Hayes Lane. We all played tennis from an early age as we all had tennis courts. Bridge parties were also held as well as mah-jong and as children, we knew everyone.

My family stayed in our house all through World War II even though we were told it was in the confines of the aerodrome. We had no air-raid shelter as my father considered that the house was much stronger and as it was we only had a few panes of glass broken and a few tiles blown off.

'Alfriston House', next door to us, was taken over by the RAF and housed its men. There was a large garage to the house and one day several lorries with boxes arrived and unloaded the contents into the garage. When I saw an airman picking apples in the garden, I put my head through the hedge and said 'Hallo'. He was taken by surprise at first and then asked about me and my family. When he realised that the family lived next door he called his sergeant over. In the evening the lorries returned and emptied the contents from the garage. At the same time my father came home and saw the operation and later told the family that the garage had been full of ammunition.

The big house that stood at the corner of Abbots Lane and Hayes Lane was called 'Abbots House' and two boys who lived there used to take part in car racing. The reason why that part of the road is wider than the rest of Hayes Lane is that one of the boys was killed there when he came out of the drive into the road and was hit by another vehicle – that was about 1930. The family name was Morgan.

One of the directors of Debenham's Store when it was in Croydon used to live at 'Marley House', now 114-118a, and another, Mr Spencer, lived at 'Morvan House' .

'St Margaret's House', now 106-110, was owned by two spinsters and they had two cousins living with them. Something happened with the relationship of the spinsters and cousins as a bit of the land of the house was given to them and the directions to the builder, who built the house, was that the lounge had to be the same size as the carpet they owned. The cousins paid several visits to the building while it was being built and checked the size of the lounge but when it was completed no one had thought of the skirting boards.

'Elmwood House' was a lovely house and the people who lived there were always very friendly and often had big parties. I remember as a child, a big wedding feast was held there and like children always do, a number of us peered through the railings which are still there. The bride saw us and came up and spoke to us. She asked if we thought she looked pretty. Of course we all said 'yes' and as she walked away, she spoke to a waiter who then brought us a tray of lemonade and cakes.

During World War II, I worked for FANI, First Aid Nursing Institution, which had very little to do with first aid. I used to travel every day to Baker Street where my job was to send teleprinter messages to the Free French resistance movement. I was at that job for just under three years.

HOUSE
AT
£800 FREEHOLD.
SIX ROOMED VILLA.
150 foot plot
Tiled surrounds and decorations to purchasers choice as per specification. Tiled Bathroom, with separate W.C.: Square Bath with panel surrounds. Domestic Boiler. Gas Copper. Electric Fittings and Gas Points. Tiled

An Estate Agent's advertisement from the 1930s

Chapter 8

World War II – 1939-1945

by Jill Tassera and Colin Burgess

The outbreak of war on 3 September 1939 brought many changes to Kenley.

RAF Kenley was not yet operational, waiting for concrete runways to be laid. The Royal Air Force volunteer reserves were mobilised and soldiers of the 12th Battalion Royal Fusiliers arrived for defence duties, along with the Honourable Artillery Company, The King's Own Yorkshire Light Infantry and the Pioneers.

RAF Kenley became the headquarters of 'B' sector in No.11 Group. 12 blast pens with an air-raid shelter at the back to protect ground staff were built around the perimeter, including four on the west side of Hayes Lane, which had been brought into the boundary. An operations room for ground-to-air control of fighter aircraft was set up (demolished in 1980).

People living within a radius of 1,000 yards of the airfield were advised to move away.

Public shelters were put up around the district. The largest was in the chalk bank at Riddlesdown, opposite Hayes Lane on Godstone Road. People booked their beds with the warden, Mr Lawrence, and took their own blankets in with them at night. A canteen supplied food and drink. There were toilets and baths for public use. One of the passages was called Sunshine Alley because the lights were kept on all night. Defence ditches were

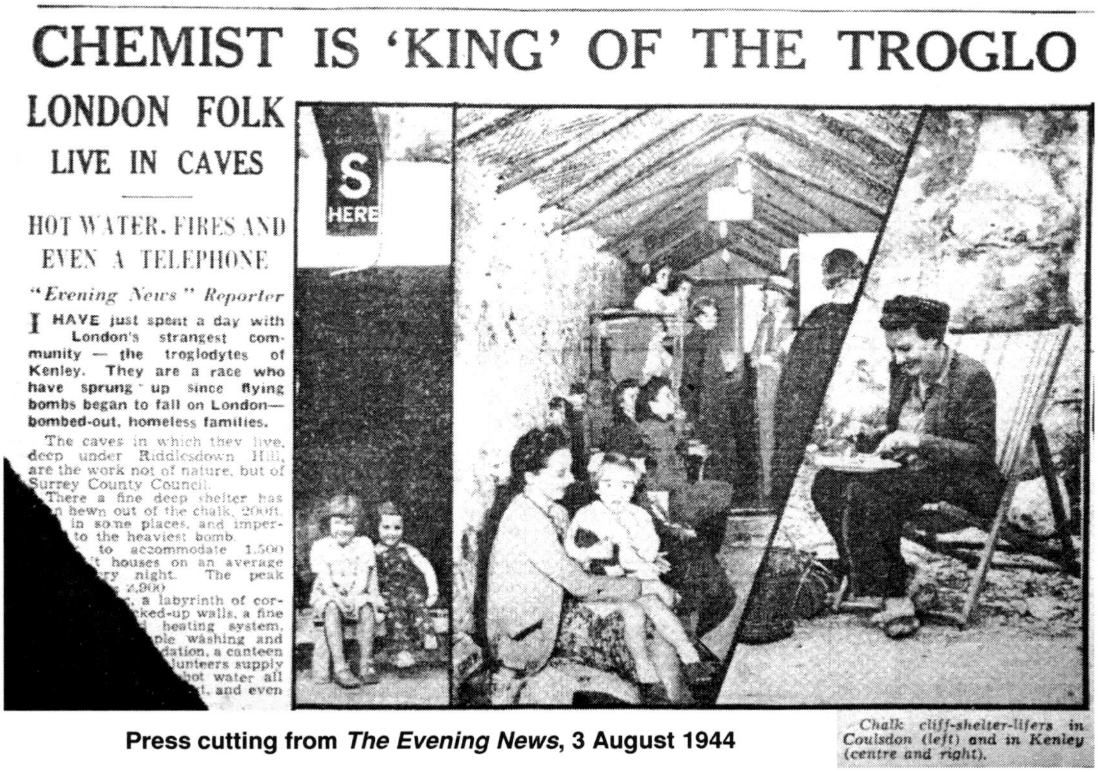

CHEMIST IS 'KING' OF THE TROGLO

LONDON FOLK LIVE IN CAVES

HOT WATER, FIRES AND EVEN A TELEPHONE

"Evening News" Reporter

I HAVE just spent a day with London's strangest community — the troglodytes of Kenley. They are a race who have sprung up since flying bombs began to fall on London—bombed-out, homeless families.

The caves in which they live, deep under Riddlesdown Hill, are the work not of nature, but of Surrey County Council.

There a fine deep shelter has ...n hewn out of the chalk, 200ft. ... in some places, and imper... to the heaviest bomb. ... to accommodate 1,500 ...t houses on an average ...ry night. The peak ... 2,900

..., a labyrinth of cor... ...ked-up walls, a fine ... heating system, ...ple washing and ...dation, a canteen ...lunteers supply ...hot water all ...t, and even

Chalk cliff-shelter-lifers in Coulsdon (left) and in Kenley (centre and right).

Press cutting from *The Evening News*, 3 August 1944

dug on Kenley Common at the top of Hawkhirst Road. Anderson shelters were dug into gardens – made of arched corrugated iron and covered with earth – and a temporary 'wooden' fire station was put up in Lower Road in Roke. Sirens to warn the public of approaching air raids were erected on Kenley police station and opposite *The Rose & Crown.*

Children used Lower Road School and the Church of England School in Garston Lane in morning and afternoon shifts. St Winifred's Boys' School in Welcomes Road closed. The former Church of England school in Garston Lane became the Home Guard HQ.

'Roseneath' at the corner of Valley Road became the headquarters of the various battalions stationed in Kenley. Soldiers coming to Kenley were billeted in the empty houses and schools. Mr Gunter's garage next to *The Kenley Hotel* was used as a food store.

Air Raid Precaution (ARP) posts with wardens whose jobs included making sure windows were blacked out were put up at various sites in the district. Mrs Martin records that there was a post opposite her house in Oaks Road and heaven help them if the wardens saw a spot of light from any house at night. They named some of the wardens Hitler No.1 or No.2 for their attitude, but the residents were often very happy for their help when a bomb fell nearby.

On 18 August 1940, a warm sunny day, the first bombs dropped on Kenley at 12.45 p.m. Group HQ at Uxbridge ordered No.615 Squadron to 'scramble'. 12 Hurricanes and eight Spitfires took off. There were many fatalities that day. Six houses in Garston Gardens and adjoining shops were destroyed. Royal Marines repairing roofs on these houses were killed. The Home Guard set up roadblocks and checkpoints after reports of parachutists seen descending from enemy aircraft. Windows at All Saints' Church were blown out. A Dornier was shot down and crashed onto 'Sunnycroft', Golf Road, and all the crew was killed. Peter Skegg who was 15 at the time remembered that as the noise subsided they went out to see what damage had occurred and in Valley Road, there was a hole of about 12" in diameter in the middle of the road where an unexploded bomb lay. The remainder of the day was spent assisting the rescue services and repair services and some time later, being consumed with curiosity, he went to watch the Bomb Disposal people working on the bomb. He has a vivid recollection of a hole and at the bottom a bomb which had then been exposed and a soldier was sitting on it – having a cup of tea! Later on 1 September a Hawker Hurricane crashed into a cornfield between Welcomes Road and Hermitage Road. The pilot baled out but his parachute failed to open properly and he was killed. He fell into the grounds of 'The Ivies' in Kenley Lane.

Peter Skegg also recalls one night at the end of 1941 when a night fighter hit a Junkers JU88 bomber directly overhead. They saw the tracer bullets and then a small red glow that rapidly turned into a large fire – the aircraft was on fire. It turned almost a complete circle and appeared to be coming straight for them but actually crashed in Town End, Caterham.

G A Burgess told of a bomb that fell in Godstone Road at the junction of Axell Hill (now Little Roke Road) that did not explode. Workmen took some time trying to find it when they dug up the road but they could not and it is there today. Considering all the traffic that passes over it and the vibration, it is surprising it has not exploded.

Mrs Martin of Oaks Road records that her father was in Heavy Rescue and posted to the Royal Oak Depot. He had to go out to buildings that had been bombed and use timber from other buildings to prop up walls and prevent the upstairs becoming downstairs. He also had to dig into bombed buildings to find out if anyone was still alive or dead, often tunnelling into the rubble. One day when he came home, as usual, covered with dust and dirt, he was very quiet and hardly said a word. This went on for three days and his wife could not stand it as he was usually a talkative man. Mr Martin sat in a chair and said it was not the family that had upset him but three days before he had tunnelled into a bombed house and found a girl about Mrs Martin's sister's age, blown apart. There was no counselling, no help, no advice – only 'you'll get over it'.

This bomb-damaged house at the top of Valley Road was the last one before the intersection; New Barn Lane being opposite. There was a bomb crater, quite small, in the front garden

Photographs courtesy of Maureen Skegg

The Martin's bungalow in Valley Road, Kenley, opposite Waverley Avenue, further down the road from the first two damaged buildings (house and bungalow)

A member of a German aircrew who had baled out of a damaged aeroplane was captured and taken to G A Burgess's house at 26 Godstone Road. The Home Guard looked after him but he was such a young boy and extremely frightened. It was the first time many had seen a 'German' – he looked such a nice lad that it seemed hard to hate an unknown person. He was taken into the lounge, as there was more space in there for all the people standing around. The airman indicated that he would like a drink and Mrs Burgess gave him a glass of water. At that moment the police arrived in force, led by a sergeant who, seeing the airman drinking, knocked the glass from his hand and demanded to know who had given him the drink. The glass went across the room and smashed in the fireplace. Mrs Burgess was livid, and verbally attacked the police sergeant, demanding to know why he behaved that way and enquiring about the broken glass. The poor lad looked even more frightened as he left. Luckily his pistol had been removed before he arrived at the house; they kept it and put it into their store of weapons.

Life had to go on as usual for the people of Kenley. Young children, including Dennis Frost, joined 'The Coggs Army'. Each was given a red armband and they collected waste paper, taking it to Dr Smith's house on the corner of Hayes Lane. Mrs Smith organised the collection. Soldiers marched along Godstone Road and 'fell-out' on the green at Garston Lane. Tea was always brought out to them by the residents there. Concerts were held in the Recreation Ground. A lorry with a stage on board was erected in the park and artists played the show called *Holidays at Home*.

Mr Wild, the owner of 'Cumberlands' had some fine gates to his house, and at the time when people had to give up railings, metal gates and pots and pans for the war effort, he was determined that his gates were not going to go anywhere. Mr Wild worked in Whitehall and had heard that in fact the metal was taken out to sea and dumped. So he instructed his gardener to take the gates down and bury them. It needed three people to take each gate down and carry it into the woods. After the war John Easton shared £50 with two gardeners for putting them back so that they swung properly, after three different builders had failed to do the job adequately.

Mrs Martin worked in a butcher's shop in South Croydon, usually walking there and back. Meat was in very short supply and most of the meat came from Argentina. It was poorly cut, boneless, and the butchers claimed that it was cut by a pack of monkeys! Her job was to cut out the ration slip – about the size of a quarter of a postage stamp – from ration books. For the slip customers were supplied with meat, which was not much, and they paid for it. The slips were put into a box on the counter, the box was taken to the council and according to the weight, the next supply of meat was ordered. There were often complaints from the council staff about the smell from the box, especially in warm periods, because accidentally pieces of pig fat would fall into the box, making it heavier. Complaints were often made by council staff that it was done on purpose but they never sent anyone from the council staff to the butcher's to check.

The Home Guard was given various weapons to try out. G A Burgess remembers 'the sticky bomb' – a glass bulb, containing explosives, on the top of a handle. The idea was to stick the bomb on a German tank if one arrived. The trouble was that if it was pushed onto the tank too hard, the glass would roll off the handle. Another was the 'Blackabomb Bar'. This was placed near the rear wheels of a vehicle and as it moved away the vehicle would touch the bar and turn it. The other wheel would set off a rocket into the petrol tank. It often misfired and the rocket went off in any direction.

1944 brought the V1 flying bomb or 'Doodlebug', a small pilotless aircraft carrying a ton of explosive. Bill Battle, a member of the Home Guard, was on duty at the Waterworks. He was standing on a concrete wall and a bomb blast blew his head off. The kitchen at Maureen Bunn's home at 1 Godstone Road was demolished by a V1 and the house suffered a lot of damage.

Both the Prime Minister and Mr Robert Menzies visited RAF Kenley. King George VI watched an entire operation plotted in the Operations Room at 'The Grange', Old Coulsdon. The security was so tight for the visit that local people were not able to welcome him, much to their disappointment.

Fragment of a German V1 Flying Bomb that destroyed the *Rose & Crown* on 3 August 1944. The fragment is behind the wall of the car park beside the present *Rose & Crown*; badly eroded over the years, little now remains.

Photograph (below): Robert Warner November 2001

Parts of pontoon bridges for the D-Day landings were made by J B Edwards & Co. at 'Kenley House' in Kenley Lane. Mr Macdonald wrote from Canada that remains of one of the pontoons lay in the brambles in the grounds of 'Kenley House' as late as 1957 when he left Kenley.

Just before D-Day, or as the local people used to say 'The Day', Godstone Road and the bypass around Caterham, filled up with all types of military vehicles. They parked under large metal hoops draped with camouflage, in three lines, one on each side and one in the centre of the road. The roads were closed, except for emergency vehicles, by the Military Police. The Memorial Hall and several church halls did a marvellous job of providing tea and meals. Miss Barbara Cooper, along with every female in Roke, Kenley and surrounding areas, came down to speak to the troops to have a smile and a giggle because everyone knew that many of the men would not return and it was as if all the women wanted to give the men a last pleasant thought of home as they left. Suddenly, overnight, they all left, leaving only scuff marks from the tanks and gun carriers on the road.

The Cooper family moved to 48 Higher Drive just before World War II and Barbara lived there all through the war with her mother. Looking down Higher Drive towards Purley, their house was on the left-hand side, overlooking Brighton Road and the railway. During the war many of the houses on the opposite side of the road were destroyed and many people were killed, yet on their side they only had a few tiles missing and a few window panes broken by blast.

Barbara Cooper remembers that she and her mother used to watch the Luftwaffe flying into London following the railway tracks; when they came back they followed the same route but their flying was not the same. Many bombers had their glass broken and the pilots were in the open trying to fly home, many flying low and often another aeroplane would fly behind to cover them and probably give encouragement. As the aircraft flew past Coulsdon many would lose height and crash into buildings or onto open land. Mrs Cooper often wondered why fighters from Croydon and Kenley were never around to finish off the aircraft in trouble. After the war she spoke to a pilot who told her that the Kenley squadrons often waited just past the North Downs and the Croydon squadrons would wait just over Reigate. They knew that the wind in the valley from Croydon would change

METROPOLITAN POLICE FORCE
KENLEY STATION

1939 In Memoriam 1945

Police Sergeant 32/107799 Herbert Charles Paisley

Born at Newtown, Lancashire, 19th December 1891, joined Cheshire Constabulary 6·4·1912. Served in the Grenadier Guards during the Great War. Joined Metropolitan Police 1918; served in "D", "W" and "Z" Divisions.

About mid-day on 25-9-1940, he went with P.S. Winckles to the scene of an unexploded bomb in the Woodcote area of Purley. One man was brought out and was tended by Sgt. Winckles while Sgt. Paisley continued the search. While he was so engaged, the bomb exploded.

War Reserve 01972 Kenneth Colin MacDonald

Alas, all too little is known of Mr. MacDonald. On the 11th October 1940, at his home in Coulsdon while with his family in their air-raid shelter, all were killed by a direct hit from a bomb.

Police Constable 764/118785 Michael Macnamara

Born at Greenwich 22nd March 1905; Royal Navy 1921-29; Metropolitan Police, "Z" Division - 9·9·29, awarded Commendation for stopping a runaway horse. In 1939 recalled to R.N.V.R. and served on Armed Merchant Cruiser "Jervis Bay", 14,164 ton converted cargo ship equipped with very old guns. On 5th November 1940, she was sole escort to Convoy HX 84 from North America to Britain, when the Pocket Battleship, "Admiral Scheer" attacked. H.M.S. Jervis Bay, laying a smokescreen, ordered the convoy, "Scatter and make utmost speed", then steamed to the attack. Hopelessly outgunned, the result was inevitable; Captain Fegen had his left arm blown off, but stayed at his post until Killed. (posthumous V.C.) Out of 262, only 65 survived, many wounded. Five only of the 37 ship convoy sunk. Captain Krancke said "God knows - those men have put themselves in their Country's debt". Many decorations were awarded - the Admiralty citation read "There must have been many more whose gallantry, were the whole truth known, who deserved decoration"---

LEST WE FORGET

Memorial Board, Kenley Police Station

when it met the wind from the Downs and aircraft in trouble would be unable to cope. They would crash and their escort would then fly up and the RAF would meet them.

Everyone dressed up when they went out for the evening, usually either to *The Imperial Ice Rink,* Purley or to Croydon. There was a great deal of friendship amongst people and it was very noticeable as they walked home from Croydon. There was no fear of meeting a strange person and they all walked along often speaking to people as they walked, including to many servicemen – and it was pitch black.

Saturday night dances were held in the Memorial Hall – quite a few young men and women married after meeting there.

The Imperial Ice Rink was used for ice hockey as there were many Canadians at the airfield, billeted in the many empty buildings in the area as well as those camping. Some Kenley girls married Canadians. Most wanted a white wedding but as there was rationing it was very difficult to buy the right material, but it was marvellous what could be done. Some Canadians never returned – dead they said, but it was better than the truth – but many did and quite a few Kenley girls went to live in Canada.

At *The Imperial Ice Rink* they used to put boards over the ice and held many flower competitions there, and also dances in the evening. Mrs Martin remembered some American and Canadian bands.

Young boys collected the shrapnel that had fallen around. Children, including Bridget Belcher from Hawkhirst Road, waited at Kenley Station for the soldiers to arrive and helped to carry luggage for 3d. The uniforms of some soldiers were ironed with flat irons by her mother. Little Sybyl Breach, aged 3 years, always ran indoors relaying the messages to her mother that everyone in Kenley could hear coming over the tannoy from the airfield.

The VE Day party held in the park was thrown by Harry Cousins from the General Store in Godstone Road.

At the end of the war RAF Kenley was used for the repatriation of Canadian soldiers. While they were waiting to be demobbed, many RAF men made ashtrays and vases from anti-tank shell cases there.

There are only two memorials to the men who lost their lives in World War II. On the St James' World War I memorial, their names have been added. About half of the list were Kenley men. The board in Kenley Police Station shows the names of three.

SOURCES

FLINT, Peter (1985) *RAF Kenley* Terence Dalton

Local residents, including Katherine Abbott, Maureen Bunn, G A Burgess, Barbara Cooper, John Easton, Mrs Martin and Peter Skegg

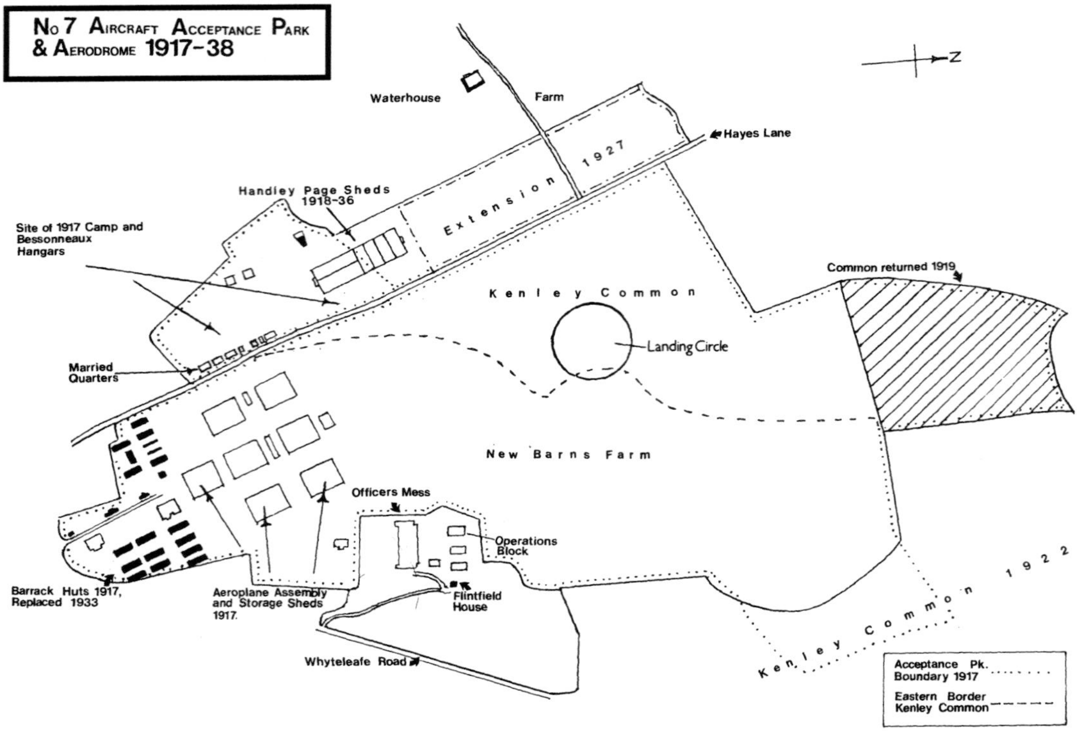
No 7 Aircraft Acceptance Park & Aerodrome 1917-38
Z
Waterhouse
Farm
Hayes Lane
Extension 1927
Handley Page Sheds 1918-36
Site of 1917 Camp and Bessonneaux Hangars
Kenley Common
Common returned 1919
Landing Circle
Married Quarters
New Barns Farm
Officers Mess
Operations Block
Barrack Huts 1917, Replaced 1933
Aeroplane Assembly and Storage Sheds 1917.
Flintfield House
Whyteleafe Road
Kenley Common 1922
Acceptance Pk. Boundary 1917
Eastern Border Kenley Common

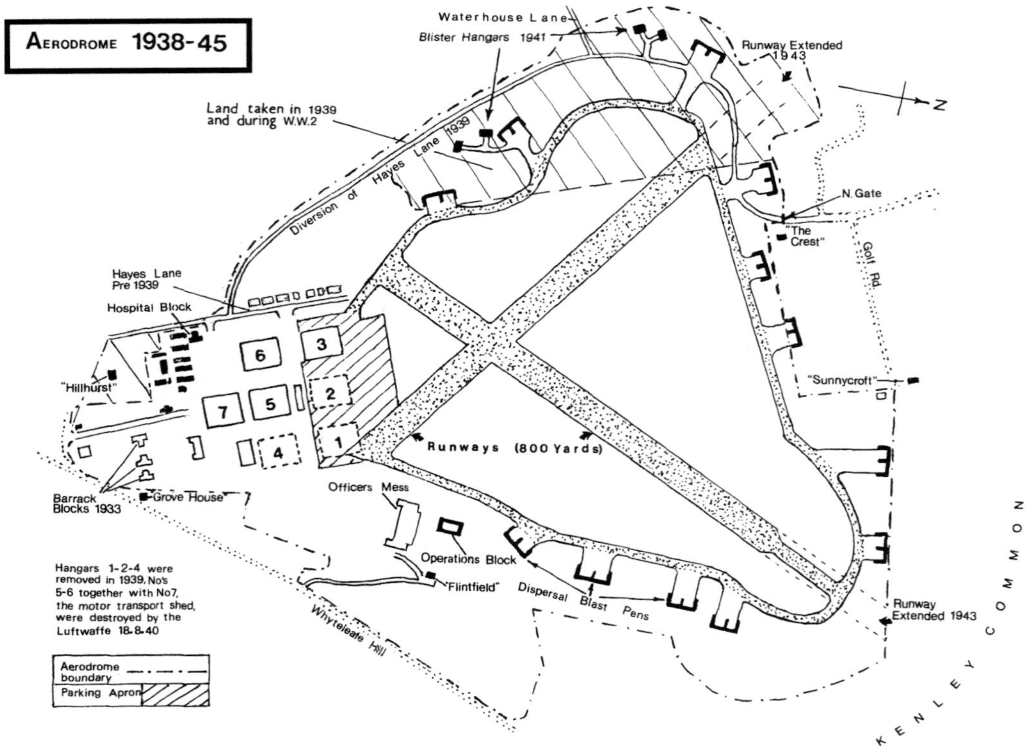
Aerodrome 1938-45
Waterhouse Lane
Blister Hangars 1941
Runway Extended 1943
Z
Land taken in 1939 and during W.W.2
Hayes Lane 1939
Diversion of Hayes Lane
N. Gate
"The Crest"
Golf Rd.
Hayes Lane Pre 1939
Hospital Block
6
3
"Hillhurst"
7
5
2
1
4
"Sunnycroft"
Runways (800 Yards)
Barrack Blocks 1933
"Grove House"
Officers Mess
Operations Block
"Flintfield"
Dispersal Blast Pens
Runway Extended 1943
Kenley Common
Whyteleafe Hill
Hangars 1-2-4 were removed in 1939. No's 5-6 together with No7, the motor transport shed, were destroyed by the Luftwaffe 18.8.40
Aerodrome boundary
Parking Apron

Chapter 9

RAF Kenley

by Robert Warner

In 1985 the late Peter Flint, a member of the Bourne Society and the Croydon Airport Society, wrote his R.A.F. Kenley, *subtitled* The Story of the Royal Air Force Station 1917–1974. *With a few alterations and additions, this narrative is condensed from Peter's authoritative book.*

Beginnings

In 1914 Conway Jenkins had moved to 'Glen Cottage' in Hillbury Road, Whyteleafe. He had proved himself to be an efficient organiser with the Army Service Corps, and when someone was required to set up Aircraft Acceptance Parks he started work at Hendon. Jenkins rose rapidly to become Lieutenant-Colonel and Assistant Director of Aircraft Equipment, and when the search for further Acceptance Parks began, he exercised his local knowledge by appraising Kenley Common with its golf course wandering among spinneys and trees.

The first that local people knew of the presence of an Acceptance Park to assemble and test aircraft entering service on their doorstep was when men of the Canadian Forestry Corps started felling trees and clearing scrub – a shock that they shared with Kenley Common's Keeper. Public outcry, and questions in parliament, followed, but the land was taken under the Defence of the Realm Act. Public opinion became more acquiescent (especially in light of the bombing of London, Croydon and Purley), and work on the aerodrome that was to become No.7 Kenley Aircraft Acceptance Park began in early June 1917. Apart from the Common, the Royal Flying Corps also took over the adjoining New Barn Farm to the south and a substantial area of Waterhouse Farm where it joined Hayes Lane to the west.

It was in the fields along Hayes Lane that all the initial activity took place. The site mushroomed rapidly, until eventually 18 Bessonneaux hangars – the standard RFC portable hangar comprising a heavy canvas cover stretched over a buttressed wooden frame, together with over 70 bell tents, marquees and other portable buildings, were standing on a site that a few days earlier had been farmland. Within a matter of days, the first aeroplane was completed and tested. Continuing use of Hayes Lane by the public caused the RFC headaches, aggravated by an ever-increasing flow of sightseers. The problem was only solved after the introduction of bye-laws restricting its use to *bona fide* users, who were issued permits.

The disadvantages of having virtually an aircraft factory thrust upon them soon became apparent to local residents. They complained about the noise, not only from the aircraft, but also from the heavy lorries running a shuttle service from the local railway stations at Upper Warlingham, Whyteleafe and Kenley transporting aircraft parts, and constant whirring of aero-engines run up on test. The matter was further aggravated by the construction of seven large permanent Belfast-type aircraft sheds, 170 ft x 160 ft, and ancillary buildings.

The guiding hand in running the Acceptance Park was the Commanding Officer, Major Thom. He was followed by Major McCallum, a production specialist, who swiftly established a first-class, efficient unit. At this time, SE5s, Sopwith Camels and Sopwith Dolphins were produced. The now Brigadier-General Conway Jenkins was a frequent visitor, flying his own special BE2C, which he kept on the aerodrome. After America entered the war, an American Air Force unit came to Kenley to train as mechanics. One of its memorable moments was when it went on strike over the food – Australian rabbits that were rather 'high'! Americans refused to eat them, but the British didn't – they were just too hungry. Tea was usually hard biscuits and jam.

The Sopwith Camel was one of the most famous aircraft that passed through Kenley. Nearly 300 were received from Tom Sopwith's factory at Kingston. The Camel gained notoriety as a difficult aeroplane to fly, and a number of inexperienced pilots were to be killed by its idiosyncrasies, but in expert hands it was a highly manoeuvrable, formidable opponent. Later the Camel was superseded by the Sopwith Dolphin, a faster multi-gunned machine.

Sopwith Camel

After testing, this aircraft went on to serve with No.45 Squadron

Lieut.-Col. F A G Noel & Peter Flint

During 1918 several bomber squadrons were mobilised from Kenley. No.88 Squadron, flying Bristol Fighter F2Bs, departed for France in April, and in July No.108 Squadron, flying DH9s, left for Cappelle. At the end of August, No.110 (Bomber) Squadron left Kenley for Courban Depôt and then on to Bettancourt, the CO, Major H R Nicholl, having in his charge a complete squadron of Liberty-engined DH9As presented to the RFC by His Serene Highness the Nizam of Hyderabad. This was the last completely new squadron to go to France.

When the Armistice was declared at 11 a.m. on 11 November 1918, Major McCallum announced the news to a full parade. Later a triumphant march, led by an American band, left Kenley to wind its way to Croydon. At the end of 1918 construction of the very large shed on the western side of Hayes Lane was under way. Designed for Handley Page and Vickers Vimy long-range bombers, it measured 180 ft x 510 ft, and was completed in 1919.

Between the Wars

After the war, communications flying throughout Europe was being operated on a large scale by 86 (Communications) Wing, with No.1 Squadron – which had been formed earlier at Hendon – flying from Kenley, its principal occupation being transport of dispatches and persons involved in the Versailles Peace Conference. For this purpose on average two Martinsyde Scouts, 20 de Havilland 4As and eight Handley Page 0/400s (large, heavy bombers) were kept in commission; some were converted to carry passengers. By mid-1919 the squadrons had flown 3,500 hours, carrying 670 passengers and 750 mail bags. No.1 Squadron dropped leaflets advertising the Victory Loan over London and other cities, and also delivered mails during the railway strike.

By 1919 Kenley had effectively become a Stores Park. With demobilisation, the hangars were chock full of aircraft, standing perpendicularly to save space. While steps were being taken by the Royal Air Force to dispose of the surplus, 12 Whyteleafe boys 'did their bit' – and ended up in court accused of stealing 22 wheels, tyres, covers, axles and other parts from the Kenley 'unserviceable dump', valued at £15. One of their parents remarked that as dozens of these wheels and axles were in use on barrows and trucks in the village, he naturally thought that they were being given away at the aerodrome!

It surprised local residents to see the aerodrome taking on a greater air of permanency. A petition was presented and questions asked. In a written reply, Winston Churchill said that a large amount of money had been spent on the aerodrome, its situation made it of great importance for air defence of London, and that therefore it should be retained as a permanent RAF station. Thus RAF Kenley came into being. Churchill was, incidentally, quietly receiving flying lessons at Kenley.

In 1920 Kenley became the home of No.1 Group, Inland Area, commanded by Group Captain H C T Dowding CMG, who later became the distinguished leader of Fighter Command during the Battle of Britain. No.24 (Communications) Squadron moved to Kenley from Croydon in January 1920. The squadron flew Avro 504Ks, DH9As, Bristol Fighters, Sopwith Snipes and Fawns. One of its flight lieutenants was J M Robb, who went on to become Air Chief Marshal Sir James Robb, GCB, KBE, DSO, DFC, AFC – one of the great men in RAF history. On 16 May 1921 the squadron was visited by Crown Prince Hirohito – later Emperor Hirohito – of Japan. The squadron remained at Kenley until January 1927.

Bristol Fighters of No.24 Squadron flying over the former Warlingham Golf Course (now Manor Park, Whyteleafe) in 1921

Air Chief Marshal Sir James Robb & Peter Flint

1923 marked the end of the post-war rundown, and the start of expansion of the RAF, including the building-up of the Home Defence Force. World War I fighter squadrons were re-formed, and one of them, No.32, eventually to be equipped with Sopwith Snipes and commanded by Squadron Leader T E B Howe AFC, made its home at Kenley. Initially the squadron was short of aircraft, and in December had just three Snipes and two Avros.

In May 1926 No.6 Group became 'Fighting Area' under a new command known as Air Defence of Great Britain. Soon after the change Air Vice-Marshal H R M Brooke-Popham CB, CMG, DSO, AFC took over the Group, remaining at Kenley for a short time before moving his headquarters to Uxbridge, where it later became No.11 Group. Air Chief Marshal Sir Robert Brooke-Popham recalled that during the General Strike Nos.24 and 32 Squadrons were used almost exclusively as an air communication service, carrying official mail and the official newspaper, *The British Gazette*. He also remarked that since he had arrived at Kenley to take over No.6 Group to form 'Fighting Area', so it is right to say that Fighting Area, and so Fighter Command, was born in one of Kenley's wooden huts.

No.32 Squadron's obsolescent Sopwith Snipes were gradually replaced in 1926 by Gloster Grebes. The older machines could easily out-manoeuvre the later ones, but the superior speed of the Grebes compensated for this. The Gloster Grebes could also carry four 20 lb bombs in under-wing racks. One evening, practising for the following day's bombing competition, four Grebes took off. Over Caterham, one of the pilots was astonished to see Pilot Officer Montgomery's machine release a bomb, which fell on Allen's baker's shop in Caterham High Street. The bomb passed right through the rear of the building, causing considerable damage, and giving the residents, Mr and Mrs Colman, quite a shock. On return the aircraft was thoroughly inspected, but nothing was found to be wrong with it or with the bomb release.

On 14 December 1931 P/O D R S Bader of No.23 Squadron flew with two other Bristol Bulldog pilots from Kenley to Woodley aerodrome, near Reading. On leaving Woodley, attempting a low roll over the grass airfield, a wingtip clipped the ground, and the Bulldog crashed and Douglas as a result lost his legs, and very nearly his life. His battle to overcome his adversity, his courage, indomitable spirit and exploits as a World War II fighter pilot and as a prisoner of war made him a legend and an inspiration in his lifetime.

Members of No.23 Squadron aerobatic team in front of a Gloster Gamecock, 1931

(Left to right) **– Douglas Bader, Harry Day, Geoffrey Stephenson (Reserve)**

10 years later they were to meet in a Prison Camp in Germany

Surrey County Libraries

In 1931 J B Edwards of Whyteleafe commenced a rebuilding programme that would establish Kenley as a fighter station, maintaining two permanent squadrons. Flying ceased for some 20 months, and Station Headquarters was re-formed in 1934, with Nos. 3 and 17 Squadrons, both flying Bristol Bulldogs, moving in from RAF Upavon. June 1936 saw the formation at Kenley of No.615 Squadron, Royal Auxiliary Air Force, titled *County of Surrey*. Winston Churchill agreed to become its honorary Air Commodore, and by the end of the Battle of Britain the squadron earned the epithet *Churchill's Own*. Several other squadrons came into being by budding off flights from existing ones, including the re-formed No.46 Squadron and No.80 Squadron. During this period the large hangar alongside Hayes Lane, which had become little used and a hazard to fighter pilots, was demolished, leaving the western boundary unobstructed.

A vertical photograph of Kenley taken by Flt.Lt. James Robb, DFC, from a Bristol Fighter of No.24 Squadron in 1921

Hayes Lane runs diagonally from bottom centre to upper left, and the large hangar, demolished in 1936, is seen to the left of it.

Air Chief Marshal Sir James Robb & Peter Flint

In March 1938 No.3 Squadron became the second squadron to receive the Hawker Hurricane – the eight-gun monoplane fighter that was to prove, along with the Supermarine Spitfire, the salvation of the nation, and indeed the whole world, in the Battle of Britain. These early Hurricanes were equipped with two-bladed, fixed-pitch wooden propellers that necessitated a long take-off run, resulting in the aircraft barely clearing the trees at the end of Kenley's grass runway. Two fatal crashes forced the conclusion that the airfield was too small, and the Hurricanes were withdrawn in July, to be replaced again by the Gloster Gladiator biplane.

Hawker Hurricane Mk IIc LF363

This aircraft first flew in January 1944 and saw active service at RAF Kenley. LF363 appeared in the film 'Angels One Five', and later in the TV series *War in the Air* and the film *Reach for the Sky*, and became a founder member of the RAF Historic Flight in 1957. It survives in airworthy order, with the Battle of Britain Memorial Flight based at RAF Coningsby, Lincolnshire.

Photograph courtesy of BBMF

At the time of the Munich Crisis in September 1938 preparedness of the resident squadrons was questionable. No.3 Squadron had trouble camouflaging its Gloster Gladiators through not having the paint to do so – overcome by sending to Whyteleafe for some household distemper!

The Empire Air Days that had started at Kenley in May 1934 became increasingly popular annual events, culminating in the display on 20 May 1939, attended by a very large crowd, and heralding the end of the biplane era. Shortly after the display No.17 Squadron moved to North Weald; No.3 Squadron had already moved to Biggin Hill, and Kenley was left with just No.615 Squadron with its Gladiators. Work was put in hand for extensive alterations and extensions to the airfield to enable Hurricanes and Spitfires to operate safely and effectively. Hayes Lane was diverted in a wide loop to the west, Waterhouse Farm having been purchased for this purpose, and concrete runways and a perimeter track laid. Three of the seven 1917-vintage hangars were demolished to allow for the runway extensions.

World War II

At the declaration of war on 3 September 1939, Kenley – the sector controlling station – was non-operational except for the control room. Fortunately, during the 'phoney war' construction continued without interruption although hampered by the severe winter of 1939/40. At the end of January 1940, before construction work was completed, No.3 Squadron, flying Hurricanes, returned to Kenley to fly on Channel patrol duties. It was joined in May by 'B' Flight, 604 Squadron's Bristol Blenheims, and for a short time by No.253 Squadron's Hurricanes. Not until 16 May, when No.64 Squadron arrived, was RAF Kenley considered suitable to receive Supermarine Spitfires.

Vertical photograph of RAF Kenley in May 1941
Note the camouflaging of both the runways and the buildings

A HISTORY OF KENLEY

After the fall of France and the Low Countries the first major clashes between the RAF and the Luftwaffe took place over the English Channel, where the RAF was concerned with providing air cover for allied shipping. A Dornier bomber made a reconnaissance of Kenley on 3 July 1940 and scattered a few bombs nearby. It was intercepted near Maidstone on its way home by No.32 Squadron. Changes were made to improve the station's security. The Scots Guards took up residence in two houses to the north-west of the airfield. One, 'The Crest', next to the north gate, had a high roof on which they set up a Lewis gun post. August 1940 started quietly, followed by attacks on convoys and coastal installations. On 12 August the Kenley Sector radar station at Pevensey, Sussex, was bombed and put out of action for some hours.

On 15 August Croydon aerodrome was bombed in the first really big raid in the area, killing 63, mostly civilians working in nearby factories, and injuring many more. Kenley's turn was to come on Sunday, 18 August. At 12.45 p.m. coastal radar reported a high degree of hostile activity, and No.615 Squadron's Hurricanes were scrambled, followed shortly by No.64 Squadron's Spitfires. Shortly after 1 p.m. nearly 60 enemy aircraft crossed the coast. The German plan was that Kenley should be attacked in three waves – the first, of 12 twin-engined Junkers 88 dive-bombers, would 'soften' the airfield's defences, followed by high-level bombing by 27 Dornier 17s, and culminating in a very low-level attack by nine Dornier 17s of 9 Staffel Kampfgeschwader 76, a specialist low-level attack unit. The Dorniers swept at sea level across the coast near Beachy Head, 'hedge-hopped' across country to Bletchingley, over the escarpment of the North Downs to Caterham and thence to Kenley. At about the time that the Dorniers crossed the coast, No.111 Squadron's Hurricanes at Croydon were scrambled.

The Dorniers, in three groups of three, sweeping towards the southern boundary of the airfield, found that the timing of the raids had gone seriously wrong. The main force, which should have softened the defences, had not arrived. Nonetheless, they poured their low-level bombs into the hangars and buildings, and across taxiways, runways and dispersals, and shot away with machine-guns and cannon at any worthwhile targets. Three hangars were blown to pieces and engulfed by fire, and a number of other buildings damaged or destroyed, including the hospital block. As the leading group approached the northern boundary, a line of rockets shot in front of them, dragging steel cables into their path – the Parachute and Cable (PAC) defence system. One Dornier collided with a cable, and disappeared towards Whyteleafe trailing the cable and parachutes. The cable came off and the aircraft survived. A Dornier of the western attacking group reduced 'The Crest' near the north gate to rubble with a perfectly-aimed bomb, silencing the Scots Guards' Lewis gun. One of the Dorniers, riddled with bullets by the defences, struck one of the PAC cables, collided with a tree and broke up, the major part of it falling on a bungalow, 'Sunnycroft', at the end of Golf Road. Only two of them eventually landed at their base at Cormeilles-en-Vexin.

Smoke and flames from Kenley clearly indicated to the Junkers JU88 aircrew that the timing had gone wrong, and that their purpose was already achieved. They therefore turned away for Manston, their alternative target. Kenley, and the surrounding district, was showered by bombs from the high-level Dorniers. As the aircraft flew away, church bells – the recognised signal of invasion – could be heard. Someone had mistaken the parachutes of the PAC defences for enemy parachutists.

Casualties were light considering the severity of the attack. 10 personnel were killed and a further 10 injured. 10 aircraft, including six Hurricanes of No.615 Squadron were destroyed or damaged beyond repair. The most vital building on the airfield – the Operations Block – was undamaged. By the following day RAF Kenley was fully operational again. Bomb damage in the surrounding district, mainly from the high-level raid, was widespread, and disruption was caused by a large number of unexploded bombs.

On 22 August 1940 the Prime Minister, Winston Churchill, visited the aerodrome, and saw a demonstration of the Parachute and Cable system, which during the raid had been used for the first time on an airfield. The demonstration and the successful deployment of the weapon during the raid convinced him to continue PAC production, which he had been about to terminate. On the same day the five German aircrew of the Dornier that crashed at Golf Road were buried at Beddington.

The raid on 18 August had highlighted the vulnerability of the Sector Operations Block, and it was quickly moved into a disused butcher's shop at 11 Godstone Road, Caterham, where it was officially known as Camp 'B'. While it was in use, a large house, 'The Grange', at Old Coulsdon was converted for the Operations Centre, Camp 'C'.

By 1941 the Battle of Britain was over, and the RAF began to turn to the offensive. Night raids continued, and successes against them with non-radar equipped aircraft were rare. By early summer the Hawker Hurricane had largely given way to the Supermarine Spitfire. The Spitfire itself had evolved into a more powerful and better armed machine in the Mark Vb than the earlier types used in the Battle of Britain. In the Spring and early Summer several squadrons came to Kenley for short stays, but in July Kenley Wing stabilised on three Spitfire squadrons – No.452 (Australian), No.485 (New Zealand) and No.602 (City of Glasgow), which stayed for the next eight months. Several VIPs visited Kenley, including Winston Churchill, Robert Menzies, Lord Nuffield and King George VI.

From mid-1942 Kenley Sector became dominated by Canadian squadrons which remained through to D-Day in June 1944. Six squadrons participated, Nos. 401, 402, 403, 412, 416 and 421. In March 1943 J E ('Johnnie') Johnson was appointed leader of the Canadian Wing at Kenley, flying the latest Spitfire, the Mark IX, which favourably matched the Focke Wulfe Fw.190. The highest-scoring RAF fighter pilot to survive the war, Johnnie Johnson shot down 38 enemy aircraft over western Europe between June 1941 and September 1944. Air Vice-Marshal J E Johnson died aged 85 on 30 January 2001. He was just one of many distinguished 'aces' to have served at RAF Kenley.

On 19 April 1944 No.421 Squadron (RCAF) left Kenley for Tangmere, prior to D-Day, and for Kenley it was the end of an era. In March 1944 Kenley Sector had been taken over by Biggin Hill. As the war moved away, Kenley was no longer so important to home air defence. In September 1944, with the end of the war in Europe approaching, plans were made for disarming the Luftwaffe. At Kenley No.8302 Wing was formed to become the Disarmament School. By December about 300 officers and 1200 men had passed through the school.

By the end of the war the Gloster Meteor jet fighter was beginning to replace the piston-engined types. It required much longer runways than Kenley could provide, perhaps the most important consideration in transferring control of the sector to Biggin Hill. In September 1945 a small detachment of scientists arrived to arrange the reception, storage and evaluation of captured German aircraft equipment. Air transport became the prime employment during the months after the war, but in 1947 HQ No.6 (Eastern Reserve) Group moved in from Rickmansworth.

Post War

In 1949 a Royal Auxiliary Air Force Air Observation Post Squadron, No.661, was formed at Kenley, flying De Havilland Tiger Moths and Austers.

A film unit used the aerodrome for outdoor scenes of the film *Angels One Five,* and another company made parts of the film *Reach for the Sky* – taken from Paul Brickhill's biography of Douglas Bader.

For many years flying activity was light, with mostly small aircraft coming and going. A French Vautour jet, mistaking Kenley for Biggin Hill, landed on the shorter runway, and ended up in the bushes at the Whyteleafe end. After repairs it was flown away. A Gloster Meteor and Hawker Hunter attempted emergency landings, with rather similar results. From the early 1960s the station was steadily run down, and by the 1970s it was little more than a dormitory for MOD personnel serving elsewhere. The Officers' Mess was closed in 1974, remained derelict and was vandalised. In 1979 the DTI bought it and it was converted into a radio technology laboratory, its position in an area of low electrical interference making it ideal for the purpose.

In 1955 No.615 Squadron Air Training Corps Gliding School took over the work of No.143 Squadron School and was based at Kenley. On 23 October 1978 fire broke out in the remaining 1917 hangar, in which the gliders were stored. All the gliders and equipment were lost and the hangar gutted, but by February 1980 Slingsby Sedburgh gliders were once again airborne over Kenley, housed on the ground in a portable Bessonneaux hangar of similar design to those that had been erected at the Air Acceptance Park in 1917. Gliding continues to this day, the Air Training Corps sharing the airfield with the civilian Surrey Hills Gliding Club.

Gliders of the Air Training Corps Gliding School at Kenley in 1984
Photograph: Peter Flint

The Royal Air Force Association's Portcullis Club – which takes its name from RAF Kenley's badge – keeps alive the Royal Air Force 'presence' at Kenley. The club, run by the Kenley & Caterham Branch of the RAFA, organised a fund-raising air show in 1976 to aid victims of the IRA public house bombing in Caterham. Further air shows were held in 1978 and 1980 in aid of RAF charities.

In the late 1990s part of the airfield was sold for redevelopment. Concern was expressed at the Portcullis Club that a suitable memorial be erected before it was too late. A committee of the Kenley Residents' Association and RAFA Kenley & Caterham Branch was formed, and after much hard work, a memorial was erected in one of the former blast pens. It was dedicated on RAF Tribute Day, 19 August 2000, 60 years and a day after the station had been so heavily attacked by the Luftwaffe. The memorial was unveiled by Air Chief Marshal Sir Anthony Bagnall and later a Hurricane, Spitfire and the Lancaster *City of Lincoln* of the Battle of Britain Memorial Flight swept over the airfield in tribute. Once again 'dogfights' between Hurricanes, Spitfires and Messerschmitts filled the skies over Kenley – but this time between radio-controlled models flown by members of Croydon Airport Model Flying Club.

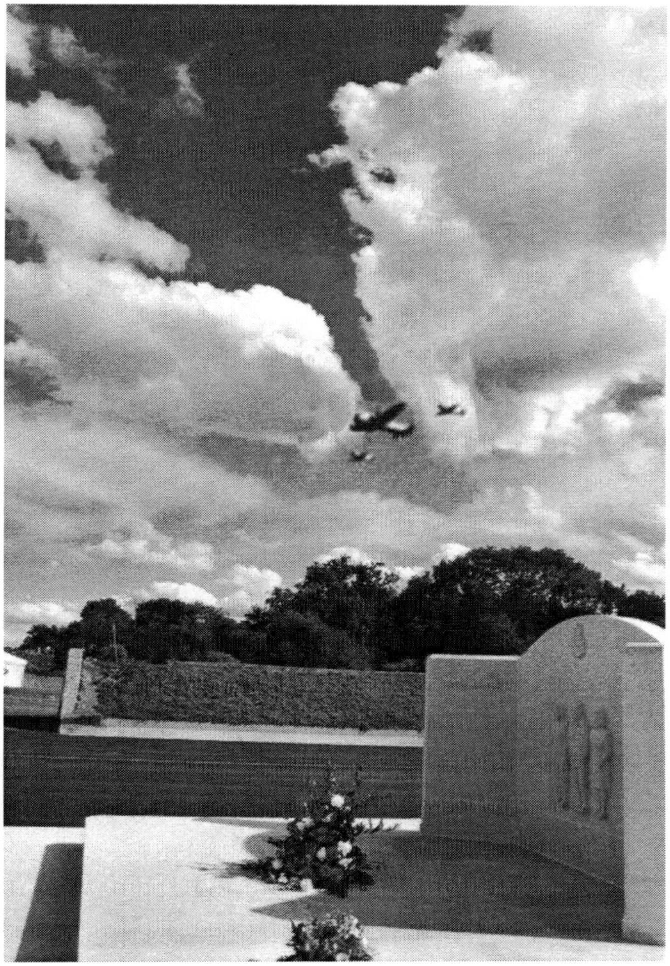

RAF Kenley Memorial
RAF Kenley Tribute Day 19 August 2000
Photograph: Grahame Brooks

SOURCES

Battle of Britain Memorial Flight 2001 Souvenir Booklet BBMF

Bourne Society **Bulletin 182** (November 2000) and **Bulletin 185** (August 2001)

BRICKHILL, PAUL (1954) *Reach for the Sky* Collins

FLINT, PETER (1985) *R.A.F. Kenley* Terence Dalton

PILKINGTON, LEN (1997) *Surrey Airfields in the Second World War* Countryside Books

PRICE, Albert (1980) *Battle of Britain: The Hardest Day - 18 August 1940* Granada Publishing

RAF Kenley Tribute Official Souvenir Brochure (2000)

TURNER, JOHN FRAYN (1998) *The Battle of Britain* Airlife Publishing Ltd

'Longwood', home of Mr & Mrs Simpson, photographed in 1987. Shortly afterwards it was sold for development. The site has become Summerswood Close. ***Photograph: Grahame Brooks***

Summerswood Close November 2001
Photograph: Gwyneth Fookes

Chapter 10

The Last 50 Years

by Jane Ruffle & Jill Tassera

The most radical event was the post-war publication of the Government White Paper of 1961 which proposed, amongst other boundary changes, the integration of Coulsdon & Purley Urban District Council (which included Kenley) into the London Borough of Croydon. In 1962 a campaign was launched by the Coulsdon & Purley Petition Committee to try to prevent the locality becoming part of the London Borough. In Kenley ward around 70% of the electorate signed the petition but the Minister of Housing and Local Government rejected all protests and the changes came about. The Residents' Association petitioned to have Kenley transferred back to Surrey but the appeal was turned down following a public enquiry in 1966.

Most residents will agree that the only benefit that this has brought about is the issue of Freedom Travel Passes to pensioners.

Until party politics entered local government the Kenley ward had been represented by the Whyteleafe and Kenley Residents' Association. In the late 1960s it was decided to merge with the Roke and East Purley Residents' Association and on 1 January 1970 the Kenley & District Residents' Association came into being. The Association continues to be a great influence on the well-being of Kenley, particularly in dealing with the local authority regarding amenities and road safety measures. Very importantly the Association vets all planning applications and has been instrumental in saving the area from overdevelopment.

The next most important change to life in Kenley from the 1950s onwards has been the demolition of many of the houses built in the 19th century and early 20th century to be replaced by (in some cases quite large) housing estates. To name a few: 'Cumberlands', 'Oaklands', 'The Towers' and 'Watendone Manor'. It is amazing to think that the whole of the Cumberlands estate was built on the site of one house and garden. Part of the old boundary wall can still be seen in Church Road. A number of other Victorian and Edwardian houses have been converted into flats or nursing homes. Even houses built in the second half of the 20th century are now being demolished for more development and in many cases blocks of flats are being built. All this development is making the Kenley roads more crowded, and commuting more difficult.

One area saved from all the development by the Green Belt Act in 1937 was Hawkhirst, a 35 acre area of woodland adjoining Kenley Common. The fate of Betts Mead was less fortunate – despite having been part gifted to the public and part purchased by the then Coulsdon & Purley Urban District Council before World War II, in the 1970s it was substantially filled with rubbish and was later relandscaped.

Hayes Lane in part still resembles a typical, rather narrow country lane, but in fact a large number of new houses have been built on either side of it and the surrounding plateau has been the site for a number of modern developments, including Pondfield Road, Wattendon Road and Wheat Knoll. To counteract the speed of the ever increasing number of cars, speed humps – or sleeping policemen – have been built into Hayes Lane, Welcomes Road and Park Road .

Roke County Primary Junior Mixed and Infants' School moved to the bottom of Hayes Lane in 1994.

The outlook along Godstone Road at Roke has been modernised with the erection of several office blocks and industrial units, such as Kiddicraft and Secom.

In 1903 Station Road was the home of Peter Prior, who ran the local slaughterhouse and Francis Webb, who built carriages for the local gentry

Postcard courtesy of Roger Packham

The original site of the Marn Service Department behind *The Kenley Hotel* had been cleared for development in July 1997

Photograph: Grahame Brooks

In April 1998 five mews houses were being built in Station Road

Photograph: Grahame Brooks

THE LAST 50 YEARS

Particular landmarks to disappear over the last 50 years were—

- the last Friesian herd and bull vanished from Kenley Farm some time after 1962 and the pigs from Golf Road went during the 1973 outbreak of swine vesicular disease
- the library, which was built at the same time as Purley, Coulsdon, Selsdon and Sanderstead libraries in 1936. They had dispensed 302,616 books in their first eight months of operation. Kenley Library was closed for economic reasons in 1975 and the property is now a private house. A mobile library takes its place
- the local authority incinerator in the mid-1960s – which was replaced by a small industrial estate
- the bowls club which was closed in 1962 and the tennis club, closed in 1969
- the waterworks was rebuilt in 1989
- the former St Winifred's School – latterly the home of The British Paper & Board Industry Research Association
- the boating lake in the Recreation Ground – now Bourne Park – to be replaced by a playground
- The Cliff House Hotel in Godstone Road which had been used by the Residents' Association as a venue for fund-raising during World War II was replaced by flats
- Lloyds Bank which had operated next door to the present Village Stores since 1905
- Kenley, Purley & District Horticultural Society
- The Scout hut in Lower Road in 1990s

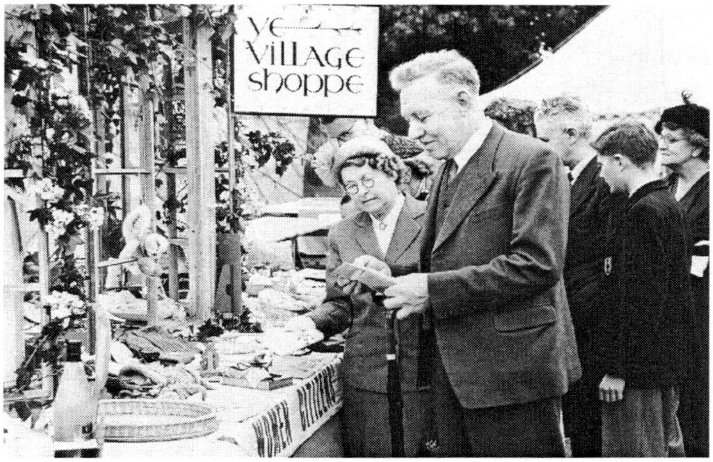

Councillor and Mrs Willis at the Kenley & Purley Horticultural Society Flower Show held at the Rotary Field, Purley , 24 July 1954

Photograph courtesy of Purley Library

A landmark which nearly disappeared was the Police Station which has existed since 1896 and was responsible for an area of 27 square miles. However, after wholesale protests and petitions it survived, albeit on a restricted basis, opening from 11a.m. to 7p.m. weekdays.

There was the welcome return of sheep which had been removed when the urbanisation of the area started encroaching onto the Commons. Prior to that time they had grazed on the same site since time immemorial.

Also welcomed was the opening of an observatory in 1979 – off Waterhouse Lane – which is open to the public by prior arrangement. Figures provided by it have appeared in the national press – sometimes Kenley having the highest rainfall in the country!

One of the most exciting events to happen as far as historians are concerned was the archaeological dig on the site of 'Watendone Manor' in 1966. The site covered 10 acres which involved a great deal of work for many people. However all the hard work had a happy conclusion in that traces of the 'lost' village of Watendone were found (See Bourne Society *Local History Records* VI).

***The Rose & Crown* on**
21 August 1956

Photograph courtesy of Purley Library

The Rose & Crown
November 2001

Photograph: Gwyneth Fookes

In August 1986 Kenley Lane was badly flooded by very heavy rainfall (though not from the Bourne on this occasion)

Photograph: Grahame Brooks

THE LAST 50 YEARS

As far as modern history is concerned the refurbishment after years of neglect of the Memorial Hall saved from demolition by Frank Tasker and rededicated by Group Captain D R S Bader in November 1975 was important as it has now become a focal point for many activities.

Kenley Airfield (where Douglas Bader served for a time) saw changes. The Officers' Mess closed in 1974 and became a radio technology laboratory testing goods from China, Taiwan etc. The Surrey Hills Gliding Club opened in 1979 making good use of the runways, and an Air Cadets Gliding School was formed in 1956. This school was made up with personnel from four schools, including Hamsey Green. In 1978 the main hangar (together with the entire fleet of gliders) was destroyed by fire. The Gliding School reopened in 1980.

The Portcullis Club (a club for ex-RAF and the Caterham area RAFA) which had met in a hut behind *The Whyteleafe Tavern* since its formation in 1947, moved to its present premises at the airfield in 1978.

RAF Kenley was used as a location for several films in the 1940s and 1950s, the best known being *Reach for the Sky*.

A day for celebration was the centenary of the opening of the railway line from Purley to Caterham. The occasion was marked by a steam engine pulling three passenger coaches carrying local dignitaries from Purley to Caterham and back on 6 August 1956. As with the other stations on the line, Kenley was packed with train enthusiasts to cheer the old engine.

Arthur Stanners from Dorset related that in the 1970s he was in the police dog section and they used to train their dogs on the airfield. One day, whilst exercising his dog, he used his newly acquired metal detector on the disused tennis court of a war-damaged building and found a silver identity bracelet bearing a Canadian officer's name and his mother's. They were from Winnipeg. The hallmark was for the year 1916. Mr Stanners wrote to the Mayor of Winnipeg to try to trace the officer, but he was last heard of in 1926. The Veterans' Department for the Canadian Army said that the bracelet and letter would be kept on file.

On a happy note, the original railway stationmaster's house which had become rather dilapidated, in 1999 became the home of Little Angels Play-Station, thus providing an activity centre for Kenley children as well as restoring an important building in the history of Kenley. In 2000 the Bourne Society erected a plaque commemorating its building in 1856.

Like the stationmaster's house, the air raid shelter in Godstone Road has found a new lease of life, first as a mushroom farm and, from 1967 as an optical works. Apparently the stability of the temperature of the underground site makes it ideal for such a factory.

The only public building to have been rebuilt after the war was *The Rose & Crown* public house which had been destroyed by a flying bomb. *The Rose & Crown* was long ago described in an advertisement in 1856 as being in 'the prettiest spot in Surrey'. The current building is the third to have been built on the site.

December 2000 saw some of the worst flooding of the Bourne for many years and at times Kenley Cricket Club's field was under water when prolonged rain added dramatically to the flow. Godstone Road was closed for 26 days.

SOURCES

Bourne Society *Local History Records*

Croydon's Parks – an Illustrated History (1988)

Purley Reference Library

Local residents

(Right): **All Saints' Church, Kenley**
c.**1905**

Postcard courtesy of Roger Packham

(Opposite page): **All Saints' Church seen from Hayes Lane, with Welcomes Road in the foreground and 'Hillside' centre right.**
13 April 1886

Photograph courtesy of Purley Library

(Below): **A painting of All Saints' Church at a rather later date.**

Print courtesy of Mrs Pam Cooper

Chapter 11

Religious Life in the Parish

by Roger Packham

Prior to the construction of All Saints' Church, many Kenley residents worshipped at St John's Church, Coulsdon and several of them are recorded in the graveyard there. St John's still has a schedule of the pew rents in which the owners of 'Hayes House', 'Kenley House' etc are prominent.

An interesting link between Kenley and Coulsdon is provided by Canon Henry Granville Dickson. He was rector of Coulsdon from 1896 to 1929 and before he moved into the Bradmore Green rectory, he lived at 'St Ruan', a big house standing until 1973 at the junction of Hayes Lane and Abbots Lane. His parish included much of what is now Purley and Kenley and he travelled many miles by foot. Canon's Lane, Old Coulsdon is named after him.

The churches and schools have all played their part in the religious life of Kenley and some of the establishments are included in the following—

All Saints' Church, Church Road

The development of Kenley in the 1860s and the distance from the parish church at Coulsdon soon gave rise to the need for a local church. By the end of the decade a meeting took place with John Young of 'Kenley House', R J S Joyce of 'Cumberlands', Mr Robins of 'The Cottage', Welcomes Road and Revd G H Bourke, rector of Coulsdon. They promised £535 towards the cost of a new church and Mr Young gave an acre of land.

The foundation stone was laid by Lord Hylton on 17 November 1870 and the church was opened for worship on 2 November 1871 by Rt Revd Samuel Wilberforce, Bishop of Winchester, having cost £3,500 with 200 seats. A debt of £1,230 was paid off by J W Wark of 'Yewbank', Church Road. A local newspaper described the opening:

> This usually quiet parish (Coulsdon) was the scene of some excitement on Thursday last, the 2nd inst. on the occasion...of the opening of a new church at Kenley. The Bishop of Winchester officiated...Kenley is some two miles distant from the mother church from which it is separated by a deep valley, so that the inhabitants of this rapidly growing place have long felt the difficulty of attending Divine service, which in bad weather becomes almost an impossibility unless by a carriage drive of three miles. Through the exertions of the rector, the Hon and Revd G Bourke, supported by liberal subscriptions from the landowners and inhabitants of the neighbourhood, an elegant and commodious structure has been erected on a commanding site near Kenley Station...A numerous and respectable congregation including most of the important families of Coulsdon and Caterham filled the church some time before the bishop arrived...Between the services a splendid cold collation was liberally provided for those who came a distance by J Young Esq at 'Kenley House', where the Bishop was placed in the seat of honour and amused all present by a happy and humorous speech.

The church was designed by J W Fowler of Louth, Lincolnshire and the builder was G W Booth. In 1873 Mr Joyce donated the organ which, after good service, was sold to the parish church of Brockenhurst. Later, Mr Young donated three bells and in 1904 a belfry clock by Gillett & Johnston was added. The church has ornamental brick arches, stone pillars with elegantly carved capitals and windows dedicated to former Kenley residents. It is in the Early Geometric style.

In 1888 the parish of Kenley was created and the church was no longer a chapel of ease to Coulsdon. The Bishop of Rochester, Dr Thorold consecrated the church in 1888, and in 1889 Revd L H Squire commenced his ministry which continued for 29 years. Prior to Squire's incumbency, Revd J G Lloyd MA, is shown in directories as the curate living at 'Longwood'.

There were enlargements to the vestry in 1894 and an extension in 1897 before the church was completed in 1902 with a baptistry and porches. The modern church hall was built in 1960.

The war memorial in the church is unusual in that it records all the local men who served as well as the ones who did not return. Until recently there were no names for those who fought in World War II.

The parish magazines for February-April 1932 provide a description of the stained glass windows at All Saints' by F G Cole, churchwarden. Some of these were destroyed in World War II.

St James' Church, St James' Road

St James' Church has its origins in the building at the north end of Little Roke Avenue – now its church hall. In 1899 the rector of Coulsdon, Revd Dickson wrote to local residents expressing concern about their pastoral situation. It is not known how many of the Roke residents attended All Saints' Church and whether there was a social divide. Following Dickson's letter, a site in Little Roke Avenue was made available by James Monger and it was agreed that the proposed building could seat 140 people and be used for services and a Sunday school. The cost of the building was over £800 and the church was dedicated by the Bishop of Rochester in 1903 as a mission district taken from St John's, Coulsdon.

Following a visit to the crowded church by Bishop Burge of Southwark in 1913 it was decided to rebuild and Stanley Croft became secretary of the building fund. In the same year the site of St James' was purchased and the cutting of the first sod was reported in a local newspaper of 27 November 1914. The first half of the church was built and consecrated in 1915 at a cost of £4,385. It is in the 15th century style with three bays of the nave and 300 sittings.

***(Left):* Temporary Church of St James, Little Roke Avenue *c.*1909**

Photograph: Miss E Tucker
Courtesy of Purley Library

***(Right):* St James' Church in the early 1920s**

Postcard courtesy of Roger Packham

In 1925 the *parish* of St James', Riddlesdown, was created and the church was completed in 1931 at a cost of £8,500 and consecrated by Bishop Garbett of Southwark. The architect had also designed St Andrew's Church, Coulsdon and a tower on similar lines had been planned for St James' but was never built.

Kenley Methodist Church, Sylverdale Road

On 13 May 2001 celebrations were held to mark one hundred years of the Methodist movement at Kenley. In about 1899 a Methodist society was formed at Gardner's Pleasure Resort, Godstone Road and Mrs Gardner became a class leader. In 1901 the Croydon Wesleyan Circuit accepted responsibility for the mission and, according to the circuit plan for April-June 1901, the first official Methodist service at Kenley ('Gardner's Resort') was conducted on 28 April by Mr J Relf of South Croydon and in the evening by Revd George Skerry of Woldingham Park.

Kenley & Purley Methodist Church in May 2001

Photograph: Grahame Brooks

In 1903 a temporary iron building was presented by Arthur Lewis and it was hoped to stage an official opening in December at a site near the railway bridge in Godstone Road. Sadly the building was unsuitable for re-erection and the project was abandoned.

After some good attendances a permanent building (the present church hall in Sylverdale Road) was begun in 1906 when Mrs Gardner laid one of the foundation stones. The others are still visible and they include one by C C Wakefield, later Lord Wakefield. The site was purchased for £287.2s.6d, and before the new church was opened Sunday services were held at the Commemoration Hall. A local resident, Frederick C Potter was an enthusiastic preacher at this time and Sir Horace Marshall of Chipstead presented £50 to the building fund.

The opening ceremony was held on 3 October 1906 when Mrs Potter (senior) received the key from the architect and at the evening meeting of the new church, Mr Potter was able to announce that the building had opened free of debt. Slide shows and a slate club were introduced and within three years of the opening, an extension was carried out by E J Saunders for Sunday School work and this opened on 29 November 1909.

Numbers declined slightly during World War I but an organ was installed during this period at a cost of £90. In 1929 a proposal to build a new church in Christchurch Road, together with a manse, was abandoned but an extension fund to the existing church led to the building of the present church with its distinctive tower on the adjoining site. It was opened for worship in May 1936 and the manse in Selcroft Road was purchased in 1948. A golden jubilee of the church was celebrated in 1956.

St Mary's Church, Watendone

In 1966 the demolition of Watendone Manor, Hayes Lane, led to the Bourne Society undertaking a rescue excavation to establish the site of the 'lost' village. The mediaeval field name 'Le cherche-dene' was used to identify the probable site by referring to Messeder's Fieldbook of the Manor of Coulsdon 1762, and superimposing a modern Ordnance Survey map. It thus became possible to trace the site of the church mentioned in Domesday Book and the mediaeval burial ground. Further excavations revealed the wall footings of the church and remains of small mediaeval houses.

The church was a substantial flint building and continued in use after the village was abandoned in about 1400. In 1453 Henry Gerbregge was rector of Coulsdon with responsibility for the church at Watendone. He lost his benefice in 1465, however, but in that year Thomas Bassett declared in his will that he wished to be buried in St Mary's Church, Whadyngdon. This is the only reference to the church's dedication.

The church was later converted to a barn and was burned down in about 1780.

St Peter's Hall, Hayes Lane/Pondfield Road

St Peter's Hall was built in the early 1900s as a chapel of ease to St John's Church, Coulsdon. It was built for the convenience of residents of Hayes Lane and nearby roads, perhaps surprisingly since All Saints' Church was not very distant. A lay reader Mr (later Revd) Kelk held evening services at the hall in the 1920s and 1930s; Mrs Weston played a portable organ and Miss Nellie Parsons and others were involved with the Sunday School. Miss Parsons also captained the local company of Girl Guides (2nd Kenley Company) which was based at the hall.

Another leading figure in the life of St Peter's Hall was Deaconess B Evans who is thought to have moved into the district in the early 1930s. A local benefactress, Miss Hayles, funded the building of a bungalow for the deaconess in her own grounds in Hayes Lane, opposite the entrance to Pondfield Road.

There are local memories of the hall which disappeared along with the allotments opposite in about 1950 to be replaced by residential development. It was popularly known as 'The Tin Tabernacle' and children's parties, sometimes with a magician, were an attraction in the 1920s.

Revd Kelk, who lived at 'Osgarthorpe', Downs Road, Coulsdon, died in 1947 but he is commemorated by a stained glass window in the old chancel at St John's, Coulsdon, for his work in the parish.

Mr Kelk, Lay Reader at St Peter's Hall, *c.*1937

Photograph courtesy of Mr S Lucas

St Winifred's School Chapel, Welcomes Road

There is a prospectus in Purley Library for St Winifred's School, dated 1914. It was a preparatory school for boys seeking entry to the public schools and the Royal Navy and it had a chapel dedicated in 1901 by the Bishop of Rochester, whose diocese at that time included Kenley.

Records show that the celebrated company of Morris & Co supplied two stained glass windows in December 1907 and July 1908 respectively and there has been speculation whether the windows may have been designed by Burne-Jones. Research has shown that one window was designed by Henry Dearle, art director of William Morris & Co 1896-1932. Dearle came to live at 'The Copse', Welcomes Road *c.*1904 but had moved to Woking by 1909. The 1907 window was dedicated to him by his son Duncan William Dearle (1893-1954) though it was presumably designed by Dearle senior, who is also thought to have been responsible for the 1908 window.

When St Winifred's School was later occupied by the laboratories of the British Paper & Board Industry's Research Association, the chapel became a caretaker's cottage. By 1958 the two panels had passed to one of the Association's employees who had hoped to include them in the rebuilding of a war-damaged church in East

Dulwich. These hopes were thwarted and in 1966 the custodian of the panels died and they were sold to a dealer in the Portobello Road. Their present whereabouts is unknown.

St Winifred's School Chapel, Welcomes Road c.1900

Courtesy of Roger Packham

The Assemblies of God Bible College occupied 'Hillside' in Welcomes Road during the 1950s

Photograph courtesy of Purley Library

SOURCES

All Saints' Kenley – A Brief History (July 1992)

All Saints' Kenley, Parish Magazines

BROADBENT, U & LATHAM, R *Coulsdon Downland Village* Bourne Society 1976

Coulsdon & Purley Weekly Record 1914

Croydon Advertiser 1871

Kelly's Directories

NEWALL, W G

Purley Library

Kenley & Purley Methodist Church – *Centenary Service Programme 2001* (courtesy Mrs M Tullett, Coulsdon)

Chapter 12

Kenley Memorial Hall

by John Bishop

The armistice signed on 11 November 1918 brought a huge sigh of relief from wives and families in towns and villages throughout the country. Many were unaware of the terrible slaughter that had taken place and it was only when those men that had survived returned home that the awful truth sank in that so many of their neighbours' fathers, husbands and sons had perished. Kenley was typical of those times; so many able-bodied men had willingly volunteered and so many had fallen. It was the shared grief amongst the Kenley residents that initiated a very strong feeling that a lasting memorial should be erected to commemorate all those local men and women who had served their country. It was then that the idea of a Memorial Hall was first mooted.

On 26 March 1919 an executive committee of 10 was formed with the powers to raise funds, to authorise the design and erection of the hall and to negotiate the purchase of a suitable plot of land where the hall would have a permanent site. Fund raising began – this was done by personal subscription to the committee, by social functions, concerts and entertainment held in the private homes of the residents and by no less than 60 volunteers with collection boxes. It is a great credit to the Kenley residents that by 30 June 1923, out of a population of only about 2,000 people, £3,116 was donated. By July 1921, as the money started to come in, the committee felt confident enough to approve the design of the hall and to authorise the start of its construction. The site was agreed to and an approach was made to the owner for the purchase, but Sir Charles Morgan of Welcomes Road, who had lost a son in the war, defrayed the £400 cost – a generous gesture since he had already donated £100 to the original fund. Other Kenley residents gave generously. The Misses Eleanor and Emily Young each gave £200. The Tufnell family who had also lost a son and were involved with the original concept of the hall gave a total of £169.

The original foundation stone
Photograph: Paul Sandford

Construction work by H W Pullen & Co. commenced towards the end of 1921 to the design submitted by the architects Flemming & Sharpe. Their design catered for a large hall but with sections that could be omitted should the funds be insufficient at the time. The committee felt it wise to take advantage of this flexible design, and the first hall to be built was without the cloakrooms and toilets, the Institute Room on the left from the front, the Parish Room on the right and a section of the hall. The first building therefore had a hall only 48 ft long seating 155 people in a fixed seating plan. Mrs Carleton Tufnell, a member of the executive committee, laid the foundation stone on 3 December 1921 and the hall was completed ready for an official opening four months later.

On 8 April 1922, with much splendid ceremony, Major-General Sir C E Pereira KCB, CMG General Officer Commanding the 56th 1st London Division attended the opening ceremony. He was accompanied by Lieut-Colonel Langworthy-Parry, CO of the Queen Victoria Rifles. Captain C E Winter M C and Captain Hamilton, both of the 56th division, were in the group. They were all received with a general salute sounded by Sergeant Ellis and two bugler riflemen. Revd F Powell in his vestments as an army chaplain led the prayers and afterwards handed the key to General Pereira who then officially unlocked the main door and entered the hall.

THE GREAT WAR
THIS HALL WAS ERECTED IN
OF KENLEY WHO GAVE THEIR
1914 1918
PROUD MEMORY OF THE MEN
LIVES FOR THEIR COUNTRY
ERNEST·E·BAILEY
WILLIAM·BARKER
LEONARD·H·BROWN
RICHARD·F·FRENCH
CHARLES·GILDER
CHARLES·H·A·GODFREY
ALBERT·GRINHAM
EDGAR·HARRINGTON
VICTOR·KNIGHT
WILLIAM·W·MORGAN
CHRISTOPHER·D·MURRAY
KENNETH·D·MURRAY
HAROLD·R·RODWELL
HERBERT·SAWYER
EDWARD·SELLS
JOHN·W·SHILCOCK
ERNEST·G·SLEMMONDS
WALTER·C·SMITH
CARLETON·W·TUFNELL
FREDERICK·C·VERNER
CHARLES·R·WAYLING
Jesus said I am the Resurrection and the Life

The original memorial plaque is still on view to visitors to the hall.

Photograph: Paul Sandford

The General unveiled the memorial tablet to 21 men who had died. At the same time Gifford Cole unveiled the tablet to Lieutenant William Watkins Morgan, the son of Sir Charles. Both of these tablets were the work of Mrs Moore Brown. A service of dedication then followed conducted by Revd Powell. At the end of the ceremony, a collection was made to fund the extensions. It is a further credit to the people of Kenley that, having given so generously before, another £150 was collected that day. In particular, the Misses Eleanor & Emily Young gave £80 to add to the £400 they had given previously.

By 1923 the cloakrooms, toilets, Parish Room and the 19 ft 6 ins. hall extension had been completed. It was only the Institute Room on the left of the main hall that has never been built. The hall we see today has therefore an asymmetrical appearance owing to the missing Institute Room. The join between the hall extension and the short hall can be seen today as a straight line across the hall floor.

The hall was legally held by the vicar and wardens of Kenley parish church by a deed drawn up on 21 December 1921 making them the trustees. However, the trustees act as leaders of the Kenley community at large and not as a representation of the parish church. This is the unique position of Kenley Memorial Hall and its relationship to the people. In 1939 the trust was transferred to the Charity Commissioners whereby the vicar and wardens became *ex-officio* members of the management committee.

The original design drawings can now be seen at the Local Studies Department of Croydon Library in Katharine Street. These plans show that initially '1921' was the date to be displayed high up on the front façade, but this was subsequently altered to '1914-1918', which we see today. Handrails guard the steps down from the Godstone Road pavement. These were erected in October 1981 in memory of and gratitude for Mrs Dorothy Pattison for her devotion over many years to the interests of the residents of Kenley. She was a councillor on the Coulsdon & Purley Urban District Council and served on the Kenley Residents' Association committee for 28 years.

During the next 18 years from its opening in 1922 the hall was booked regularly by local groups which soon showed that they were keen to make use of its facilities. The Kenley Football Club and the Old Coulsdon Cricket Club both held dances. The Water Company held socials. The Women's Institute and the Women's League for Health & Beauty had regular bookings. The social committee ran whist drives and badminton was played weekly. Towards the end of 1938 and up to the outbreak of World War II the bookings were of a different nature. The Navy League and the Sea Cadets started to hold regular meetings. The Air Raid Precautions (ARP) held lectures.

Sir Charles Morgan, CBE, who donated generously to Kenley Memorial Hall, died in 1940 and was buried in St Luke's Churchyard, Whyteleafe, where his wife's memorial is to be found.

Photograph: Robert Warner

This continued until November 1940 when the War Department requisitioned the hall. Its offer of £130 per annum as compensation was accepted in March 1941 by the then vicar of Kenley, Revd Jackson. The use of the hall then became the responsibility of the War Department and as such, no detailed local records of its use survive. However it is known that it was used as an ARP post and, intriguingly, as a Troop Rehabilitation Centre. This continued until 1947 when the War Department handed back the hall to the Kenley Hall Trustees.

No essential maintenance was done during the War Department's tenure and the hall had now started to show signs of disrepair. This sorry state of affairs continued for the next 27 years during which time further deterioration occurred. The roof leaked and although structurally sound, much redecoration needed to be done. This rather derelict-looking hall then became the focus of developers and in May 1973 the Charity Commissioners posted notices that the site was to be sold. Developers submitted several plans proposing that the hall be demolished and replaced by shops and maisonettes together with a car park to the rear. A smaller Memorial Hall was to be repositioned as a two-storey building tucked away in the furthest south-west corner of the site.

At the end of 1972 an awareness of this dire situation surfaced and was being discussed amongst some Kenley residents. It was apparent that, unless urgent action was taken, Kenley was on the point of losing its hall. It is to the credit of one man who was convinced that the restoration of the hall was a worthwhile project – Frank Tasker – that it was saved. His confidence in raising public awareness and his ideas for raising the necessary funds set in motion the most remarkable turnaround in the hall's short history. The trustees convinced the Charity Commissioners that their scheme was a viable one. A management committee was set up in July 1973 to start looking at various fund-raising schemes. News bulletins, starting in January 1974, were printed and distributed

The Dilapidated Memorial Hall before restoration began in 1973

Photograph courtesy of John Bishop

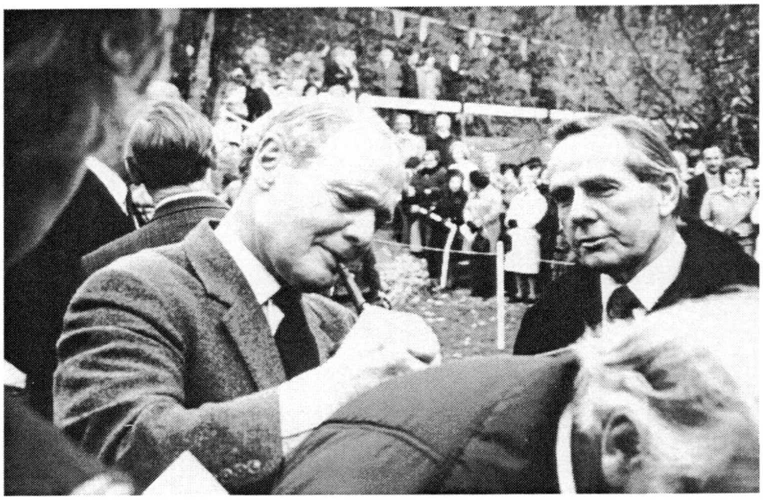

Guest of Honour Group Captain Douglas Bader signs an autograph at the rededication ceremony on 8 November 1975

Photograph courtesy of John Bishop

Many residents came to the re-opening of the Kenley Memorial Hall on 8 November 1975

The crowd watch Group Captain Douglas Bader sign autographs

Photograph courtesy of John Bishop

free of charge with the Sunday papers by the local newsagents. The restoration costs were estimated at £10,900 – of which £8,175 was promised (but not 100% confirmed) by Croydon Council's Education Department. Local fund raisers were set the target of £5,000. The enthusiasm of this one man brought together people from all walks of society. By the end of 1973 many tons of waste paper collected fetched the sum of £366. By 1974 15 tons of waste paper was moved and loaded within three hours by an army of 30-40 helpers. A total of 49 tons of paper was collected during the restoration crisis. Miss Jones made over 100 jars of marmalade which sold for £17. Socials and dances were held. Jones' Dairy, J Sainsbury, Bucklands and Scoble – the two local newsagents – Pudney & Sims, Roy Bélanger of British Rail, The Bourne Society, Kenley Police and Kenley Residents' Association were some of the many that contributed towards this very worthwhile project.

On 31 July 1974, 20,000 new tiles were delivered. They were off-loaded from Godstone Road and stacked in front of the hall by the scouts of the 7th Purley group, taking 12½ hours to complete this arduous task. Many had very sore hands at the end of the day. The re-roofing began on 1 August. Croydon Council eventually confirmed the advance of the £8,175.

The Marchioness of Anglesey agreed to become a patron. Her uncle was Sir Charles Morgan, the man who had so generously defrayed the cost of the land in 1921. An elderly lady resident in Purley contacted the management committee and requested information about the restoration. She also became a patron and it was found out later that she was Miss Olive Fremlin Squire, daughter of the first vicar of Kenley and a member of the War Memorial committee set up in 1919. Scouts and guides volunteered for all sorts of menial tasks, one of which was the digging of a 2 ft 6 in. deep trench for the new water supply pipe. By the spring of 1975 the hall had been freshly decorated and re-plastered and was ready to be officially reopened.

It was very fitting that the opening ceremony should be conducted by no less a national personality than Group Captain Douglas Bader – knighted in 1976 – who was stationed at Kenley airfield for a period before the war. The ceremony took place on Saturday, 8 November 1975, when 200 local residents gathered in the hall to witness the unveiling of the plaque. Many more listened to the proceedings outside. Representatives from the embassies whose forces operated aircraft from Kenley during the war were also present. On Sunday 9 November Revd M Vonberg held a service of remembrance in the hall, and later the Kenley Women's Institute planted a tree to commemorate the reopening. The hall was now again ready to serve the Kenley residents. As a tribute to the man who fought to save this unique building, the parish room was subsequently renamed 'The Frank Tasker Room'.

Today the hall is a well administered centre used for badminton, table tennis, Tumble Tots, Karate, stamp collecting, jumble sales, the Community Market, the Residents' Association and many other activities. It serves its people well.

SOURCES

The Pollard Machin archives

Local Studies Library Purley

Local Studies Library Croydon

Archives held by the Trustees

Notes & memoranda by F Tasker left to the Trustees

Photographs from the Trustees' archives

NOW IN OPERATION....

A New BLUE BELLE

SERVICE BETWEEN.....

CATERHAM-ON-THE-HILL *and* LONDON, VIA CROYDON

Residents of Croydon now have a BLUE BELLE SERVICE of their own. Starting from the Guards Depot, at Caterham-on-the-Hill, these Luxury Coaches depart frequently for London via Croydon, covering the entire distance in the average time of 70 mins. You are invited to travel the BLUE BELLE way—the way of comfort, safety, punctuality and economy.

DAILY SERVICES

Saturdays and Sundays included

LEAVING GUARDS DEPOT
(CATERHAM-ON-THE-HILL)

7.30 a.m., 8.30 a.m., 11 a.m., 1.30 p.m., 4 p.m., 6.45 p.m., 10 p.m.

Note.—Coaches depart from CROYDON for London approximately 20 mins. after above times.

RETURNING FROM LONDON
(Victoria Embankment—R.A.F. Memorial)

9.50 a.m., 12.20 p.m., 2.50 p.m., 5.20 p.m., 6.20 p.m., 8.15 p.m., 11.30 p.m. (Theatre Car).

Note.—Coaches arrive CROYDON approximately 35 mins. after above times.

ROUTE FOLLOWED

Guards' Depot
Asylum
Golden Lion (High St.)
Burntwood Lane
Whyteleafe Hill
Whyteleafe
Kenley Purley
CROYDON
Thornton Heath
Norbury
Streatham
Brixton,
Victoria Embnkm't
(R.A.F. Memorial)

Travel to London on the Blue Belle

BLUE BELLE MOTORS, LTD.
43-45 ACRE LANE, S.W.2
Phone: BRIXTON [illegible]

An advertisement for a Blue Belle Coach Service from London to Caterham via Kenley that commenced on 1 October 1930

Chapter 13

Travelling through the Valley

by Gordon Newall

During the reign of Elizabeth I (1564) a new form of transport, a horse-drawn coach, was introduced from the Netherlands. Less than 100 years later Captain Bailey, a retired sea captain, offered for hire the use of four 'Hackney' horse-drawn coaches. In the year of Oliver Cromwell's second term as Lord Protector (1657) 'a coach service began running three times a week between London and Chester'. Space does not permit elaboration on the 'Flying Coach' (1745 – London to Birmingham); the 'Flying Machine' a stage coach (1764 – Leicester to London in a single day); or George Pocock's 'Kite Carriage' (1827 – faster than the Bristol mail). In 1829 George Stephenson entered his steam engine 'Rocket' in a competition and was awarded first prize for the best engine, and George Shillibeer opened the first 'omnibus' service in Britain between Paddington and the Bank of England. This conveyance was a French invention, horse-drawn, and carried 22 passengers.

Riddlesdown, Kenley, appeared early on the map of stage-carriage routes using the old Roman road across the downs which formed part of one of the London to south coast alternatives. At its junction with the present Godstone Road stands *The Rose and Crown*, a former coaching inn. Stage-carriage routes proliferated across London and radiated out into the suburbs in the 19th century. The horse and carriage gradually gave way to trains.

Much later two forms of public road transport emerged – modern omnibuses, with relatively short routes and many stops/fare stages; and express coaches with longer routes and fewer stages.

Express Coaches

The chief operator in the capital was the London General Omnibus Company (LGOC) and its successors. LGOC separated the two forms, retaining buses and registering the coaches in July 1930 as Green Line Coaches Limited. Some routes were operated by former rivals, including Autocar Services and the East Surrey Traction Company.

On 29 September 1930 a Green Line service was inaugurated from Godstone Green through Kenley to Oxford Circus. East Surrey's all-weather 'Regal' stage carriages were used, extended in November to East Grinstead and still run by East Surrey – 'Reliances' leased from LGOC replaced the 'Regals'. Blue Belle Motors Ltd in competition from East Grinstead routed through Kenley, past Croydon Airport to Victoria Embankment. It was bought out by LGOC in 1932.

Pre-World War II routes were distinguished by letters. Reinstated after the war, routes were numbered, the 'H' through Kenley becoming '8' to which 700 was soon added. The 708 had arrived.

Expecting immediate and heavy air raids following the declaration of war on 3 September 1939, the Government had plans prepared to deal with the emergency. On 31 August 1939 all Green Line Coaches were called in. On 1 September they were stripped of seating and name boards and fitted with stretcher racks to serve as ambulances. The 'phoney war' ensued, and this together with the sudden loss of transport – particularly in East London and Metropolitan Essex – by the above action led to 153 coaches being reinstated.

In the post-war years East Grinstead remained the southern terminus but 708s crossed London to Hemel Hempstead. During the Green Lines Coaches' expansion period double-deckers displaced the former coaches; and driver-only RFs entered service in 1976.

When on 1 January 1970 London Country Bus Services Ltd – based at Reigate – took over, the number of persons using Green Lines was in decline, due largely it is thought to the greater use of the motor car for work and leisure journeys.

London Country inherited an ageing and mixed fleet of vehicles. The need to replace them was an opportunity to standardise the types of double- and single-deckers and to evaluate the routes, particularly their extremities, in order to maximise income. Route 708 was withdrawn on 1 April 1978. The 719 took over, and ran from Victoria to East Grinstead via Kenley.

Omnibuses

Whilst express services had been evolving, buses had long since been running to and through Kenley along the A22 Godstone Road. Commencing on 16 June 1912 the first motor bus 61 ran from Brixton to *The Whyteleafe Tavern* on Sundays only. Its *raison d'être* was to enable Londoners south of the Thames to escape from 'the smoke' to two of the commons purchased by the Corporation of the City of London – Riddlesdown and Kenley.

Almost annually numbers and destinations changed, but all listed here passed in turn through Kenley: No.61 became No.100 but from Stockwell, Sundays with Saturdays added mid-June to October 1913. On 22 March 1914 the 152 took over on Sundays to Godstone but terminated at Caterham on weekdays. Then 59A linked Caterham with Camden Town.

Tillings acquired route 59A, being based at the new (1914) LGOC's South Croydon garage from January 1916. This accounts for the TC (Tillings Croydon) garage nameplates, contrasting with the plates of other garages: TH Thornton Heath, SP Sidcup, SW Stockwell and SF Stamford Hill.

Subsequent changes are too many to detail here, (See King & Newman, 1974). Suffice to mention that twice *The Kenley Hotel* was honoured by being the southern destination of the 43 route from Muswell Hill, April 1919 and 269 from Edmonton, July 1929.

Rivalry was minimised from 1 July 1933 by the formation of the London Transport Passenger Board (LTPB). During the 1930s the 75 route through Kenley linked Caterham with Woolwich. In 1940 the 197 took over the southern section – Caterham to Norwood Junction Station.

Fuel shortage in 1942-1944 curtailed the 197 service cutting out Sunday mornings; and also caused the running of this route's buses on producer gas – actually anthracite activated by sodium carbonate – carried on a small trailer towed by the bus. No other bus routes out of Croydon garage were gas-fuelled, 197s being the last London buses to join the scheme. In 1944, whilst still gas-fuelled the 197, owing to a V1 flying bomb incident along Godstone Road near Bourne View, was diverted along Beverley Road, Valley Road and Oaks Road – Kenley Station's bridge being too steep on its eastern side for successful operation.

During the blitz Croydon lost 70 buses out of the 110 based there when South Croydon Garage was bombed. Deficiencies were temporarily made good by buses from north-west England and the eastern counties.

Conductors on the 75 route had been required to 'clock in' like factory employees at both the outward and return journey clocks at Warlingham, (now Whyteleafe South), on Godstone Road. These clocks did not survive into the driver-only bus era.

One further service passing through Kenley was the 115 terminating at *The Whyteleafe Tavern* having travelled from Thornton Heath along Purley Way and through Purley during the 1950s and 1960s, providing a service for Purley Way's factory workers.

Today only the 407, formerly run by South London Buses and presently by Arriva, is scheduled to run through Kenley. Flooding of the Bourne towards the end of 2000 caused a temporary diversion at *The Whyteleafe Tavern* up to Hamsey Green, Mitchley Avenue, Sanderstead and Downs Court Road rejoining the route at Purley

A Thomas Tilling petrol-electric bus, route 59A, in Croydon, *c.*1916, *en route* from Camden Town to Caterham via Kenley

Photograph courtesy of Croydon Local Studies Library

A 59A motor bus passing the *Kenley Hotel* *c.*1923

Postcard courtesy of Roger Packham

A London Transport ST1031 bus, route 75 out of Croydon Garage, opposite the Kenley Hotel, destination Caterham Valley. *c.*1930s

to its destination at Sutton. Complementing this, once Godstone Road became passable between Purley and *The Rose and Crown*, a shuttle service, 407A was introduced to cover that part of the route inaccessible from the Whyteleafe side.

Trains

Although two lines pass through Kenley only one serves local residents, namely the Caterham branch line.

In 1854 an Act of Parliament authorised the building of a railway from Caterham to the main line at Purley, then known as Godstone Road. The scheme was to build a railway connecting the firestone mines to the south of Caterham to the existing London to Brighton railway. Firestone was a very valuable material used for lining chimneys and furnaces and that found beneath the chalk of the North Downs was of high quality and sent all over the country. The countryside along the valley where the railway would run was almost uninhabited and it was therefore necessary to try to generate traffic by encouraging speculative building. The new residents, if they were shareholders of the company, would receive 21 years' free railway travel.

The line was built as a single track, which it was to remain until the end of the century. Stations were built at Kenley (named Coulsdon until December 1856) – the Bourne Society celebrated its historical significance by unveiling a plaque on the building on 29 August 2000 – and Warlingham (later renamed Whyteleafe South). The building of the railway was completed by September 1855 but it was not opened until 4 August 1856. This long delay was caused by disputes between the two main line railway companies, the London, Brighton & South Coast and the South Eastern. One of the difficulties was that Godstone Road station (renamed Caterham Junction in 1856 and Purley in 1888) had been closed in 1847 by the LBSCR which owned that part of the main line. The LBSCR refused to reopen the station until an injunction was obtained by the Caterham Railway Company.

The Caterham Railway Company experienced financial difficulties at an early stage of the construction, but neither LBSCR nor SER was keen to purchase the line. SER did eventually – in 1859 – become responsible following a Court ruling. Agreement had, with difficulty, been reached that LBSCR would stop four trains a day at Caterham Junction Station for the transfer of SER passengers. This was fraught with obstructions by LBSCR requiring the transferees to hold LBSCR tickets and the stopping trains were so scheduled as to leave insufficient time for the purchase of the tickets before departing for East Croydon. Also, physical restraint was used to hinder SER passengers. The quarrels between the two companies did not end until *The Times* published a leading article on the subject following readers' letters.

The first through train service from Caterham to London began in 1866. During the late 1890s the line to Caterham was doubled and a new station was opened at Whyteleafe on 1 January 1900.

In 1923 all local lines were absorbed by the Southern Railway. 'Third rail' electrification of the Caterham branch was installed by March 1928.

Steam locomotives were still to be seen after World War II, hauling the coal trains to Caterham in the morning and returning during the afternoon. In addition to the terminus, both Kenley and Whyteleafe were provided with pairs of sidings where the coal was transferred to large bunkers and the empty wagons were marshalled for the return journey. The Kenley sidings now contain Elgar, Sullivan and Purcell House.

A further siding survived after World War II, spurred from the 'down' track immediately before it entered Whyteleafe station. This line extended back to buffers at the site of the former level crossing – vehicles and pedestrians – between Old and New Barn Lanes, Kenley. A branch served the former Gas Company site occupied during the 1930s by Cohens (part of the 600 Group). With a footbridge having been built as a safe crossing for school children from Godstone Road to Kenley Primary School (opened January 1936) and the vehicle crossing having been fenced off, the siding was later extended to the Coulsdon & Purley UDC waste disposal depot, branching into two tracks, for the collection of scrap metal, some of which was 'cubed' in the manner of motor cars.

Kenley Station and Staff, *c.*1905
Postcard courtesy of Roger Packham

The 'Caterham Centenarian' that went through Kenley on 6 August 1956
Photograph courtesy of Purley Library

There was and still is a pedestrian level-crossing at Bourne View where, pre-war, several fatal accidents occurred. In spite of this and the deaths of dogs that strayed onto the live rails, no bridge was provided. The footbridge at Roke was built following a death just after the war.

The other railway is a short section of the Oxted line coming south from Sanderstead, which traverses Kenley on emerging from the Riddlesdown tunnel. Running along the western slope of the downs parallel to Godstone Road, it then crosses the former Riddlesdown Chalk Quarry by means of a viaduct. The line leaves Kenley heading for Upper Warlingham station. This section of line was opened in 1884, although Riddlesdown station was a later addition. During the construction of the Oxted line there were the usual disputes between would-be operators, irregularities relating to the purchase of land, delays, and even a riot when Belgian labour was used to assist with the construction of the Edenbridge section.

A collision occurred in Firbank's newly constructed Riddlesdown tunnel in August 1882. Two engines were completely smashed and a number of men sustained serious injuries. They were treated by Dr Diver and removed to Croydon General Hospital and Caterham Cottage Hospital. The driver of one of the engines, Burgess, was thrown completely off his engine and onto some trucks; his fireman, Lamb, was seriously scalded and Lee, the most seriously injured, was crushed.

Electrification was approved only as recently as 13 May 1985 and completed in 1987. To bridge the gap after the withdrawal of steam, diesel locomotives were used, replaced in turn by diesel-electric trains.

Although not directly related to Kenley but which would have opened access towards the east was the application by the Southern Heights Railway for the approval of a light railway to be spurred off the Oxted line south of Sanderstead with the following eight stations: Mitchley Wood, Hamsey Green, Chelsham, Westerham Hill, Cudham and Biggin Hill, Downe and Keston, and Green Street Green – and connecting with the main Dover line south of Orpington. This venture was abandoned. Today these centres of population still have no rail service.

Nationalisation of public transport was brought in during 1948, but recent privatisation of buses and trains has resulted in an ever-changing fragmentation in the process, almost a case of the wheel turning full-circle although whatever competition there is takes a somewhat different form.

Aircraft

Kenley, of the villages in this series, is unique in having its own airfield – the former Royal Air Force fighter station. Today only glider flights take place. However, immediately post-war Kenley was one of the bases used by Westminster Airways Ltd.

The company was registered on 5 June 1946, its directors being a group of Members of Parliament led by Air Commodore A V Harvey. Operations commenced at Heston with a Percival Proctor; in July a Consul was added (converted from the twin-engined Oxford military trainer and known as the Airspeed AS65) which was frequently seen landing at Kenley that autumn. Captain B A Powell was chief pilot for the company.

A fleet of 18 aircraft was built up. Croydon, where an office was opened in the terminal building, was used concurrently with Kenley, the latter housing the Maintenance Division which was later, April 1947, removed to Blackbushe.

As far as is known no scheduled flights originated at Kenley. Charter flights included passengers and freight – national and international. Two of the most outstanding of these involved overseas working. First there was the evacuation from Prague to the United Kingdom of children who had been inmates of Auschwitz concentration camp. The other was Westminster's contribution to the Berlin Airlift. At least five of its aeroplanes were involved (2 Dakotas, 3 Haltons), flying a total of 656 sorties.

A Westminster Airways Ltd Handley Page Halton (Converted Handley Page Halifax Mk.8 bomber) similar to the three that flew on the Berlin Airlift. ***c.*1949**

Photograph courtesy of Philip Jarrett

SOURCES

Bromley Reference Library, (through Biggin Hill Branch Library)

Croydon Local Studies Library

DENDY MARSHALL, C F (1936) *A History of the Southern Railway*

Fly Past Magazine Jan 2001

GAMMELL, C J (1986) *Southern Branch Lines*

JONES, D W K, *Greenline 1930-1980*

JOYCE, J (1988) *London Transport Bus Garages since 1948*

KING, J T & NEWMAN, A G (1965) *Southbound from Croydon* Omnibus Society/Bourne Society

LEONARD, A (1980) *A Chronology of Railway Stations in Greater London*

London Transport Museum, Covent Garden

MARTIN, Gavin (1990) *London Buses 1929-1939*

MERTON, A C. *British Independent Airlines since 1946*

PEARCY, Arthur (1997) *Berlin Airlift*

SKINNER, M W G, *Croydon's Railways*

SPENCE, J (1986) *The Caterham Railway* Oakwood Press

WAGSTAFF, J S (1968) *The London Country Bus*

WARREN, Ken (1979) *Fifty Years of the Greenline*

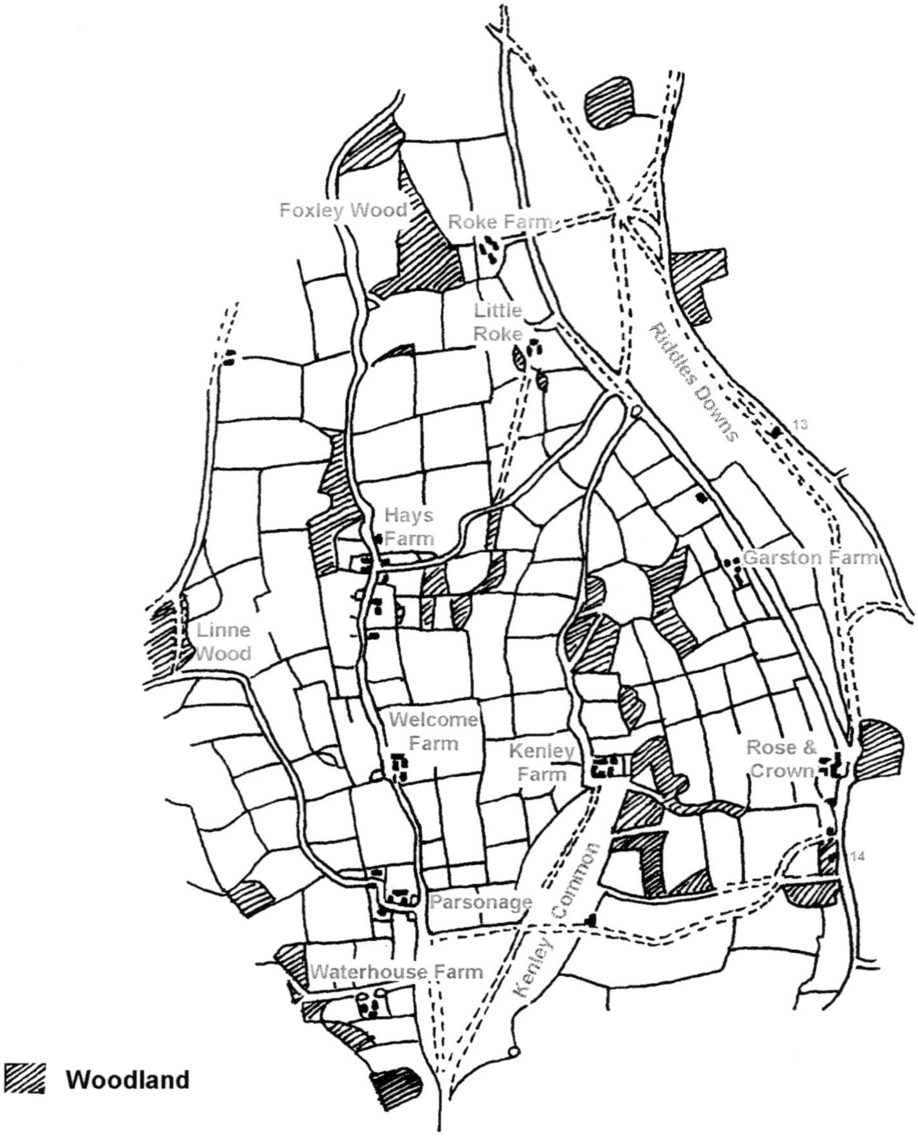

Kenley Farms

as they appeared on the Ordnance Survey surveyors' maps of 1805

Extract about 2½ inches to one mile

Chapter 14

The Farming Scene

by John Carr

Six farms were working the land of Kenley at the beginning of the 1800s, three of them situated along the Riddlesdown Valley, with a new road cut out of the hillside dividing their fields. The other farms occupied the plateau that runs from the junction of Hayes Lane and Park Road and extends to the south side of the airfield, formerly part of Kenley Common.

Water was essential, and early settlers naturally chose sites where water was readily available. The Bourne did not flow constantly through the valley, so wells had to be sunk and water was collected from cottages and farm buildings and conserved in large butts. Farmers dug saucer-shaped ponds in most strategic fields – these were about 30 ft across and excavated to a depth of eight to 10 feet to minimise evaporation, then lined with compounded clay. Cottages tended to have surface wells, many operated by a hand pump, but these would dry up in continuous hot spells. Farms had very deep wells. When some years ago 'Kenley House' was being refurbished the old farm well was discovered. Measurements were taken that showed it has a total depth of 300 ft, with 70 ft of water. George Tucker, wellsinker, born near Hungerford in the 1790s, lived in Hayes Lane and was still working into his late 60s.

Not everyone took adequate precautions in drawing water, and on Christmas Day 1853 Harriet Attlee and her three young children died of typhoid fever at Garston. A few days later her husband, William, a farm labourer, also died. It was said that the family had drunk pond water.

When Greenwoods, the London firm of surveyors, compiled a book of the residences of *Nobility, Clergy and Gentry of Surrey* in 1823, they described the little hamlet of Kenley as—

> 'Wholly agricultural; the land, on which some sheep are fed on turnips, is arable, with some woodland, let in large farms.'

While not the most flattering description, it was nevertheless accurate. The total area covered about 1500 acres, of which about 10% was common land.

Farmers generally preferred to keep sheep. There were two saleable products, meat and wool. Sheep required less labour and housing than cattle, they ate roots and corn grown on the farm and produced the best manure.

At Welcomes Farm Tom Johnson and his 11 year old son, George, both shepherds, managed a large flock. The farm covered 300 acres and they had common land rights as well. This was the 1860s and all feed preparation had always been done by hand. Winter feed involved cutting root crops like turnips to the size of chips with a knife to make them suitable for sheep to eat. Straw was also cut into short lengths, all very labour intensive. Then machinery started to transform the farm and within a decade devices for cutting, threshing and milling grain were being used. They started to grow kale as the winter feed supplement allowing the sheep to graze it.

In 1879 disaster struck due to a countrywide outbreak of diseases that continued until 1883. First foot rot, then liver fluke followed by foot and mouth disease. By the end of the century the sheep population was still 20% below the number prior to the outbreak.

Arable farming declined between 1875 and 1900 due to imports from America. Prices were so low for home-grown crops that the only justification for growing them was as a source of straw for bedding.

Cattle fared no better. At the Croydon Farmers' Club Annual Dinner in 1884 the president, R W Fuller, referring to the import of live cattle, said that the home growth of cattle had declined and only 72% was being supplied, but the Government's policy was to adhere to free trade and leave the farmers to fend for themselves. The final blow to meat production came with the introduction of chilling and refrigeration ships, allowing supplies to be transported 12,000 miles from Australia and New Zealand. Now many of the owners of large farms became importers – William and James Hall, of Kenley, became Miller & Hall Provision Merchants and others followed.

As the 19th century drew to a close great changes had taken place. The railway had created an opportunity to convert agricultural land into building land. The owners, most of whom were the large farm owners, lost no time in converting it. Most of Roke Farm had gone, with artisan housing covering the fields. Welcomes Farm was reduced to 50 acres. 'Kenley House' was offering large plots for building substantial residences.

Tenant farmers who had seen most of the traditional markets collapse were forced to convert to dairy farming. The demand for fresh milk in London – 9 million gallons in 1870 – had grown to 53 million gallons. Ayrshire or Friesian cattle were the most popular breeds as they gave a high milk yield. Other small farmers preferred the dual-purpose shorthorns which produced both good meat and milk. Soon more small dairy farms started to appear.

Such was the change in agriculture that on the eve of World War I the country was only supplying 42% of all food consumed in the UK. The Government then set up War Agricultural Committees for each county, responsible for the supply of farm labour, reporting and promoting the cause of greater food production.

In World War II the Women's Land Army and the Ministry of Food were established. Many parks and open spaces such as Betts Mead were all dedicated to the production of food. Animal feed was rationed, milk production was seen as a priority, the sheep and pig population was reduced so that feed could be directed to dairy herds.

Today farming in Kenley is part of the leisure industry.

Waterhouse Farm

Coulsdon Court Roll of 1580 makes reference to Thomas Bassett of the Water. This refers to the nearby spring. It is said that the well was never known to run dry. Even at times of severe drought, local farmers would visit to fill water carts.

Lord Folkestone, head of the Bouverie family, owned the freehold in 1688 and in 1782 the title was purchased by the Byrons of Coulsdon.

A Coulsdon widower, John Walker, with his five-year-old son, became in 1837 the tenant of the large mixed farm of 170 acres with sheep and arable crops. Later son John also worked the land and seven labourers were employed. In 1861 they moved out. Thomas King was the next tenant, in 1866, and a year later the farm – being part of the freehold and manorial domain of Coulsdon Court – was offered for auction. Nothing changed and Tom King continued until 1876.

A farmer from Nutfield, John Budgen, signed a 10 year contract with Edmund Byron in 1878, renewing it again on the 10th anniversary. He agreed a fixed rent of £150 a year for the 184 acres. A strange clause was added to the contract – stating that he could only kill rabbits between 15 January and 15 February, using no guns, no snares or traps and one labourer with only ferrets and nets. He retired in 1903.

Mr Martingell, who was born at Old Lodge Farm, recalled Waterhouse Farm. He had lived in one of the cottages for 13 years and was a friend of Bill Weedon, the then tenant. He kept cows, sheep and chickens – he grew mangolds and wheat for animal feed.

The Royal Flying Corps, using the Defence of the Realm Act, introduced by-laws restricting the use of Hayes Lane to holders of permits in 1917. Joe Hoare, a small dairy farmer, was constantly troubled by the noise of aircraft. Sydney Lucas of Golf Cottage recalls having fresh milk delivered in a churn on a pony and trap driven by Joe's daughter.

The farm was flattened when the aerodrome runway was extended and the road rerouted in 1939. A short stretch of Waterhouse Lane has survived with a new bungalow near the farm site.

Kenley Farm (later known as 'Kenley House')

Deeds show that Robert Lucas purchased the lands from Lord Viscount Folkestone in May 1750, but the farm is considerably older than that. The famous oak tree standing in front of the house is reputed to be over 800 years old.

Joseph Hodgkins, Cripplegate, London, became the next owner. It was he who had commissioned Isaac Messeder to draw up a plan of the estate in 1762 showing the size, location and usage of the 114 acres of land.

In May 1792 the estate was sold to John Pitter and others for £2940. It was Pitter who demolished the farmhouse and built 'Kenley House' after 1816, and in 1823 when Greenwoods published *The Seats & Residences of Surrey*, they make reference to his fine house.

Thomas Frederick Marson of Cumberland Terrace, Regents Park became the new owner in July 1839 in a deal which included Garston Farm near Godstone Road. He in turn sold the total estate in December 1853 to George Drew, a director of the proposed Caterham Valley Railway Company, who having built the track across much of the land he owned, sold the rest off to Francis Fuller, a land and estate agent.

The house and farmlands were auctioned on 13 July 1863. The new owner, John Young, son of a brewer and maltster from Bedale in Yorkshire, paid £9,950. He was a wealthy Australian merchant and in June 1865 he acquired the 100 acre Kenley Park Estate which included Hayes Farm buildings and land. The tithe map in 1866 records him as the owner of 250 acres of land, some in the most desirable development areas where large houses were being built. He was the instigator of many changes in Kenley.

A fine horseman and an active member of the Old Surrey Hounds, he rode two or three times a week as did his son Henry. He died aged 79 and was buried at St John's Church, Old Coulsdon on 18 February 1893. The value of the estate left to his wife and two sons Henry and John was £389,273. The family continued to live at 'Kenley House' until Henry died in 1912 and all was left to Eleanor Young, the eldest sister, of Queen Ann's Mansions, SW1. A spinster, she died in February 1933 aged 88 and also lies in St John's churchyard.

For some years the house remained empty, but was later used as a nursing home for military personnel between 1917 and 1923.

Sold at auction in November 1927, it was turned into flats until acquired by public works contractor J B Edwards & Co (Whyteleafe) in the 1940s. Sydney Lucas worked for the company from 1933 until 1940. He still remembers the owner, Job Wild, giving him a test before offering him a position. He had to tidy up the large yard near Whyteleafe Station, burn all the rubbish and stack up the materials. He started the next week in the joiners' shop with 25 other carpenters. The job was to take him to army camps all over Surrey and Hampshire.

The company built complete army and RAF bases. When fires at Whyteleafe caused by incendiary bombs burned down the part of the workshops building pontoons for the D-Day landing, work was transferred to 'Kenley House'.

After the war Mr Wild had 'Kenley House' lands used as a farm. By then he had purchased 'Cumberlands'. He had cows, pigsties for 48 beasts and a large number of horses.

In 1962 Kenley still had a herd of Friesians, with a bull in a bullpen. Milking was in the long building along Kenley Lane – since demolished and rebuilt in replica.

By 1964 'Kenley House' was part of the Cumberland Estates Ltd, purchased by Micro Consultants in May 1979 for Quantel Ltd until Gardner Merchant (now Sodexho) acquired it in April 1988. Extensive changes have taken place to the old farm buildings, but the house looks little different from when it was built.

Hayes Farm - also known as The Hayes

In 1869 a small fire started at Hayes farmhouse. Purley and Caterham brigades were called, but neither would turn out – Kenley was outside their jurisdiction and the house burnt to the ground. The house and grounds were on the east side of Hayes Lane and started at The Hayes School, following Hayes Lane down to Firs Road to the junction with Cullesden Road, a total area of 30 acres.

It was rebuilt, as 'Hayes House' in 1876 and William Mosse Robinson, a Croydon banker and linen merchant, lived there until 1891. A keen cricketer, he helped form the Kenley Cricket Club in 1880. Blanchard Montel was the next owner. He changed the name to 'The Hayes'. Little is known about him or the next two residents.

Then in July 1912 the house went up for auction. By now it had developed into a substantial gentleman's house. The sale catalogue contains photographs of the lavish interior.

When Lieutenant-Colonel Charles Hopkins sold it in 1924, it had 17 bedrooms and two lodges, stables and pasture lands. The new owners employed a pig farmer to run the estate.

Having suffered considerable damage the house was demolished after World War II. Job Wild who also owned 'Kenley House' became the new owner and used Hayes to graze the herd of 30 Ayrshires he kept. However, debris from bomb blast damage covered the meadows and a number of cows suffered 'hardware disease'. They had eaten small bits of wire with the grass, which would be fatal if they reached an animal's liver. The local veterinary surgeon would examine a cow's stomach with a metal detector, locate the objects, open up and push his hand inside, holding a potato, feel for the wires and push them into the potato. Once stitched up the animal made a full recovery.

Alan Taylor started work as a farm hand at 'Kenley House' farm in 1953, assisting Mr Freestone the ploughman. The farm had two Fordson tractors, one with solid rubber tyres, the other with metal spiked wheels for working on heavy soils. Wooden blocks like snow shoes had to be fitted each time it took the road for The Hayes. Most of the fields were sown with cereal crops at this time.

By the late 1950s, Steyning Close, Wattendon Road and Chertsey Close had been built and bungalows started to appear, along with The Hayes Primary School.

Welcomes Farm

The farm was first recorded in 1395, when Thomas Bassett passed the freehold to his son Thomas. In 1450 Thomas and John Basset were amongst those pardoned after Jack Cade's rising in Kent. In 1595 Welcomes and Lawrences referred to lands on each side of Hayes Lane.

Much development took place after 1816 under the ownership of John Keen and later his son Thomas. It was he, together with Thomas Marson owner of 'Kenley House', who covenanted to build a new road to Kenley and Welcomes, made and kept in repair by and at their equal expense. This is now Welcomes Road.

Gabriel Lovelock was farm bailiff. He managed the 300 acre mixed farm until his death aged 67 in 1858.

When in May 1862 the estate, now some 316 acres, was auctioned, it was said to have a superior homestead containing five bedrooms, a range of buildings consisting of stabling for 15 horses, fatting shed (adapted for 24 beasts), cattle sheds, pig sties, granary etc, also six cottages. These included Welcomes Cottages and the pair of

November 21st, 1896.

THE WELCOMES
Residential * Estate.

18 CHOICE BUILDING SITES,

OF FROM 1 TO 5 ACRES, ON HIGH GROUND

— ALSO —

The Residential Hunting Box,

With extensive Modern Stabling, Model Farm, and well-matured Grounds of 11 acres.

Messrs. ASHURST, MORRIS, CRISP, and Co.,
Solicitors,
17, Throgmorton Avenue,
London, E.C.

Messrs. C. and F. RUTLEY,
Surveyors and Auctioneers,
11, Dowgate Hill, E.C., and
"Birchwood," Caterham Valley, Surrey.

Left—
Sale particulars 1896

Below—
'Milking Time'

Goddard & Sons, Welcomes Farm. Early 1900s

Photograph courtesy of Croydon Local Studies Library

flint cottages at the junction of Hayes Lane and Golf Road. In addition it came with common rights. It sold for £16,000.

George Cutt, the new owner, a director of the Guildhall Agricultural Society, continued to improve the farm, planting orchards and building a 30 stall cowhouse. John Hough, a Yorkshireman, worked the farm with nine men and three boys.

In 1881 a young Scot, John McKercher, took over. He had 11 men and four boys helping him run the farm. By the mid 1890s the farm had been reduced and land was sold off for development. Uplands Road was built with large plots being sold.

Offered for auction in November 1896, the farm now known as 'The Welcomes' covered 50 acres – divided into 18 plots, along Hayes Lane and the top end of Welcomes Road.

In 1902 Edmund Woodland (known in racing circles as 'Teddy the Hendon trainer and horse dealer') became the new owner of 'The Welcomes'. For 10 years previously he held a stud farm at Bradmore Green, but it was his son, Percy Woodland, who achieved great fame. Riding his first winner aged 13, he went on to become one of the greatest jockeys ever.

In April 1921 'The Welcomes' was burnt down and the owner, Ernest Dyer, who had a friend named Eric Tombe, experienced financial difficulties. Wanted by the police on a charge of fraud, Dyer went on the run and Eric Tombe went missing. Tracked down by police in November 1922 after checking into the Old Bar Hotel in Scarborough, Dyer, thinking they were after him for the murder of Tombe, shot himself. Eric's mother had a vision and appealed to Scotland Yard to search Welcomes Farm. The body of Eric Tombe was found in a cesspool. He had been shot in the back of the skull.

This story has always been quoted as fact until, in 1985, a bundle of papers was sold at auction. It was the property of the late Dennis Wheatley, one of the most popular crime writers of the century. Among the papers was an unpublished 35,000 word memoir, together with letters and cuttings entitled *Eric Gordon Tombe*. The sensational story of Ernest Dyer, Dennis Wheatley and his very close friend Eric Gordon Tombe was published in *The Sunday Times* Magazine of 17 March 1996. The full story is covered in Chapter 21.

Major Charles William St John Rowlandson, resident of Welcomes Farm in 1932 found himself in a financially hopeless position and shot himself in a taxicab in St James' Street, London. He owed £68,000.

Returning from an assignment in Russia in the spring of 1934 a Yorkshire couple Henry and Edith Metcalfe decided to buy the now dilapidated farm. Their three boys had been at boarding school in Kenley 30 years before and the eldest son had his first riding lessons at Welcomes. They set themselves five years to restore the farm. By now three of the farmbuildings had been converted to houses. It was put on the market at the early part of World War II and Air Commander Harry Broadhurst lived there when based at Kenley Aerodrome.

Today more of the buildings have been tastefully converted into desirable homes. Houses now stand on the former tennis court and paddock.

Great Roke Farm

Following a brief mention of a tenement named 'Le Roke' in 1334, Dr Madge, local historian, traces its history from a court roll of 1359, when Adam atte Roke was living in the area cleared for farmlands opposite Riddlesdown. Early maps also refer to it as 'Standing Lodge'.

In 1762 Roke Farm as it was then known, is recorded as one of four farms belonging to Sir John Stanley, a major landowner in the area. It was let to Robert Lucas and consisted of 165 acres.

By 1841 Henry Rowland farmed the lands which then covered 600 acres and the census of 1861 shows that Stephen N Rowland, aged 35, had increased the acreage to 750 and had 17 employees.

Great Roke Farm
(Bourne flow *c.*1897)
Mr Stuchberry's Farm

Photograph courtesy of Croydon Local Studies Library

Great Roke Farm *c.*1889
This farm stood on the site of the original Junior and Infants School at Roke

Photograph courtesy of Purley Library

Said to be Little Roke Farm, *c.*1900

Photograph courtesy of Purley Library

Albert Brown held the tenancy in the 1870s of a greatly reduced farm, and was followed by Edward Stubbington. It was auctioned in July 1889. By then it only had 130 acres of farmland as much had been sold for development. Thomas Stuchberry, the last tenant, took over in 1891 and like most of the other farmers found that dairy farming was the only growth area. He gave up in 1901.

By 1905 the great barn and most of the farm buildings had been demolished and Roke School soon stood on the historic site. The farmhouse survived until 1936.

Little Roke Farm

The farmhouse or collection of houses was on the south side of Little Roke Road (known as Axell Hill by the locals in Victorian times, because Amos Axell, a builder's foreman, had a house on it). The farm shows on the 1805 Ordnance Surveyors' map and records going back to 1841 show that it was always part of Great Roke Farm and was used as labourers' houses.

Garston Farm

Garston Farm was part of Sir John Stanley's estates in 1762, when 28 acres were let to Mr Gibson. He grew six acres of oats, which suggests he had a number of horses.

Haymaking at Garston Farm *c.*1890

A view from the railway, looking over to Riddlesdown

Photograph courtesy of Dorothy Tutt

Thomas Marson obtained the freehold in 1837 just prior to purchasing 'Kenley House'. Drew purchased the Kenley estate in 1854, together with Garston farmlands as they were crucial to his railway line. When 'Kenley House' was auctioned again in 1863, John Young became the new owner of Garston.

Its position between Godstone Road and the railway line with a threat of the Bourne flooding its land, could have been the reason tenants were constantly changing.

By 1901 it became W Coates Dairy, then in 1912 it was Goddard & Sons Dairy Farmers. At about this time it was also referred to as Welcomes Farm Dairy.

Garston farmhouse was offered for sale in June 1931. It had six bedrooms and grounds of 1½ acres and the asking price was £2,650, but the owner, Mrs Leonard had no takers until January 1936, when Harry Plummer offered £2,500.

It was sold in October 1937 and demolished for residential development.

Garston Farm House
***c.*1920**

Photograph courtesy of Purley Library

Garston Hall

In the reign of Henry III in 1269 Joel de Garston and Philippa his wife had a house in the manor of Whatendone in today's Old Lodge Lane.

A distiller from Cripplegate, Joseph Hodgkins became the owner of Garston Hall in 1750. He also purchased Kenley Farm and in 1762 commissioned Isaac Messeder to produce a map of his estate. This is the oldest known document of its type that relates to Kenley.

After a succession of owners, the Byron family of Coulsdon acquired the title in 1826. 10 years later it was to become known as the home of 'The Old Surrey Fox Hounds'. Sir Edmund Antrobus of Cheam, master of the hunt, lived at the hall, as did the huntsman and stud grooms. Others like the whippers-in lived at the surrounding cottages. William Mortimer was joint and later master until 1877, then Edmund Byron took over the role until 1902.

The best known character was Tom Hills (1796-1873) who was described as 'the best huntsman who ever lived'. Born in Godstone he worked in the Godstone quarries, and at the age of 20 he was appointed huntsman to the Old Surrey, a very important post, which he held for 45 years with the exception of a short break. Tom had five sons, three of whom were huntsmen.

In 1861 Sam Hills took over from his father and held the position until 1892. By then much of the open countryside was under development, making it more and more difficult to hunt and in 1902 the pack amalgamated with the Burstow.

Unoccupied during World War I, Garston Hall soon began to show signs of neglect. In April 1932 it was sold, but the 5½ acres of land was let to a statutory tenant for £25 a year. Mr Fordham, the last tenant, stayed until April 1939, when the hall was sold to the council. Damaged during World War II, it was demolished in the 1950s.

Elm Grove Farm

The farm is an old-world cottage residence, built of brick and flint with a weather-boarded elevation and a slated roof, situated on the end of Old Lodge Lane.

It was first recorded in 1837 when the owner, William Hewitson, had a few acres of land to the rear and sides of the house. The boundary line was what is now *The Wattenden Arms* public house. He also owned the plot opposite.

In 1904, Elm Grove Cottages were built in the field between the farmhouse and pub.

Elm Grove Farm was auctioned in 1920 for £1,275 and again in 1926. Features included nine pigsties, cowstall, cartshed, fine paddock, orchard and tennis lawn, about 3 acres.

Sidney Cornwell owned the place from 1933 to the mid 1950s. He had a few pigs and Sydney Lucas recalls him driving the cows up and down Hayes Lane to a field rented just past Welcomes Farm.

Sunnycroft Farm

The land formerly part of Welcomes Farm Estate was sold in 1862. A local directory for 1917 records that Charles Ponting was living at 'The Bungalow', Golf Road. By 1931 the Shakelly family were the new owners and they changed the name to 'Sunnycroft', but by 1938 they had gone.

When the Army commandeered 'The Crest' in Hayes Lane for an aircraft defence post the owners, Mr and Mrs Turner-Smith, moved to 'Sunnycroft'. On Sunday, 18 August 1940 one of the Dornier aircraft attacking Kenley aerodrome crashed in flames onto 'Sunnycroft' killing its crew. Inside the bungalow the Turner-Smith family were saved by a wall that held firm.

In 1953 Cyril Jones acquired the property, named it 'Sunnycroft Farm' and for many years it was known for its herd of Jersey cows. Though related to Jones' Dairies he was independent and sold milk to them. The farm had about 12 acres, but the field and the cow sheds were rented from 'Kenley House'. It was sold in 1977 to the present owner. Today the farm covers 16 acres and has a small flock of thoroughbred Suffolk sheep, horses, chickens, peacocks and 'Cat's cottage'.

A few years ago a young German student called at the farm and asked if he could stand on the lawn for a while in memory of a relation, a cartoonist before the war, who died aboard the Dornier.

SOURCES

BANNERMAN, W Bruce (1910). *Parish Registers of Coulsdon.*

Caterham Valley Library

BROWN, Jonathan (1987) *Agriculture in England.* Manchester University Press

Croydon Local Studies Library

GREENWOODS (1823) *Nobility, Clergy & Gentry of Surrey*

HAINGE, F T (1962) Bourne Society *Local History Records* Vol I

LUCAS, Sydney, of Hayes Lane

PORTER, Valerie (1992) *Life Behind the Cottage Door.* Whittet Books

Purley Library

Surrey History Centre, Woking

TAYLOR, Humphrey R (1906) *The Old Surrey Foxhounds*

TAYLOR, Alan, of Wattendon Road

TRING, Les, of Welcomes Farm

WILKES, Peter (1978) *Illustrated History of Farming*

Chapter 15

Industry and Utilities

by Grahame Brooks

Since the coming of the railway in 1856, Kenley has continued to develop as a mainly residential area, firstly with several large private estates, often with a lodge for the gate keeper, and sometimes a cottage in the grounds. This was followed in the last hundred years by the sale of areas of farmland, that were then used for a growing development of houses, mostly within easy reach of the station.

In the last 40 years, many of the original mansions have been pulled down and the land used for so called executive housing. More recently, a number of older houses have been converted into nursing and residential homes, to care for the growing number of ageing senior citizens. Despite these developments, and the growing reliance on motor cars, which has increased road traffic dramatically, creating additional parking problems, Kenley has remained a relatively pleasant place to live.

In the last half of the 19th century, the main utilities – water and gas – followed in the early 1900s by electricity, developed their supplies to cope with the increasing demands from a growing population. From 1870, the works of the **Caterham & Kenley Gas Company** near *The Rose & Crown* supplied the mansions of Kenley with gas for their lighting and stoves. The gas holder seen today was completed in 1953. In 1905 the **County of London Electric Supply Company Limited** was given implicit powers to supply Kenley when the southern border of its statutory area of supply near South Wimbledon was extended southwards by the Croydon Rural Electric Lighting Order. However, the exact date when a public supply became available in Kenley remains unknown. It seems Kenley aerodrome must have had its own generators until 1928 when an agreement was made for its supply.

In more recent times some light industry has been established in Kenley, and to describe these and the various utilities a journey is proposed through the district –

Commencing on Godstone Road (A22), from the direction of Purley, even before reaching Kenley, there are the milk floats owned by **Jones' Dairy (Purley) Ltd,** based in Sunnydene Road. The Dairy moved here from Court

Mr Alfred Jones outside the Dairy in Sunnydene Road, Purley. His son, Cyril, is in the rear van

Mid 1930s

(Cyril later owned Sunnycroft Farm in Golf Road)

Photograph courtesy of the Jones family

In the 1960s the original St Winifred's building was the headquarters of the British Paper & Board Industry Research Association

Photograph courtesy of Purley Library

'Kenley House', built in the early 1800s on the site of the original Kenley Farm, is today the home of Sodexho, formerly Gardner Merchant

Photograph: Grahame Brooks

Godstone Road in the early 1950s, showing the former Kirkham's Garage site, which was taken over by Pudney & Sims in 1953

Photograph courtesy of Purley Library

Farm, Warlingham, in 1932 but has supplied homes in the area since 1928. Shortly after entering Kenley, a turning to the right is Lower Road, and at No.33 **C F Denyer & Co** commercial printers, has been in business since 1946. In the 1930s, the butcher **Gooda's,** who had a shop at No.40 Godstone Road, had an abattoir at the rear of his premises, with its entrance off Lower Road. Returning to Godstone Road, a Bourne Society plaque at No.23 marks the site of **Gardner's,** a tea gardens very popular in the early 1900s. Just opposite in a late 1950s building, now named Legion House, **Kiddicraft,** a toy manufacturer was in business until the 1980s. Further along the road, on the right hand side at No.50, stands Secom House, home of **Secom plc,** a company specialising in security systems, which moved here in the early 1990s. Just behind this area lies Roke Close and the premises of **Turner Electronics Ltd,** who no longer manufacture but are agents for cable equipment.

Returning to Godstone Road, opposite the junction with Hayes Lane, **Optical Surfaces Ltd,** an important manufacturer of optical lenses, is tucked away in the cliff face. The underground area in which the company has its workshops was used during World War II as an air-raid shelter. The company moved here from Coulsdon in 1967 and found the conditions, with almost constant temperature (+/-1°F) and freedom from vibration some 100 ft below Riddlesdown, ideal for the very specialised work it undertakes for the space programme and observatories etc. One of its clients, the European Space Agency, uses lenses made to an accuracy of a millionth of an inch for its Earth Observation Project research.

A block of flats on the right hand side of Kenley Lane, named 'St.Winifred's', is built on the site of the school of the same name, which later, in the 1960s, was the headquarters of the **British Paper & Board Industry Research Association.** At the top of the lane is 'Kenley House', built in 1820 for John Pitter (see Chapter 14). 'Kenley House' is now the home of **Sodexho,** formerly Gardner Merchant, and one of the world's leading catering and support services organisations. In the UK and Ireland the company has 53,000 employees delivering services to millions of people in business and industry, education and healthcare. Previous occupants of 'Kenley House', have included **J B Edwards & Co,** the building and engineering contractor, which used it as its Head Office during World War II, and **Micro Consultants**, which bought the estate in 1978 as an administrative headquarters for **Quantel Ltd.**

No. 139 Hayes Lane is known as 'The Old Forge Cottage'. This area was originally the site of three old cottages, adjacent to which the village **blacksmith** worked. The forge, run by Austin Killick, continued operating until the 1950s, when it became a small general store that closed in the late 1960s. Next door at No.135 is **L Parsons Ltd,** Builders & Decorators, which has been in business here since 1963, although the site had for some years previously been used as a builder's yard. Further down Hayes Lane at Station Approach and the junction with Station Road, in 1903, were the premises of **Francis Webb,** who built carriages for the local land owners, and **Peter Prior,** who ran the local slaughter house. On the land that is now occupied by **Alldays** convenience store, which opened at Easter 1999, there was a car showroom operated by **Marn,** which took over the premises from **Pudney & Sims,** who opened a garage in 1953. Prior to that it was **Kirkham's Garage**, which sold cars, petrol and ran a taxi service. The rear of the site was used for a time by the **Chemical Pipe and Vessel Company.**

In the early 1900s, the **Kenley Fire Brigade**, made up of volunteers, based its fire engine in the chalk pit opposite *The Kenley Hotel*. The horse that pulled the engine was supplied by Mr Skeel, the greengrocer, who had premises in Little Roke Road.

Along Godstone Road, past *The Kenley Hotel* and the shops in Norfolk Terrace, which were begun in the late 1800s, No.6 in 1924 was occupied by **Furs Unlimited**, a manufacturer of powder puffs. Behind the police station (see separate section) in the 1930s was the premises of **Kenley Engineering Works**, owned by W J Wallis.

On the right hand side is the site of the **Kenley Water Treatment Works,** now part of the Sutton and East Surrey Water plc operation. The first piped water was supplied by the Kenley Waterworks Company, which was incorporated in 1869. It supplied Kenley, Sanderstead, Purley, Coulsdon and Woodmansterne. The original

This worker's cottage was on the site of the original waterworks *c.*1912

In 1906 Mr Burston was at No. 1, Mr Borer at No. 2 and Mr Hall at No. 3 Waterworks Cottaages

Postcard courtesy Roger Packham

works was established at Kenley in 1881, prior to the opening of the Purley Waterworks. The Purley site was vacated in 1989, to be followed by the building of a Tesco supermarket. All the treatment and pumping of water from boreholes at Purley, Smitham and Kenley is now carried out at the Kenley site, which was modernised in 1989. The Kenley Treatment Works now supplies an average of 5 million gallons of water a day!

Further along Godstone Road, in the vicinity of Gomshall Gardens, is the original site of Garston Farm, which was the home of **Welford's Surrey Dairies Ltd** and which supplied milk in the early part of the 20th century. Until 1967 printers **J & N Moverley** operated from premises at No. 169 Godstone Road.

Continuing along Godstone Road, and in the area opposite *The Rose & Crown*, the **lime-works** was in operation from the early 1800s by James Atkins and his sons. Into the 20th century it had two limekilns, when it was owned by Frederick G Nichols. During World War II prisoners-of-war were employed in the quarry under its ownership by the Riddlesdown Lime Company. In 1953, the land was purchased by the Blue Circle Cement Company, which continued to operate the quarry until 1967, when the site became derelict. In 1975, a car-servicing centre opened on the site, which today is occupied by builders' merchants.

Several firms occupy premises in Bushey Close off Old Barn Lane on a former railway sidings area - **Postfield Systems Ltd (Datacom Cables), Maxon (Ceramic tile distributors), Maecenas Music Ltd, GSS Security Consultants, Ann Summers, GSP and Duplex Electric Tools Ltd.**

Kenley Police Station

In 1805, long before Kenley had its own police station, a Patrol Station was set up at Sanderstead, on Limpsfield Road, close to Kings Wood. From here, the Bow Street horse patrols were sent out to apprehend robbers & vagabonds in Kenley and the surrounding area! The Metropolitan Police Act of 1839 extended the Metropolitan Police District out to Kenley and environs. The following year, Kenley was placed under the jurisdiction of the 'P' or Camberwell Division (Croydon Sub-Division). In 1847, Kenley and the surrounding district were transfered to the Carshalton Sub-Division, and in 1865, it was placed under the new 'W' or Clapham Division.

On 22 May 1886 the Home Office authorised the Receiver to purchase a freehold site at Kenley for a police station for the sum of £400. The land was compulsorily purchased from William Taylor on 25 March 1887, the new station was erected and business commenced on 6 July 1896 and formed part of 'W' or Clapham Division.

The Kenley Police Station did in effect replace the Patrol Station at Sanderstead, but for some years this was used as a section house for single police constables based at Kenley.

Prior to the outbreak of World War I discussions had taken place as to the formation of a new Division with headquarters in Croydon. Talks resumed after the war and the new Division to be known as 'Z' or Croydon

Looking down on the Waterworks from Riddlesdown in the early 1900s

Postcard courtesy of Roger Packham

Looking towards Riddlesdown, this view of the original waterworks *c.*1907 shows the Church of England School on the far right of the photograph

Postcard courtesy of Roger Packham

A View of the Pumping Machinery in the Original Waterworks *c.*1910.

In 1906 the Engineer at Kenley Pumping Station was Mr E Borer

Metropolitan Police 'Z' Division, Kenley Station – Sepember 1928
Photograph courtesy of the Metropolitan Police Historical Museum

Division came into being on 28 February 1921. In 1963, the Secretary of State authorised a re-organisation of the Force designed to relate police boundaries to the new local authority boundaries created by the London Government Act, 1963. Kenley 'ZK' remained a Sectional Station of Croydon 'ZD' Sub-Division situated in the new London Borough of Croydon.

On Saturday 6 July 1996, Kenley Police Station celebrated its Centenary, with a splendid Open Day attended by many local residents, the Mayor of Croydon and the Chief Commissioner of Police.

In the year 2000, the future of Kenley Police Station had a question mark over it! In the spring of that year the dog-handling unit was moved from Kenley to Catford, and residents feared that any more reduction in staff strength would eventually lead to closure of the Station.

SOURCES

Bourne Society journals

BIRD, M, Metropolitan Police Service

Coulsdon & Purley Advertiser

Croydon Local Studies Library

Local directories

Metropolitan Police History Society

PIPE, E J (1996) *Electricity Supply in Caterham & District from 1900-1992*. The Bourne Society

Purley Reference Library

Sutton & East Surrey Water plc

Chapter 16

Early Notable Houses

by John Carr

Before 1866

Only the long-established farmhouses and cottages were recorded in the 1861 census, but by the time the revised tithe map was published five years later in 1866, the following six houses were shown – 'Cumberlands', 'Elmwood', 'Hayes Court', 'Hillside', 'Oaklands' and 'The White House'.

However, for a total picture of this period the farms section, Chapter 14, should be read as many residents were gentlemen farmers whose farmhouses were grand mansions.

'Cumberlands'

Surrounded by a large estate, the house, formerly off Kenley Lane, was built for **Richard James Joyce**, a gentleman merchant.

'Cumberlands' c.1950s
Photograph courtesy of the Wild family

He was a member of the committee that decided to build All Saints' Church and when it was finished he donated the organ. Together with John Young of 'Kenley House', he presented the church with three bells. The family moved to 'Hazeldene' in Valley Road in 1897.

William Henry Verner and his descendants occupied the house until 1922.

Local businessman **Job Longson Wild** of J B Edwards & Co carried out considerable improvements over the next 30 years. He always travelled by chauffeur-driven black Bentley, and when his son Roger became RAF squash champion, he built a court in the grounds.

Sydney Lucas recalled building a verandah along the rear of the house, using the finest teak timber.

Mr Wild was very keen on showing Hackney horses and kept 12 at Kenley House Farm which he also owned. He won the Hackney Horse Society champion cup in 1948 at White City, and the 'best horse' and many other major events. Though he loved the horses he seldom watched them perform.

The house was demolished *c*.1960 and Cumberlands Estates built the houses seen today off Kenley Lane.

'Elmwood'

Stephen Neate Rowland like his father Henry, moved from Ramsbury, Wiltshire, to take charge of Great Roke Farm. A major landowner by 1886, he built a 10-bedroomed mansion in grounds off Hayes Lane, with two staff cottages and a coach house. In 1874 he sold it to **Thomas Laughford**, a London stockbroker.

'Elmwood'
c.1897

Photograph courtesy of Croydon Local Studies Library

Mrs Jackson, widow of a Ceylon tea planter, lived at 'Elmwood' with her two adult sons for a few years, then sold the house by auction in late 1897 to **Henry Hales**.

A sugar merchant Hales and his wife were renowned for their generosity. The 10 acre grounds annually hosted the Summer Horticultural Show, always opened by the local MP. All the gardeners from the big houses would show there, and there was dancing on the lawn in the evening to the Life Guards' Blues Band.

Leslie Farrow, a director of Wiggins Teape, with his wife and three daughters lived at 'Elmwood' from 1931 to 1949.

It is said that film tycoon **J Arthur Rank** had lived, or had close connections with the house, at this time, but extensive research has failed to confirm this.

The house was divided into three flats in 1951. **Robert Simpson** lived in one. He worked in the City for Hudson Bay Company. He turned part of the grounds into a market garden. **Alan Taylor** who lived close by remembered him growing chrysanthemums commercially.

Over the next few years land was sold off to build Cedar Walk. By now the old house had deteriorated and in the 1980s it was demolished to make way for Lawford Gardens – named in honour of Councillor Lawford who lived in Abbots Lane.

'Hayes Court' – originally 'Little Roke House'

William Hall, like his older brother James, was a provisions merchant (Miller & Hall), a director of St Louis Beef Canning Co and farmer of some 150 acres. He named his new residence 'Little Roke House'. It stands at the junction of Hayes Lane and Park Road.

'The Hayes'
***c*.1924**
The grounds extended to approx. 30 acres

Photograph courtesy of Purley Library

He was a widower with three small children and he married Emily 17 years his junior in the mid-1870s.

William Hall was famous for his victorious law suit in 1877 against Edmund Byron, lord of the manor, over the encroachment of commons. Following his death in 1887, Mrs Hall moved a short distance away to 'The Oaks', Firs Road.

When **Pering Castle-Smith** bought it in 1892, he renamed the house 'Hayes Court'. He was a solicitor from St Pancras and his great enthusiasm was showing dachshund dogs.

Arthur Steward became the new owner in 1909 and lived at the address until the 1920s. Little is known about him or **Oscar Faber** who vacated the house when it was requisitioned by the RAF in 1940 and used as an officers' mess. It suffered damage to the roof when it was hit by a fire bomb.

In 1946 **Sutton Council** commandeered the building as a home for displaced children of pre-school age. The council sold off the land as building plots, then offered the house for auction in 1965.

It was converted into **Hayes Court Nursing Home** in 1966 and it has belonged to the same family ever since.

'Hillside'

The house was built in Welcomes Road for **Edward Whitford**, a stockbroker in the City. His wife Elizabeth's father was coroner in the Maria Marten – Red Barn murder case.

Only one of their 10 children married and she in turn had 10 children.

Charles Whitford, the eldest son, was appointed clerk to Coulsdon Parish Council in 1895. He was involved in the case for provision of a burial ground for Kenley. One proposed site was between Hayes Lane and Old Lodge Lane, but after objections from Reedham Orphanage because of its concerns over contamination of its water supply, the House of Commons rejected the proposal and instead St John's churchyard, Coulsdon, was extended.

In 1903 **George Turner** purchased the house and the stables and cottage that were built on the opposite side of Welcomes Road. These can still be seen today. The paddock was sold and two new houses built in the 1990s.

The house had a number of owners and has been known as **'Hillside Hotel'** and later **Assemblies of God Bible College** *(see page 96)*. Detached houses now occupy the site.

'Oaklands'

'Oaklands' was built in 1865 for **James Hall** of Miller & Hall, provision merchant and farmer. It was formally set in three acres at the bottom of Hayes Lane and Park Road. The coach house and stables, now converted into houses, are a short distance away in Oaklands Gardens. It had a two acre paddock with the ancient oak trees which gave the house and surrounding area its name.

'Oaklands'
***c.*1950s**

photograph courtesy of East Surrey Museum

1877 saw victory for his brother, William, over Edmund Byron in the encroachment upon commons. His own case had collapsed some years earlier. It must have taken its toll on his health and he died in 1882, aged 50.

The family moved to 'Sherwood Oaks' in 1882 and Mr Hall tried to let 'Oaklands' with its 10 bedrooms, advertising in *The Croydon Chronicle* a substantial house at a rent of £180 p.a.

Sir Joseph Lawrence, the new owner in 1892, was born on the Island of Zante, Greece. He was a very successful businessman in the newspaper industry, chairman of the Linotype & Machinery Company, sheriff of the City of London in 1900-1, JP, Alderman of Surrey County Council and Conservative MP for Monmouth from 1901-6. He was instrumental in the building of the Commemoration Hall, Kenley, in celebration of Queen Victoria's Diamond Jubilee.

After his death in October 1919 Lady Lawrence retired to 'The Bungalow' they had built just off Hayes Lane 10 years earlier.

Exactly what happened to 'Oaklands' is not clear. It was unoccupied for most of the 1920s, and then converted into 10 flats, but it became dilapidated. Ron Monger, a local builder, recalled carrying out general maintenance and finding that one elderly resident had ivy growing through the wall of her lounge, so trained it all round the picture rail.

'Oaklands' was eventually demolished and a number of blocks of flats, which have retained the name, were built by the local council.

'The White House' – originally 'Copenhagen House'

The house standing at the junction of Kenley Lane and Hermitage Road was originally known as 'Copenhagen House'. **James Nichols**, an East India merchant, lived there with Maria his wife and their six children until 1877.

For the next 36 years it was the home of **Cecil Price** a marine insurance broker. He decided to change the name to 'The Ivies' in 1900. He also made a career change, moving into the family business of City vintners, White & Price of Mark Lane. A fine memorial stained glass window, dedicated to Mrs Ada Louisa Price who died in 1910 can be seen in All Saints' Church.

In early 1921 'The Ivies' was bought by **Walter Robert King**, a retired solicitor, and remained in his family until the outbreak of World War II.

About 1960 another solicitor, **Humphrey Bowles**, a senior partner in Bowles & Co of Epsom, purchased the property as an investment. The house was divided into two wings, much of the land was sold off for development, and it was renamed 'The White House'.

The house was the subject of the book *Tracing the History of your House* by Peter Bushell, which gives an in depth account of the occupants over the past 140 years.

From 1867

Between 1867 and 1900 considerable improvements were made to the roads and railways and many prosperous business people found it feasible to commute to London. This created a significant demand for grand houses. The following residences give some impression of the type of people who lived in the district at that time – 'Hazelshaw', 'Kenley Park House', 'Kenmure', 'Sherwood Oaks', 'The Towers', 'Watendone Manor' and 'Woodhurst'.

Most had large domestic staffs – cooks, coachmen, maids and full-time gardeners.

'Hazelshaw' – later 'Ravens Wold', Hayes Lane

Master bookbinder **William Charles Straker** owned the house in 1874. He was born in London where he established a publishing company employing over 300 people.

Ernest, his son, a director of the company, took a great interest in the local area. He was an active member of the Croydon Microscopical & Natural History Club. He delivered a paper in 1888 on his 10 year study of birds, flowers and other wildlife in his garden. Many of his early photographs and writings on Kenley are held at Purley Reference Library.

The family sold 'Hazelshaw' to **J F Junkin** in 1915. The new owner changed the name to 'Ravens Wold' and lived there until 1939.

'Hazelshaw'
***c.*1900**
Later renamed
'Ravenswold'

Photograph courtesy of East Surrey Museum

During that period it is said that Joachim von Ribbentrop was a frequent visitor at social events held there. It is not clear if these were connected with Ribbentrop's business interests as a wine exporter or as a guest of the Anglo-German Fellowship while he was German Ambassador to Britain.

A substantial house in picturesque grounds, it was purchased by Pendale Property Company and Wallington builders Clifford Rawling Ltd developed the site in the late 1960s, building eight houses and several more bungalows in the secluded grounds.

'Kenley Park House'

Lady Lawrence moved to 'The Bungalow' in 1920 when Kenley Park Estates was formed to develop her former home 'Oaklands' and the extensive lands that surrounded the bungalow at the top of Hayes Lane. An ambitious development which proposed to build 65 houses between Hayes Lane and Old Lodge Lane was rejected and some years later the company went into voluntary liquidation, eventually being auctioned off in 1931.

'Kenley Park House' in the 1930s. The small rear building was the billiard hall of 'The Bungalow'

Photograph courtesy of Purley Library

The bungalow and grounds not part of the development was sold to **Leonard Balls**, a local veterinary surgeon in 1924. An accomplished horseman, he would canter over the common very early every morning with his young daughter, much to the annoyance of the keeper. However, Mr Balls provided the keeper with a large turkey every Christmas and their relationship blossomed.

Some years later the bungalow was demolished, but the large billiard hall which it had incorporated was preserved and became part of the new 'Kenley Park House'. The billiard hall became a very popular respite from duty for local police patrols and the servicemen who operated the searchlight mounted in Old Lodge Lane during World War II.

Prior to the war the old dairy which was built into a bank was converted into an air-raid shelter. Five bombs fell in the grounds – missing the house, but one blasted the shelter, blowing in the door and scattering those inside.

Just after the war the house was sold to **Mr Beard** who divided the five acre grounds in two and built himself a new home called 'Top Level'.

'Kenley Park House' was eventually bought by **James Gardner**, who moved in with his six daughters in 1963. It was he who sold the house for development in 1988.

'Kenmure'

The house was owned by **Alexander Donaldson**, a Scottish born Australian merchant. He probably first named the house in 1878. It stands at the junction of Park Road and Oaks Way.

Mrs Donaldson, a widow by 1885, moved away but let the eight-bedroomed house to a retired surgeon, **George Stunt MD,** who stayed for 10 years and then decided to move to 'Birchin' in Hayes Lane.

A prominent local builder, **John Edmund Saunders**, purchased the house in 1900 and spent a considerable amount on decorating each room to a very high standard. The grounds which included an orchard, covered four acres. The gardener lived in 'Kenmure Cottage' off Oaks Way.

Saunders built many notable buildings including Purley Ice Rink during the 50 years he lived at the house.

In 1955 the house was divided into two and when the cottage and lands were sold, it became neglected.

The present owners purchased the major part of the house and restored it to its former splendour. A developer, who owned the other portion and a lot of land, planned to convert his section of the house into flats and build a new house in the grounds. After long negotiations he sold out and the house is now one again.

'Sherwood Oaks', Frensham Road – was known as 'Lissadell' until 1898

The house was built for **James Hall,** the land owner and provisions merchant, who moved from 'Oaklands' in 1882 and died within the year. His widow, Mrs Annie Hall, continued to live in this large house with her two daughters and three sons.

'Sherwood Oaks'

***c.*1924**

Photograph courtesy of Purley Library

It was built of red brick with a fine stone and terracotta ornamentation, and the great feature of the house was its large turret room overlooking the grounds and across Riddlesdown. All the rooms were of generous proportions and the hall was open up to the roof.

Close by and in keeping with the house was the detached stabling with a double coach house, harness room, bays for three horses, loft over the stables, with a two bedroomed living accommodation.

In 1899 **Mr and Mrs Biddell** became the new owners. Concerned that the local parish church was some distance away, they, together with the rector of Coulsdon, Granville Dickson, and others, held a meeting at 'Sherwood Oaks' on 14 November 1899. Little Roke was being covered with houses with a considerable population increase every month. Provision for spiritual needs of the people and for the religious teaching of the children was deemed necessary. James Monger had donated a large site at Little Roke Avenue, and £600 was raised to build a mission schoolroom there – now known as St James' Mission Hall.

The house was unoccupied from 1921. Mr Welham who lived at the stables was caretaker for many years.

Auctioned unsuccessfully in May 1924 it remained unoccupied and was offered again for sale in November 1928. The house and 30 acres of land were sold in August 1931 for £14,500.

T G White, a landowner and businessman from Purley, was the last owner. The area is now developed and the land is known as Kenmore Road, Burwood Avenue and Frensham Road. The house and stables still exist.

'The Towers' – formerly 'Kilmarnock House' 1900-1908

The house was built in Park Road by the prosperous **William Hall** family, who lived in the adjoining property 'Hayes Court'. The family never lived in it but rented it to various tenants between 1874 and 1901.

A South American merchant, **Jacob Walter**, born in Barbados but resident in Brazil for many years, used the house as his London base in 1881.

Jeremiah Colman of J & J Colman, the famous mustard manufacturers, used it as a temporary home from 1886 to 1888. He then outbid a development syndicate for Gatton Park Estate by offering £82,000.

For most of the next 10 years, the house seems to have been left empty. John Johnson the gardener, acted as caretaker. **Dr Boyd**, the new owner in 1900, changed the name to 'Kilmarnock House'.

Eventually **Joseph Sawyer** bought 'Kilmarnock House' in 1906, soon changing the name back to 'The Towers'. An architect of great repute, he designed Gamage's Store in Holborn and the Cecil Hotel, Victoria Embankment, the largest hotel in Europe, when opened in 1886 boasting 800 bedrooms. It was demolished in 1931 to make way for Shell-Mex House. Sawyer was a keen horseman who rode each morning. The stables and coach house are still standing and now make an attractive house in Park Road.

During World War II the house was occupied by the Guards Armour Division as HQ. Local people recall the grounds being covered with bivouacs and tracked vehicles clattering down Hayes Lane.

The house was demolished in the early 1950s and most of the properties that occupy the site were built in 1959.

'Watendone Manor'

Carleton Fowell Tufnell purchased 10 acres of land in Hayes Lane, once the site of Hayes Farm. Three flint cottages were still standing and these he refurbished for his staff. The 12-bedroomed mansion, finished in 1900, occupied the medieval site of Watendone. It was a grand house with heavy gilded ceilings and ornamental carved mouldings to the hall with its grand staircase and to the reception rooms.

Tufnell was an ardent cricketer. He captained Kenley Cricket Club and was president from 1909 until his death in 1940. A member of the MCC and Surrey CCC committees, he played for Kent. His son also distinguished himself playing for England on the tour of South Africa in 1910.

Charles Gamage was appointed head gardener in 1924 and a year later his daughter Dorothy was born. She recalls when she was aged about eight 'I was watching Dad digging a deep bean trench when he found some human bones, then a large floor tile. I washed it in a bucket and it was beautiful with a blue and gold design. I can still picture it 70 years later.' The British Museum was called and the finds were examined and then taken away.

Donald Grant, the department store owner, became the new occupier in 1934. Dorothy became the chamber maid and remembers having to clean five bathrooms every day and act as a silver service waitress when board meetings were held at the house.

Every evening throughout the war Mr Grant and his family travelled to Croydon and slept in the basement of his store.

After the war Dorothy's fiancé became Mr Grant's chauffeur. Dorothy married Mr Penfold and Mrs Grant made all the wedding breakfast arrangements.

In 1954 Mr & Mrs Grant found the house too big for their needs and moved to Tadworth.

The house was let for some years and demolished in 1966, when the grounds were excavated by the Bourne Society – see chapter 3.

'Woodhurst'

A metal broker, **Peter Winton Spence**, originally from Liverpool, purchased three acres of land at the junction of Welcomes and Zig-zag Road and in 1882 he built 'Woodhurst'.

The lounge of 'Woodhurst' *c.*1910
Photograph courtesy of Purley Library

In 1904 Sir Charles Langbridge Morgan moved to the house from 'Cullesden' in Firs Road. He was president of the Institution of Civil Engineers. He was appointed Lieutenant-Colonel in the Royal Engineers and awarded the CBE in 1918 for his services. An expert on railways, Sir Charles was a director of numerous organisations, including the Southern Railway Company and the Bournemouth Gas & Water Company. He was also commissioner for Newhaven & Seaford Sea Defences.

His only son, William Watkins Morgan (RNVR) was killed in action at Gallipoli in July 1915. In his memory the family donated the land for Kenley Memorial Hall.

'Woodhurst' was auctioned in 1923, most of the land was sold off, and some time later the house was divided into two and remains so today.

Also of Interest

'Ferncroft', Welcomes Road

The first bomb dropped on Kenley in World War II landed on this house at the top of Welcomes Road.

'Kingswear', Little Roke Avenue

John Monger built his – and many other houses in Little Roke Avenue – in 1893. Mrs Monger named it after her favourite holiday location in Devon and 'Kingswear' has always been owned by the Monger family.

'Old Place', Uplands Road

A fine tudor-style house designed and built by **A Jeffrey**, an architect, for his own occupation around 1909. It is said that the house was named 'Old Place' after the home which Mr Jeffrey and his wife lived in *up north* and that 'Old Place' was so built because his wife refused to move unless her southern home was a replica of the one she cherished. It was later lived in by the entertainer Des O'Connor.

'The Lady Holt', Hayes Lane

A late Georgian house, known as 'Wentworth House', stood in Dorking until the 1950s, when it was dismantled and rebuilt in Hayes Lane. Much of the lavish interior is contemporary with the outside.

'Woden Law Cottage', Firs Road

Inspired by an article in *Country Life* in 1919 headed *Building in Chalk*, Robert Mennel, assisted by a carpenter from Purley, Mr Poynter, built a bungalow in the grounds of his house in Firs Road with 18 ins. thick walls of chalk mixed with straw. The basic materials were found on his own land and the house is still lived in today.

SOURCES

BUSHELL, Peter (1989) *Tracing the History of your House*, Pavilion Books, reprinted in *LHR* **32:** 8-17 (1993)

BOURNE SOCIETY *Local History Records* **6** (1962)

Caterham Valley Library

Croydon Local Studies Library

East Surrey Museum

LUCAS, Sydney, of Hayes Lane

PENFOLD, Mrs Dorothy, of Old Coulsdon

Public Record Office, Kew

Purley Library

Surrey History Centre, Woking

TAYLOR, Alan, of Wattendon Road

Chapter 17

Schooling in Kenley

by Jane Ruffle

The first school built was **Riddlesdown National School** on the corner of Godstone Road and Downs Court Road in 1871 shared by children from Purley and Kenley (See *Village Histories 1: Purley* pp. 84/5)

This was followed by **Kenley Church of England Voluntary Primary Junior, Mixed and Infants',** Godstone Road opposite the Waterworks, which opened in 1885 as an all-age National School. 82 children enrolled on the first morning and another six in the afternoon. By the end of the first week 97 children were on the register. On 2 November 1926 the seniors moved to Roke Central School and the school became the Kenley Church of England School.

The original National School in Downs Court Road, Purley, in 1871

The School served both Purley and Kenley prior to the opening of Kenley Church of England School in 1885

In All Saints' Church there is a brass tablet to the memory of Walter Smith who died on 6 December 1915 having been Headmaster of the school for over 30 years. Walter Smith made his first entry in the school log book in April 1885 and over the years kept a fascinating record of every aspect of school life and occasionally on life outside the school. Of the many entries, the following are picked at random—

> 17 July 1885. Mumps have broken out and several children with symptoms of them have been sent home. All the Jenners are absent, Diphtheria having broken out in their home. The pupil teacher was absent on Wednesday, being too ill to attend.

Kenley Church of England School

Class B *c.*1932

The school was opposite the Waterworks

Roke School, Purley Vale, from the railway looking east, *c.*1910

Postcard courtesy of Roger Packham

A Road Safety demonstration at Roke School in 1956

Photograph courtesy of Purley Library

Purley County Secondary School, seen from Godstone Road/Lower Road

Built 1914

Postcard courtesy of Roger Packham

SCHOOLING IN KENLEY

> 20 April 1891. The children seemed very pleased school is opened again and have commenced work in earnest. A good many seem weak after their long illness. Scarcely a child in the parish seems to have escaped the complaint [measles on this occasion], and there have been several deaths through it.

> 8 Dec 1891 A violent storm all the morning, the worst, I think we have had this winter. It commenced at 8.15 just the time a great many of the children would ordinarily be starting for school. The few who put in an appearance were drenched. School was not opened, and most of the girls who were present had to be sent into the infants' room to take off their frocks, boots and stockings to dry them.

Many years later Pamela Kimberley (née Bell) writes that she attended the school at the age of 5 in 1932. Quite a few children from the new estate on Valley Road went there – trekking down Bourne View and across the level crossing four times a day as all the children went home 'for dinner'. Miss Francis was the headmistress, there were three other teachers and each Friday morning the Deaconess from All Saints' Church went to teach the whole school the Catechism. Every few weeks progress was tested by the vicar, Mr Harré.

The building was Victorian with few facilities and there was a small playground with *very open air* toilets on the far side of it. The annual sports day took place on one of the lime beds at the Waterworks. Each Ascension Day the whole school trooped up the hill to Kenley Church for a service and then had the exceptional treat of the remainder of the day off. There was also quite a celebration each Empire Day, and a party in the playground for King George V's Silver Jubilee in 1935.

At the age of 11 everyone moved on to Roke or one of the other senior schools, although Pamela Kimberley says she believed that when the school was first opened pupils completed their schooling at Kenley. In about 1936 a new school was built in New Barn Lane to serve all the new housing on that side of the railway. Many children transferred there, preferring a new building and playing fields.

At the outbreak of World War II pupils were moved to the school in New Barn Lane as they had no air-raid shelter. The school closed on 20 December 1940.

Roke County Secondary School was at one time housed in the school built for Purley County School for Boys in 1914 on the site of the Commemoration Hall at the bottom of St James' Road. At various times these buildings have also housed Purley County School for Girls, Whyteleafe County School for Girls, briefly during World War II Croydon High School for Girls, an annex to Riddlesdown High and Shaftesbury Independent School. Recently **Oakwood School** and **Treetops Nursery School** have been in occupation.

Roke County Primary Junior Mixed and Infants' School (originally called Coulsdon Roke Infants' School) was built between 1907 and 1908 on two acres of land in Purley Vale belonging to Great Roke Farm at a cost of £1050 per acre which was considered an exorbitant price.

In 1926 it was divided into Infants/Juniors and Central. The headmaster in the early 1930s was Thomas Holland. He was a well-known writer of school stories, the best known being *Bully Austin* indicating that bullying is not a modern phenomenon. In 1939 the Central School moved to the building vacated by Purley County School for Girls at the corner of Godstone Road and St James' Road. It remained there for 30 years when it amalgamated with the Junior School and returned to its original site.

In the 1950s the head was R C Loveday and a former pupil remembers playing cricket in the rear playground and that there were allotments near the railway where pupils grew vegetables. At the time disciplinarian Miss Brown was in charge of the infants. Mr Gatenby was the genial caretaker.

In the 1990s a new building for the school was constructed on the site of the former Kenley Bowling and Tennis Clubs, taking in part of the school's former playing field. The siting of the school was the subject of much controversy, viz; the demolition of garages, the felling of mature and 'preserved' trees and, in particular, the potential danger of the access road. It is interesting to note that the playing field was used by St Winifred's as a football pitch, certainly before World War I and for some time after. The new school opened late in September 1994, but it was not officially opened until 9 November 1994 by Tony Hart, the artist well known for his children's programmes on TV. Kenley Cricket Club benefited as it acquired a new Clubhouse having lost its previous one to the demands of the access road. The old school has been turned into homes by a housing association and the Edwardian façade has been retained. The former infants' school was demolished and has been replaced by new houses.

Kenley County Primary Junior, Mixed and Infants, New Barn Lane opened in January 1936 and, like the new Roke School, there was much controversy over the siting, the main disagreement being on which side of the railway line it should be built. Before 1936 children from the new estates mostly attended the Infants' School in Maple Road, Whyteleafe. As this was before the widespread use of the motor car this entailed long walks for the children - and their mothers - probably four times a day as no food was provided. The first Headmaster of the new school was H E L Green - who retired in August 1953 after 17½ years – and he was supported by four teachers. 112 children enrolled who were divided into two infants' classes and two junior classes. The school remained there during the war and in 1948 boasted 402 pupils. However it does not now cater for so many children, mainly because of the number of new schools in the district.

Kenley Primary School, New Barn Lane, taken soon after it opened in 1936

Postcard courtesy of Roger Packham

Kenley Primary School Christmas Play 1937

Photograph courtesy of Joyce Breach

St Winifred's School, Welcomes Road was founded in 1882 as a preparatory school for the public schools and the Royal Navy and closed during World War II. According to the 1914 prospectus the chief aim of the school was 'to educate not merely to teach the boys – to make them manly, reliable and industrious'. It was obviously a very strict regime. Exeats were not allowed because 'the risk of infection in railway carriages was a serious one for a school of young boys' and parents were requested not to send hampers unless they only contained fruit. Oatmeal porridge was served every day for breakfast, together with meat or fish. Revd Sidney I W Shilcock was head master and chaplain for many years, and the famous cricketer, J N Crawford, was a pupil.

The Swimming Pool at St Winifred's School *c.*1914

Photographs courtesy of Purley Library

A Riding Class outside the entrance to St Winifred's School *c.*1914

There were two stained glass panels in the chapel one perhaps designed by Burne-Jones and the other by Henry Dearle, Art Director of William Morris. In 1958 the school buildings became the laboratories of The British Paper and Board Industries Research Association and the chapel was converted into a house for the caretaker. The stained glass panels were sold to a dealer in Portobello Road, since when they have disappeared. A block of flats bearing the same name has been built on part of the site – the rest of the grounds being used for private housing.

The Hayes County Primary School was officially opened by the wife of the then MP for East Surrey, Charles Doughty, on 7 November 1958. This school was built to cater for the post-World War II development of Kenley and the first Chairman of Governors was Mrs Dorothy Pattison, a local Councillor. There was much discussion over the school badge. Finally one was designed based on the nearby Saxon settlement of Watendone.

Opening of Hayes School in November 1958 by Mrs Doughty, wife of Charles Doughty, M.P. for East Surrey

Photograph courtesy of Purley Library

The first head was Miss M M Tedder assisted by five members of staff, who oversaw its rapid growth in pupil numbers from the intended 280 to over 500. Miss Tedder used to teach the 'Eleven-plus' group – two dozen of the brighter children from the top class – in her office where they sat crowded on the floor with their 'Progress Papers' on their laps. With her hands twisted with arthritis, stiff gait and cracked voice, many pupils suspected her of being a witch!

Wattenden Primary School in Old Lodge Lane opened on 9 January 1968, its first headmaster being George Thomas. The school never achieved its capacity and in 1992 with only 83 pupils and 100 vacancies, and costing more than £300 more per place than the next most expensive of Croydon's schools, it was threatened with closure. Parents came up with their own solution and petitioned the local authority to open a nursery class to fill a gap sadly lacking in the area, which would also serve to fill the school. They were successful and the report on the official inspection of the school in November 1996 states that 'The nursery is the strength of the school'. The finding of the report was that 'the school was providing sound value for money'. ***Right: Wattenden Primary School Badge (Courtesy of Fookes Family)***

SCHOOLING IN KENLEY

The latest 'school' to have opened in the area (January 2000) is the **Little Angels Play Station** catering for both pre-school and older children after school. It is housed in the former stationmaster's house which was constructed in 1856.

These are the major schools in the district. Others that need to be recorded are—

- **Purley Preparatory School** which in the 1917 local directory is shown as being based at *'Hillview*, Godstone Road, Kenley – the first house after St James' Road'. Later shown as *'Avondale*, 19 Godstone Road, Kenley next to Gardners Hotel', Headmaster Revd Fred Bloxam. The last trace of it is in 1930 when the headmaster was still the Revd Fred Bloxam.
- In the 1920s a nameless informal school was run in 'Colescroft' in Firs Road for approximately six pupils per class up to age 11. On 7 July 1923 it suffered severe damage when a plane flying to RAF Kenley crashed on it – fortunately on a Saturday. Both occupants of the plane were killed. The children, however, were soon back at school.
- At Kenley House there was another informal school run at the end of the 19th century for children of the family and estate workers.
- **The Assemblies of God Bible College** existed from 1957-1965 at 4 Kenley Lane, the former *Hillside Hotel*, the principal living at 'The Copse', Welcomes Road.

SOURCES

The Schools and Local residents

HUMPHREYS, E P (1995 & 1997) Bourne Society *Local History Records* 34 & 36

Local directories

Purley Library

Village Histories: 1 – Purley (1996) Bourne Society

RICKETT, SMITH & CO.,
(LIMITED),
Coal & Coke Merchants,
CATERHAM RAILWAY STATION.

Orders also received at
EAST CROYDON STATION.

APPLICATIONS FOR PRICE LISTS INVITED.

H. J. JACKMAN
FAMILY + BUTCHER,
Aberdeen House,
HIGH ROAD, KENLEY.

Prime Pickled Tongues & Corned Beef,
Dairy Fed Pork, Wether Mutton.
ALL MEAT GUARANTEED HOME KILLED.

Whyteleafe Bakery
A. MEAD
(LATE RUSSELL)
FAMILY BAKER.
Vienna and Pure Home-made Bread.
BROWN, WHOLE MEAL AND HOVIS BREAD.
All kinds of Cakes fresh Daily.
CARTS DELIVER IN KENLEY DAILY.

SURREY DAIRY AND GARSTONE FARM,
KENLEY.

WELFORD'S
SURREY DAIRIES
(LIMITED)

Families Supplied with Rich New Milk, Fresh & Dorset Butter, Thick Cream, and New Laid Eggs Twice Daily.
Special Milk from Alderney Cows
Supplied for Infants and Invalids,
in Sealed Glass Bottles

'PHONE 760 PURLEY.

R. FRENCH,
Fishmonger, Poulterer,
Licensed Dealer in Game,
HIGH ST., KENLEY.

Families Waited on Daily. A Trial Solicited.
Lunch Orders Promptly Despatched.

A. WICKINGS,
Family Grocer . .
AND
Provision Merchant,
HIGH STREET, KENLEY.

HIGH-CLASS GOODS IN ALL DEPARTMENTS

Personal Supervision

Local trade advertisements in All Saints' Church Parish Magazine
January 1915

Chapter 18

Over 100 Years of Shopping

by Jane Ruffle

Before the advent of the railway in 1856 there was little need for shops as the population was very small and the farms which covered most of the area were largely self-supporting as far as food was concerned. In 1851 Waddington village had a bakery-cum-alehouse, but the nearest shops/market for goods that could not be grown or made was Croydon. The fourth quarter of the 19th century saw development of the area and it was then that commerce began.

Local directories provide information on the earliest shops in the district. The first shops on record date from 1872 and consisted of a butcher's, a grocer's and a haberdasher's. *The Kenley Hotel* is also listed. These were all in the terrace formerly known as High Street or Norfolk Terrace.

There are now three terraces of shops in Godstone Road where most of the shops are situated—

The terraces now numbered as Godstone Road were originally named – starting from the Purley end of the area – Kenley Parade, Excelsior Terrace and High Street (incorporating Norfolk Terrace). During the 20th century these shops served the daily needs of the local residents. There were few exceptions to the grocer's, greengrocer's, butcher's, tobacconist's and chemist's shops but in 1904 Mrs Carter, collar dresser, is listed. Presumably she stiffened the white collars worn by the commuters of the day to the City. Typically a gentleman wore at least one freshly starched detachable shirt collar each day and a box of them was once a week taken down to the laundry or in this case to the collar dresser.

H J Jackman's shop in Norfolk Terrace in 1906
The business continues in the same premises today

There was a fourth terrace at the end of Garston Gardens consisting of four shops housing a greengrocer (Mr Smith), a tobacconist/newsagent (Mr Williams), a hardware shop (Mrs Pearce) and a hairdresser (Kathleen). However, the terrace, together with six houses, was destroyed by enemy action in World War II and was not rebuilt. The site is now occupied by private housing.

The transport at the turn of the century for the man in the street was the bicycle and his needs were served by Mr Morris at No.8 Godstone Road from 1899. There was a cycle shop on the site until towards the end of the 20th century. The 'gentry' had their carriages built for them by Mr Webb in a workshop behind *The Kenley Hotel*

Norfolk Terrace c.1928 – Note the bus outside *The Kenley Hotel*
Postcard courtesy of Roger Packham

The Same view in the 1950s
Postcard courtesy of Roger Packham

next door to the slaughterhouse. This latter became the workshop for the garages situated on the site now occupied by Alldays supermarket.

The shop with the longest unchanged history is H J Jackman's, butchers, at No.66 Godstone Road (formerly No.4 High Street). It is first recorded in 1891 under the name of James Haggis – a not inappropriate name for a butcher! In 1893 he is shown as owning a fishmonger's shop at No.2 High Street. The butcher's shop was taken over by H J Jackman at the beginning of the century – probably 1909.

The Village Stores at Nos.86/88 Godstone Road started life in 1902 as Wickings Stores, later to become a branch of Walton Hassell & Port. The Village Stores was taken over by Mr Michael Shah in the 1970s. Thus it has served the residents of Kenley for nearly one hundred years.

Lloyds Bank opened a sub-branch next door to Wickings Stores in 1905. When it closed soon after World War II, it became a doctor's surgery and was subsequently converted into a private residence *c*.1991.

No.64 Godstone Road (formerly No.2 High Street) has seen changes. It started life as a fishmonger's, for many years was a confectioner's and is now an Italian restaurant.

In the former Excelsior Terrace (No.34 Godstone Road) Walter Bettles opened a shoe shop/shoe repairer's in the early 1930s. He was kept busy during the war repairing the boots of Canadian soldiers stationed around the area. When he died in 1961, his son John continued to run the business at Kenley until the 1980s when the shop closed. However, John transferred to the Caterham branch, which he still runs despite being over 70.

It is indicative of the times in which we live that, until the latter part of the 20th century, each of the areas had a shoe repairer – now there is none.

There are (and were many more) shops scattered around the area:

There are two shops on the east side of Godstone Road between Bourne View and *The Rose & Crown* both serving the motor industry. *Motos* was originally The General Stores which from 1941-1953 was run by the Cousins family Harry, Emma and their three children. Harry was also the local chimney sweep. Vegetables were always displayed outside the store.

The four shops in Station Approach have suffered many changes. The first recorded is the Post Office in 1889 which had previously operated from the railway station. For many years there was a succession of dairies. There was also a shoemender's shop, the last incumbent being Mr Poate. The other shops have in turn been a chemist's, a confectioner's, a doctor's surgery, a grocer's, more recently an Indian restaurant and now a Chinese takeaway. In the late 1950s one of the shops was *Minim* – selling records

The Kenley Forge in Hayes Lane run by Austin Killick was necessarily much in demand at the end of the 19th and beginning of the 20th centuries, not only by the farmers but also by the racing stables at Welcomes Farm, but as demand tailed off it became the premises of builders L Parsons Ltd.

Also in Hayes Lane was a general store called the Old Forge which existed for about 30 years until the late 1960s. Because of its proximity to The Hayes School it acted as a tuck shop for the pupils. It has now become a private residence.

A small terrace of shops was built opposite *The Wattenden Arms* in the 1930s but it came to nothing and it was very soon converted into private residences.

Before moving to Roke, mention must be made of *The Oak Cabin* on the site of the lamp room of the railway station. The cabin was originally the estate office for the newly-built houses in the late 1920s and early 1930s. It then became a sweet-shop and tobacconist's presided over by Mrs White and her Pekingese. It later became a mini-supermarket for a short while and has now reverted to its original use as an estate agent's office.

No.3 Norfolk Terrace in the 1920s

Mrs Shaw stands in the doorway. Her husband, Mr T Shaw, published many local postcards

Postcard courtesy of Roger Packham

The Roke area has had a variety of shops in Kenley Parade over the last hundred years – confectioner's, greengrocer's, general stores – but none has stood the test of time. There was a café and ice-cream parlour ('Moravonside') for many years on the corner of Godstone Road and Little Roke Road but that disappeared. The longest-lived was Grimes the baker's which is first heard of in 1882, the last owner being John Isles. Bread was sold from a shop in front of the bakery and often the bread handed over the counter came straight out of the oven so was almost too hot to handle. The wonderful smells emanating from the brick-oven lasted until the 1970s.

A J Pitman's Grocer's Shop in Little Roke Road, c.1950s

Photograph courtesy of John Bishop

OVER 100 YEARS OF SHOPPING

Although there were plenty of shops providing for the day to day needs of the residents, there were also tradesmen calling using horses and carts until the motor car became popular – greengrocers, milkmen, bakers and coalmen. Balch Bros (Dairymen) used a horse-driven milk float until after World War II.

The only shop remaining in Roke, apart from those in Kenley Parade, is the art gallery and picture framer in Lower Road.

Station Approach in June 1989. Today all the premises are occupied by different businesses

Photograph: Grahame Brooks

Mr John Poate who was born at 2 Station Approach in October 1927 remembers the Kenley shops of more than 60 years ago—

Somehow, Hayes Lane has managed to creep down to join Godstone Road. When I was a boy it knew its place and stayed the other side of the bridge. From the bridge to Godstone Road was Station Approach and consisted of two properties, No.1 a branch of the United Dairies, manageress Mrs Eagles and No.2, A J Poate boot & shoe repairer, my father.

Kenley is a village made up of parts, one of these parts was the village, and Station Approach was part of it. I was one of the village kids.

Coming from Purley the first part of Kenley is Little Roke. We always dropped the 'little' and it became The Roke. The Roke was a place one went down to. You went along Godstone Road, round the station or Valley Road, up the hill but down The Roke. The Roke was always thought of as a separate entity, a hamlet on its own, hardly part of Kenley at all and certainly not part of The Village. Kenley Village started with Heaton (Yateley) House, now gone, which fronted onto Godstone Road on the corner of the Hayes Lane turning. This was Dr Smith's surgery. On the other corner but still fronting onto Godstone Road was Kirkham's Garage and showrooms. This was quite modern and up-market. They also ran a chauffeur hire car and taxi service. The next building was *The Kenley Hotel* run, in my early childhood, by a family called West. Paul, the son was about my age and a friend. I used to play with him in the pub yard. They kept chickens, I remember. Later the pub was run by Bill White, whose dog bit me. Next to the pub was my favourite shop called The White House, run by Mr Shehan, his wife and his wife's sister. This was, of course, a sweet shop. I might say THE sweet shop. It was, in my opinion, by far the best and who would know better than a child. Mr Shehan was a very short little man but very nice. He had a practice of ringing all the silver coins on the counter to make sure they were not

A traffic accident in Station Approach in 1935 damaged the premises of A J Poate – shoe repairers

Photograph courtesy of Mrs Poate

duds. Some people said he was a Jew boy. You were allowed to say things like that in those days. I don't know if he was Jewish or not but he was always very nice to me and I saw him most days. I had to get dad's fags there and dad was a heavy smoker.

I'm not going to pretend I can remember the sequence of all the shops but next was Jackman's, the butcher's, manager Mr Burrill, who was every inch the butcher – big, round and rosy, striped apron and round straw hat. They had an errand boy who rode a trade bike nearly as big as himself, Bill Lovelace, who lived down The Roke. Bill was always whistling – it was expected of errand boys in those days. There was one other member of staff, a butcher cum van driver. I can't recall his name but can't forget the van. It was a Trojan chain drive and was deafening at one hundred yards.

The following shops included a chemist 'nice smell' (proprietor Mr Lawrence), where I bought Bismuth tablets. Dad was a martyr to his indigestion. The drapers, run by Mrs Greenstreet, a nice little lady, the ladies' gossip shop of the Village. Dad's shop was the men's gossip shop. Next, I think was Skeel's the greengrocer. I don't remember much about the Skeels. About the middle of the parade was Dilgers, high-class tobacconist's, newsagent's, stationer's, paperback lending library and toy shop and, in season, fireworks. The Dilgers were naturalised Germans. They were oldish compared to most of the other shop people and had a mature daughter living at home who quite late in life married a gentleman also with German antecedents who, during the war, became an officer in the local Home Guard. Next, I think, was the fishmonger's. My earliest memory is of the French Bros, managed by Mr Head.

We were a family that ate a lot of fish. Dad in particular was very fond of such things as kippers, bloaters, mackerel, herring and shell fish – shrimps and prawns. I got to know Mr Head quite well – he always greeted kids by name. 'Hello John, how are you and how is Jean?'. Why he was interested in my sister Jean I could not make out but he always asked. We had a cat named Tiger who was even keener on fish than dad. I used to get cod's head for him. Mum boiled them and took the bone out. It stank the kitchen out and old Tiger went balmy until he got a feed. The diet suited him and he grew into a fine cat. He was a great hunter and during the war Kirkham's Garage, or Guntrips as it had become, was used as a food store for bulk food such as rice, lentils, dried peas and food such as that. It became infested with rats and old Tiger left a rat on our back door step most mornings, sometimes two. He never chewed them up, he preferred fish.

OVER 100 YEARS OF SHOPPING

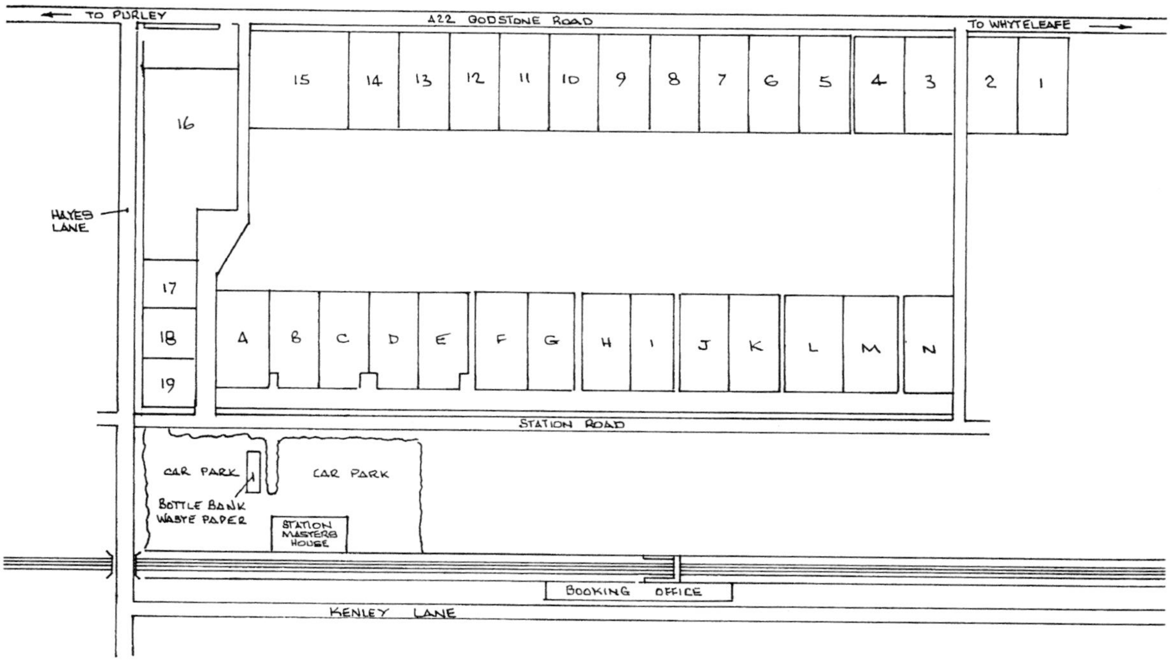

List of shops in January 2001

***The Kenley Hotel* and the parade of shops along Godstone Road – not to scale – by John Bishop**

Commercial sites

1. Private residence
2. Mr Michael Shah, Minimarket
3. Post Office
4. Studio 2, hairdresser
5. Westbourne, florist
6. Thresher's wine stores

7/8. Zina's, chemist

9. Buckland's, newsagent
10. Items, cake decorations & accessories

11/12. The Comodor, restaurant

13. H J Jackman, butcher's
14. Santini's, restaurant
15. *The Kenley Hotel*
16. Alldays, Minimarket
17. Surrey Wide, house agents
18. Chinese take-away
19. Bairstow Eves, house agents

Private houses

A-E Built 1998

F-N Original houses built *c.*1900

The other thing I associate with the fishmonger's was the great blocks of ice that were delivered at least once a week. The van man carried them in on his shoulder with a cloth wrapped round them. His hands had a pinkie-mauve look about them like Mr Head's, as if they had been playing snowballs.

Later, about 1936-37, the fish shop changed hands and the new people were the Hudsons. They came from Keswick and spoke a foreign language. When Colin and Elaine, the children, first started to play with us, we had a job to understand them but they soon learned to speak 'proper' like the rest of the village kids. The remaining shops in the parade before coming to the post office were a rather sad bunch. One was a sort of tea shop with tables and chairs. They sold teas and scones, that sort of thing. They did most of their trade on Saturday, Sundays and Bank Holidays. They also sold sweets, ices, cold drinks and, I seem to remember, souvenirs such as coloured postcards, little bits of brass and china. The name was Watkins and there was a boy, Teddy, who seemed to have access to unlimited sweets which gave him a certain popularity but he had two left feet and a finger and four thumbs on each hand and was hopeless at ball games of any sort. The tea shop closed long before the war and the premises were empty for some time. It later became a ladies' hairdresser's. The last shop but one before the post office was Mr Harrington's office. He was the local builder and carried out a lot of small building work such as painting and decorating in the area, mostly at the big houses up the hill. The shop had a partitioned section in it in which sat a middle aged lady, presumably a bookkeeper, sometimes with Mr Harrington, although he was mostly out in his car checking on jobs in hand. It wasn't really a shop at all although it did have things in the windows like hand basins, sinks and WCs, sets of taps and wallpaper pattern books and paint colour cards. It was quite interesting but as the display was seldom changed, it didn't warrant too much of a boy's attention. The shop next to the post office also had a bit of a chequered career and was empty for long stretches of time. I remember at one time it was an electrical shop that used to recharge accumulator batteries and I seem to remember it as a shop selling baby clothes and as a bike shop run by K&K, whoever they were and also a ladies' hairdresser's.

Finally, the post office which at the time of which I write was also a sorting office and had five or six postmen starting their walks from it. Next came Wickings Store and Lloyds Bank. The bank was something of a nonentity. I can't remember ever seeing anyone go into it although, of course, they must have. It was there quite a long time before it closed to become the new doctor's surgery.

Wickings store was rather special. I remember most vividly the smell, smoked bacon hanging from rails, hams on the bone on china stands for carving, butter being knocked up into shape and size, big pungent cheeses on marble shelves at the back, open boxes of a dozen or more different biscuits, sugar, coffee, dried cereals of all sorts, pepper, curry powder, nutmeg, spices of all kinds dispensed and weighed up from open containers of one sort or another, all filling the air with a pungent bouquet superimposed on the scent of pine wood sawdust on a bare wooden floor, yummy! One of the many purchases I was sent to get from Wickings was paraffin. This was kept in a big tank in the back yard, and usually you had to go and find the store man to serve you and then go back into the shop to pay at the cash desk. The only other shops I remember having a cash desk were the fishmonger and Jackman's, the butcher's.

SOURCES

Local directories

Local memories

John Poate

Chapter 19

Play Up, Kenley! – Sport and Leisure

by Roger Packham

GARDNER'S PLEASURE RESORT

Any survey of leisure in Kenley cannot over-emphasise the impact of Gardner's Pleasure Resort. It was sometimes known as Riddlesdown Tea Gardens or the Temperance Hotel and the main house survives complete with Bourne Society blue plaque, at 23 Godstone Road, almost opposite the entrance to Little Roke Road.

The entrance to Gardner's Tea Pavilion and Pleasure Grounds in Godstone Road
***c.*1913**

Photograph courtesy of Purley Library

William Gardner (see Chapter 23) was the energetic owner of the resort, having purchased the land, which extended onto Riddlesdown, from Frank Wigsell Arkwright of Purley Bury on 19 November 1892. However, he was not the first man to see the potential of a local resort. In a directory for 1876, William Edgington is listed at the Strawberry Tea Gardens, Godstone Road, Kenley and six years later he was advertising in *The Croydon Advertiser*—

> SWINGS FOR SALE: one set to carry 18, and one single –
>
> Apply W Edgington, Tea Gardens, Riddlesdown.

Perhaps the sale indicated the demise of the venture but William Gardner, although 53 years old when he purchased the land, made such a success of his pleasure gardens, that when he died in 1930 aged 91 he had run the resort for 38 years and it continued until 1934.

The existing house was the Gardner's living accommodation and the adjacent pavilions gave a frontage of 320 feet along Godstone Road. Admission was free but visitors could spend money on luncheons, dinners and teas at popular prices. Thousands of people, especially Londoners, would visit Gardner's on bank holidays to enjoy the walks over Riddlesdown and sample the pleasures of the tea gardens which included donkey rides, swings and a roundabout, hoopla and coconut shies, a museum, an aviary, curio shops selling china ornaments and a postcard and portrait saloon. Perhaps the most popular attraction with adults was the fairground steam organ and the children were enthralled with the miniature railway.

Children outside the 'Fancy Bazaar & Toy Stall' at Gardner's, *c.*1910

Note the sign on the right – 'To the Monkey House'

Postcard courtesy of Roger Packham

This two-foot gauge railway was at Gardner's from about 1893. It was made at William Gardner's foundry in Lambeth

Photograph courtesy of Purley Library

A report of a fire in 1919 describes Mr Gardner's enterprise—

GREAT FIRE AT KENLEY

GARDNER'S PLEASURE RESORT ABLAZE

SMART WORK OF THE PURLEY FIRE BRIGADE

> One of the greatest fires that has taken place in the district for some years occurred on Tuesday night at Kenley at the world renowned Gardner's Pleasure Resort at Riddlesdown. There are very few people who have not heard of these famous Tea Gardens, which have been established for many years, the proprietor Mr WG Gardner, now in his 81st year, having catered for thousands of visitors. It is a great blow to the proprietor that this catastrophe should take place in the height of the season.
>
> It appears that Mr Gardner resides at the residence with his niece, Olive Gardner, and on Tuesday he paid a visit to Croydon, and about nine o'clock Miss Gardner locked up the house to go for a walk with her friends. At this time, Mr Bowers, who superintended the donkeys, proceeded to the gardens to give them food and water, and he observed flames issuing from the back of the building, and immediately gave the alarm, and Mr Goddard, of the Dairy opposite, sent telephone messages for the brigade...
>
> By this time the flames had a good hold on the large building, known as the Children's Tea Room, which could comfortably hold 100 persons to tea. In addition there were the large tables and brewing plant and abundance of crockery and other necessities for a party from Catford which had been booked to visit the gardens, numbering between five and six hundred.
>
> The Purley Fire Brigade ... arriving on the scene, the hose was got out and a window in the upper part of the house smashed, so as to admit of the hose being inserted and directed on the flames, which were now riding to a tremendous height. To the credit of Mr Carter and his men, they fought the fierce flames admirably and were thus able to confine the fire to the back buildings, and eventually the fire was got under, but not before that part of the gardens known as the Children's Tea Room, had been destroyed, in addition to 4 bedrooms of the house, with their contents, which, we understand. are insured...

Mr Gardner, helped by his sons, restored the resort and it continued until 1934 when the land was bought by local builder, E T Brown, who retained some mementoes from this celebrated enterprise.

COMMEMORATION HALL 1897-1914

Mr Gardner's premises also accommodated some local events such as Methodist church services, and there was a concert hall and a dance hall. In 1908 it was the venue for Barber's Bijou Cinematographic Show but for many Kenley people, it was the Commemoration Hall that staged the majority of local attractions.

Sir Joseph Lawrence built the hall in 1897 to mark the diamond jubilee of Queen Victoria and an inscription survives by the horse trough on Godstone Road near the junction with St James' Road. The hall was opened on 19 June 1897 with patriotic enthusiasm and it could seat 450 people. In its brief existence it was the venue of some meetings of the Coulsdon Parish Council, a People's Mission (1899), Methodist Church services (1904), a Ratepayer's Meeting (1903), Purley Library and the annual meetings of the Kenley & Coulsdon Horticultural & Cottage Garden Society.

Mr Hainge recalled dancing and billiards at the Hall and he attended an autumn chrysanthemum show. Formal entertainments were organised by Coulsdon Parish Council and these included the appearance in 1899 of Harry

Furniss, the celebrated caricaturist who provided some 'rollicksome humour' and in the same year there was a comedy lecture by Max O'Rell and a talk by W S Caine, late Civic Lord of the Admiralty and MP for Bradford.

In 1903 there was an Exhibition of animated photographs attended by 600 people, and in 1904 there was a ventriloquial entertainment. Kenley Cricket Club held a *café chantant* in 1908 when the England Test cricketer, J N Crawford 'was in fine voice.'

Despite the hall's popularity it was converted to school premises in 1914 – presumably with Sir Joseph's approval – and its demise was noted in a local newspaper—

COUNTY SECONDARY SCHOOL

> The building known for many years as the Commemoration Hall has now been transformed into the commodious Secondary Schools, large additional buildings having been erected, the whole structure forming one of the most up-to-date County Secondary Schools in Surrey, which is saying a great deal. The school has been erected by the Surrey County Council as a Public Secondary Day School supported by fees and partly by Government grants and partly by Surrey County Council Rate and partly by local rates. The School opens on Tuesday next and already pupils have been enrolled from Purley, Caterham, Chaldon, Coulsdon, Godstone, Limpsfield, Lingfield, Oxted, Tadworth and Warlingham. This shows the need of such an institution. Mr R B Wight is the Headmaster at the school from whom all particulars can be obtained as to the terms.

So, the Commemoration Hall, parts of which are said to survive within the school buildings, gave way to Purley County School, which later became Roke Senior School, Shaftesbury Independent and Oakwood School. There were other schools to use the building and these are listed in Chapter 17. Local activities later found another suitable venue with the construction of Kenley Memorial Hall (see Chapter 12).

Sport

Kenley has been an active community. Traditionally it has been associated with hunting and in 1823 there was a meet of the Surrey Fox Hounds at *The Rose & Crown*. Later, Tom and Sam Hills, sometime residents of Garston Hall, were huntsmen to the Old Surrey for 76 seasons and Edmund Byron would attend the Boxing Day meets at *The Rose & Crown*.

The Old Surrey Fox Hounds outside Garston Hall

***c.*1900**

Photograph courtesy of Purley Library

In 1926, *The Purley Review* noted a new publication: '*Kenley Sports & Pastimes* is the title of a new 6d brochure which is reported with having met with instant success. It is a record of the activities of the games played in the locality, and is primarily issued by the Bowling Club, of which Mr C L de Wolff is secretary. Kenley sports include cricket, lawn tennis, football, hockey and Badminton Clubs, as well as Boy Scouts, local Brotherhoods, and a Rotary Club.' Some of these activities still flourish and below is a summary of some Kenley sporting and leisure activities—

CRICKET

Cricket is first recorded in the parish of Coulsdon in 1731 but the earliest reference to a match in Kenley is in 1847, when the Burstow Hunt played the Old Surrey Fox Hounds near Mr Atkins' Lime Kilns on Godstone-road near *The Rose & Crown*. In 1900, an advertisement for that public house refers to a cricket ground. After the construction of the gentlemen's houses from the 1860s it was inevitable that there would be some local cricket and W M Robinson, of Hayes, hosted a match in 1876 between the London & County Bank and the Union Bank (Chasemore & Robinson).

Mr Robinson was William Mosse Robinson, a Croydon banker and linen merchant, and he was the instigator of the present Kenley Cricket Club which was founded in 1880 after several unsuccessful attempts. He was greatly helped by the offer of a field by J Hall and over £30 was raised by donations. The first captain was Howard Houlder, later Mayor of London and an honoured name in the world of shipping.

A photograph taken during Kenley Cricket Week, 1895

C F Tufnell is at 1st slip

Photograph courtesy of Roger Packham

The cricket square was laid by Sam Apted, head groundsman at the Oval, and a groundsman/professional was soon engaged, being required to bowl to the members every day in the season from 4 p.m. A thatched pavilion was built on the Godstone Road side of the ground which lasted from 1886 until 1937 and a ladies' pavilion appeared in 1895/96 which was still used as an equipment shed until recent alterations.

The Club was given impetus by the arrival of Carleton Tufnell in 1895 (see Personalities). He was a former Kent cricketer, captained Kenley for seven years and became president from 1909 until his death in 1940. He maintained the club during World War I when cricket was suspended and three of his sons played for Eton. Carleton (junior) won the match against Harrow at Lord's in 1911 but was killed in France three years' later and

Neville toured New Zealand and South Africa with MCC, representing England in one Test Match. He later became a gentleman usher to King George VI.

In the early 1900s many famous cricketers appeared at the ground, including the 52 year-old W G Grace, who, in 1900 top scored for London County and also performed the hat-trick. The freehold of the ground was acquired in 1901 and this led to the formation of the Kenley Sports Company. This body has had to administer the different sports and in previous years allocated matches on the field on which the new Roke School stands. Cricket was played on the latter by teams such as Kenley Village, Early Risers and S E Railway but was later sold to Surrey County Council. A popular match in the Edwardian period was the annual fixture between the local grooms and gardeners ('Whips *v.* Worms').

The brothers Monger played some spectacular innings for Kenley in between the wars. H E Monger scored five successive centuries in 1925, including 129 against Surrey Club & Ground, whilst in 1927 H S Monger scored a century in just over 20 minutes, with all but eight of his runs coming in boundaries.

Kenley cricket continued during World War II despite some matches being abandoned during the blitz and good crowds attended Saturday matches in the post-war period before the advent of league cricket in 1973. Kenley won the South Thames League in 1992 under the captaincy of Roland Butcher (Middlesex and England) and in 1995 the club entered the Surrey County League in an effort to get promotion to the prestigious Surrey Championship.

ASSOCIATION FOOTBALL

In 1895 Kenley Workingmen played Caterham Village at Mr Poland's ground, Caterham, and there was a Kenley Football Club in the 1902-03 season largely made up of members of the cricket club. Friendly matches were played against teams such as Bowes Park and Westminster School and the team against the former was F H Townley (goal); C A Litchfield and T J Bruce, (backs); B D Darkin, H B Drake and E O Paterson (halfbacks); J B Densham, F S Darkin, C F Drake, W W Bruce and F R Maw (forwards). The Club sublet the second field, now occupied by Roke School. In between the wars, Kenley Wesleyan F C enjoyed some success and in the 1970s Kenley Elmwood F C was a force in local Sunday football.

Kenley Wesleyan Football Club, 1933-34.
Champions of Excelsior League, Division III, 1933-34.
A. Potter, H. Morgan, L. Clarke, (Vice-Captain) F. Stevens, A. Chadd,
B. Read, S. Lake, F. Morgan, (Captain)

Kenley Wesleyan Football Club 1933-34

Photograph courtesy of Purley Library

KENLEY & CATERHAM GOLF CLUB

The Caterham Weekly Press for 25 April 1903 reported a meeting of the above at 'The Rowans'. Miss B Cook of The Chestnuts, Queen's Park, Caterham was elected honorary secretary and treasurer and subscriptions fixed at one guinea per annum or 2½ guineas for a family. In May 1914 there was another report concerning a new clubhouse for the Kenley Golf Club – formerly the Caterham & Kenley Golf Club. The Club was formed in 1891 and its 9-hole course was situated off Hayes Lane on Kenley Common. It is remembered today by the road names Golf Road, Parfour Drive and Fairways and the Clubhouse survives as 190 Hayes Lane having originally been built in 1902 for the staff of a house situated in Zigzag Road. The golf club came to an end with the military occupation of Kenley Common in 1917.

LAWN TENNIS

Tennis was added to the activities of the Kenley Cricket Club in 1885 and a tent was pitched every day for the convenience of the lady players. Hard courts were laid down during World War II and many will remember the tennis tournaments played on five grass courts on the cricket outfield. Sadly, 1969 saw the demise of the tennis section.

BOWLS

Bowls was first mentioned at the cricket club's AGM of 1920 and a bowling green was laid at the cost of about £120. The Bowls Club became independent and were awarded a lease on the green in 1923/4. After considerable popularity, the bowls club was wound up in 1962 and the green given over to tennis.

HOCKEY

In 1925, the Kenley Hockey Club was playing at Purley Cricket Club, The Ridge. Its popularity waned and the present club takes its foundation date from 1967 when it played on the far field (now Roke School). It played on the cricket field in 1969 and started league hockey in 1972-73.

CYCLING

The popularity of cycling before the increase in traffic along Godstone Road can be judged by the two cycle makers in 1921 – H B Lee at 8 Kenley Parade (later Kipps' Cycle Shop) and F Pearce at 2 Excelsior Terrace.

SHOOTING

There is a reference to the Riddlesdown Rifle Range in 1903, perhaps one of Mr Gardner's enterprises, and, following the outbreak of World War I, the Purley & District Rifle Club was started in the East Surrey Waterworks, Godstone Road.

ASTRONOMY

Kenley residents have been familiar with the Croydon Astronomical Society's observatory off Waterhouse Lane since 1979 and a photograph of it appears in the Chronology. The 'little dome' at the observatory came from a garden in Stafford Road, Caterham, after the death of its young owner, Alan Treays. John Matthews in volume 20 of *Local History Records* tells an amusing story of Gardner's pleasure grounds being viewed by Mr Biddell from his observatory built into his house on the opposite side of the valley.

GARDENING

The present Roke Gardening Society has some well established predecessors. The Kenley & Coulsdon Horticultural & Cottage Garden Society, founded in 1883, held annual meetings at venues such as the Commemoration Hall and a field adjoining St Winifred's School. There was also the Kenley & District

Gardeners' Society in 1903. Today's Roke Gardening Society can trace its origin to 1954 when the gardening section of the Roke & East Purley Residents' Association was formed by S D V Rogers of 'Woodlands.'

BOURNE PARK AND HIGHER DRIVE RECREATION GROUNDS

Recreation areas apart from Kenley Common, Riddlesdown and Kenley Cricket Club, include Bourne Park – previously known as Kenley Recreation Ground – and Higher Drive Recreation Ground. Bourne Park was acquired by the Coulsdon & Purley UDC in 1921 and was laid out as a public park, playground, paddling pool and allotments. The park was extended in 1987. The recreation ground at Higher Drive was acquired in two stages. The upper field beside Higher Drive was purchased in 1925 by the council, having been part of the Sherwood Oaks Estate, while the lower field was compulsorily purchased in 1953 from Roke Land Ltd. Betts Mead in Old Lodge Lane was opened to the public in July 1925.

The opening ceremony at the Betts Mead Recreation Ground in Old Lodge Lane in July 1925

Photograph courtesy of Purley Library

OTHER LEISURE ACTIVITIES

Scouts And Guides. E R le Kuez, was scoutmaster for a new Kenley troop to replace a disbanded one. At Whitsun, 1913, the troop was under canvas in a field at Valley Road, courtesy of Welford's Dairies. The Roke scout hut is in Lower Road. The All Saints' troop was at one time run by Charlie Taylor, then later Ray Mears and Roy Belanger. Guides from the East End came out and camped at Cross Rigg, a piece of ground on the corner of Pondfield Road, which had a hut, water and toilets. It is still used by local guides and scouts

Guides at All Saints' Church on 24 February 1957 – hanging out of old and dedication of new colours

Photograph courtesy of Purley Library

occasionally but the hut was burnt down. It was given by Miss Connolly. There have been and are several active guide companies – 1st Kenley(Roke); 2nd Kenley (St Peter's Hall); 3rd Kenley (All Saints'); 5th Kenley (Wattenden School); 16th Purley (St James'). Brownies and cub scouts are also associated with the above groups.

A **Kenley Church Institute** was formed at All Saints' in 1912 for 'recreation, reading, games, armoury and gymnasium' for young men and its secretary was E R le Kuez.

The **Royal British Legion** has staged a variety of sports and games and in 1956 it staged the England v Wales quoits match.

The local schools have also contributed to Kenley sports and St Winifred's, under Revd Shilcock, helped the child prodigy, J N Crawford, towards being the youngest England Test cricketer. A near contemporary was Stanley Foster-Jackson who later played cricket for Shrewsbury School, football for Lancashire, and was killed in the Dardanelles in 1915.

England v. Wales at Quoits
August 1956
Photograph courtesy of Purley Library

PUBLIC HOUSES

Kenley's public houses remain a popular part of local leisure activity and below is a summary of their history—

The Kenley Hotel

The Kenley Hotel was built in 1869 for the convenience of travellers along Godstone Road and for railway passengers. Its early years were somewhat troubled and, also in 1869, it was closed and the furniture sold. The licensee, William Burbidge, was an uncertificated bankrupt and when he applied to transfer the licence to Christopher Little in 1870, he was opposed by T H Bentley of *The Rose & Crown.* In the latter year a spirit licence was granted, surprisingly supported by the vicar! In 1881 six men were charged at Croydon Petty Sessions with being drunk at the Hotel and with riotous and disorderly conduct on a Sunday. Mrs Moore was the licensee by then and in the same year she was summoned for adulterating the gin.

In 1900 the new licensee was Peter Clarke (born 1857) from Cumberland and he cut the blocks for a handsome design of shells on the floor of the private parlour of *The Kenley Hotel*, 'a redbrick building in the Gothic style of architecture that cannot fail to catch the eye.'

The Rose & Crown

The Rose & Crown is shown on Rocque's map of 1765 as *The Rose* and a brick over a window bore the date of 1723. It was built to serve the coaches on the old Lewes Road over Riddlesdown and it was demolished in 1929. The inn was of plaster and lathe and the doors were about five feet high on entering the old taproom. Its replacement was built behind the old *Rose & Crown* and opened on 29 August 1929 but was hit by a flying bomb and the present inn was built on its foundations. A plaque records the destruction caused by the bomb.

Revd Gilbert Buchanan, rector of Woodmansterne, recalled his historic visit to the inn in 1804—

> On the 29th of April, 1804, I went with the poor children of this parish, accompanied by their mothers, to *The Rose & Crown*, at Riddlesdown, on the Godstone Road and met there Mr Addington, a surgeon

Kenley Public Houses

***The Wattenden Arms* and *The Kenley Hotel* 2001**

(Photographs: Gwyneth Fookes)

***The Rose & Crown* c.1903**

(Photograph courtesy of Purley Library)

in London belonging to the Royal Jennerian Society (who) inoculated (against cowpox) the nine children following....

In 1823, a meet of the Old Surrey Foxhounds at *The Rose & Crown* was advertised and the inn also had its own cricket ground. In Victorian times it boasted tea gardens and a fun fair and it was notable for cycle runs and bean feasts and a centre for day trippers from London in their stream of vans and light carts. No doubt it was also used by the quarry workers on the opposite side of the road.

In recent times, the name of the inn was changed to *Roses* but this only lasted for a few years.

The Wattenden Arms

The Coulsdon census for 1851 recorded a beerhouse at Waddington run by George Butt, who also worked as a baker. The house was later called *The Pig & Whistle* and it is believed to have been located at the present thatched cottage near *The Wattenden Arms*. Miss Broadbent in 1976 stated that the present building retained the name of *Pig & Whistle* until recent times.

There is a local tradition that Lord Nelson (died 1805) visited the inn and that a plate said to have been used by him is preserved in the locality. In the schedule to the Coulsdon tithe map it is evident that there were two neighbouring beerhouses in the vicinity. Later, directories show that the licensees were members of the Hills hunting family of Garston Hall – Thomas in 1876 and Sophia in 1895.

The date of the present *Wattenden Arms* is uncertain but Mrs Cooke in 1962 referred to *'the old Wattenden'*. The 'Watt' served as the RAF Sergeants' Mess during World War II.

In 1968 the Bourne Society was involved with the unveiling of a new inn sign and its heraldic design. Recent patrons will recall landlord Ron Coulson before his move to *The Royal Oak*, Caterham, and the award from a London evening newspaper.

SOURCES

BROADBENT, U & LATHAM, R (1976) *Coulsdon Downland Village* Bourne Society

Bell's Life in London 1823

A Centenary History of the Kenley Cricket Club 1880-1980 (The Club 1980) plus supplement

Coulsdon & Purley Weekly Record 1900, 1914, 1919

Croydon Advertiser 1870

MATTHEWS, J D (1980) Purley's Pavilions of Pleasure in Bourne Society *Local History Records* Vol 19

MATTHEWS, J D (1981) William & Henrietta in Bourne Society *Local History Records* Vol 20

Purley Review No. 8 May 1926

Sussex Agricultural Express 1847

Ward's Croydon Directory 1921

The Wattenden Arms – New Sign Unveiled (1968) Bourne Society *Bulletin* 52

WINTERMAN, Mrs M A (1988) *Croydon Parks – An Illustrated History*. Croydon Parks Dept

A group walk amongst the tall flat-topped heads of wild carrot and dense clumps of aromatic marjoram in one of the most flower-rich areas of Riddlesdown in 1997. Trees colonised this open downland when it stopped being grazed, and to prevent this progressing further, sheep were reintroduced here in 1989.

Photograph by Andrew Scott

Chapter 20

Kenley Common and Riddlesdown

by Andrew Scott

Origins

The attractive open spaces covering the high ground at Kenley were probably cleared of their original forest cover during prehistoric times. Thereafter, the land was probably cultivated for crops until the soil fertility was exhausted and used since for rough grazing by domestic livestock. This pattern of prehistoric cultivation and abandonment was described on Farthing Down by the archaeologist, Brian Hope-Taylor, who mapped the Iron Age–Romano-British fields there. He also thought there were signs of early cultivation on Riddlesdown, where today a series of parallel banks and trackways can be seen although they have never been surveyed in detail.

Manorial Waste

During the mediaeval period both open spaces formed part of the waste land of the Manor of Watendone. Soil derived from clay-with-flints on the original area of Kenley Common, or chalk on the original area of Riddlesdown, was too poor to grow crops or grass for hay or even woodland for coppice products. The only economic use that could be made of such unproductive land was as pasture to graze livestock. However, although the lord owned the waste land he did not have exclusive use of this common land. Commoners (i.e. people who had rights in common) had legal rights to the product of the soil and in addition to obtaining pasture for their livestock used commons for gathering material for fuel (e.g. gorse), livestock bedding (.e.g bracken), roofing (e.g. heather), etc.

The Statute of Merton guaranteed the rights of commoners in 1235. The lord was prohibited from enclosing common land, which would thereby deprive commoners of their rights, unless given permission to do so by Act of Parliament. These rights were jealously guarded so land tended to be used in the same way for generations.

With the Agricultural and Industrial Revolutions the pressure on common land increased, as improvements in agricultural practices and machinery meant land that was previously waste began to be exploitable and so have increased economic value. The growth of the railways in the 19th century meant that these Commons had a new and much more lucrative value for residential development. This increase in potential earning power was too great to ignore and the Lord of the Manor of Coulsdon, Edmund Byron, enclosed and appropriated some 150 acres of Hartley Down. He failed, however, to persuade the Inclosure Commissioners to enclose the four remaining Coulsdon Commons: Farthing Down, Coulsdon Common, Kenley Common and Riddlesdown.

Edmund Byron then negotiated with the main neighbouring landowners of the Coulsdon Commons to seek their agreement to enclose them without the sanction of Parliament. He promised to give them parts of the Commons in exchange for their rights. William Hall, who owned Roke Farm by Riddlesdown with his brother James, stated in a letter to *The Croydon Advertiser* in 1883 that he refused Byron's offer (as did some other commoners) made on 23 March 1871. In 1872 Byron began to enclose sections of the Commons and strip large areas of turf, loam and gravel from Coulsdon Common and Riddlesdown.

The Hall brothers reacted by initiating proceedings against Byron in 1873. In 1877 the Court of Chancery upheld William Hall's commoner's rights (James had dropped out) by granting an injunction against Byron enclosing any part of the Commons or interfering with Hall's rights by removing soil or vegetation. Unfortunately for William Hall, he was not awarded costs and because he refused to pay his solicitor's bill in full he was taken to court. Matters were not settled until just before the start of his second (!) trial – so the action against Byron and the dispute with his own solicitor cost him the princely sum of £3510.16s.4d.

The City comes to the country

The stage was almost set for a most unlikely organisation to become involved with the affairs of Kenley. The Corporation of London, the local authority of the City of London, spent 11 years between 1871-1882 working to save most of Epping Forest from enclosure and development.

William Hall now approached the Corporation offering to sell an acre of his land for £4000 and with it his commoner's rights to the Coulsdon Commons – so the Corporation could act as it had at Epping and stand up to Byron if further enclosures were in the offing. The Corporation's solicitors thought this would not provide sufficient protection and the price was not right – 'It would be far better to negotiate with Mr Byron for the absolute ownership of them'. This took place and eventually Byron agreed to sell to the Corporation the freehold of 347 acres of the four Coulsdon Commons for £7000 plus his legal expenses.

Unfortunately, William Hall was not satisfied with this as he believed that the Coulsdon Commons consisted of 480 acres and not the 347 dealt with by the Corporation with Byron – the difference representing the sale of common land made to adjacent landowners – 'Of course Mr Byron did not attempt to sell to the Corporation what he had previously purported to sell to others'.

The sale was completed on 5 February 1883 and the Lord Mayor dedicated them officially on 19 May. Donovan Dawe's account (1968), based on contemporary newspapers, vividly captures the day's atmosphere, beginning with a procession from Caterham Junction (Purley station), past the foot of Riddlesdown where the City flag was hoisted at its summit, to Kenley and Coulsdon Commons where memorial trees were planted.

Kenley Common and Riddlesdown were acquired under the powers of the Corporation of London (Open Spaces) Act, 1878, which enabled the Corporation to acquire land within 25 miles of the City 'for public recreation and enjoyment' and 'to preserve the natural aspect'. The Act gave the Corporation powers to make bylaws to regulate and maintain the open spaces. One of its first actions was to appoint a Coulsdon Commons keeper, James Simmons, to enforce the bylaws. He lived in a cottage near Kenley station and knew 'every inch of the ground as he has made it his pleasure for years past to follow the hounds on foot'. A local carpenter, Jabez Barley, made up boards to display the bylaws in the local train stations and on each common. William Hall complained about the position of the board on Kenley Common, saying it was dangerous to anyone driving or riding at night, and asked if it could be removed.

William Hall also asked the Corporation to use its influence to persuade the South Eastern Railway Company to provide a shelter at Kenley Station 'it is really distressing to see those poor *ill-clad* and *ill-fed* children who are out for a *'Day in the Country'* standing an hour or more in the pouring rain'. The General Manager, Mr Fenton, gave instructions for this to be provided in September 1883.

In December, the keeper, James Simmons, was given a Christmas cake by his employer worth £1.10s.0d – five shillings more than his weekly wage!

In 1884 the Corporation built a thatched 'rustic shelter' on Riddlesdown (in front of the present car park?), ruling out an adjoining keeper's lodge because it was too expensive (the one there now was not built until 1958). A polished granite commemorative stone was set in the concrete floor at the entrance in 1885 and the planned inscription was—

Coulsdon Commons

Acquired by the Corporation of the City of London 1882

Dedicated to the public use 1883

This shelter erected for the public use 1884

KENLEY COMMON AND RIDDLESDOWN

H Hicks 1882}
R C Halse 1883} Chairmen of the Coal and Corn and Finance Committee
C H Stewart 1884}

This committee governed the Corporation's work on its open spaces outside the City. The shelter burnt to the ground in 1901 and the commemorative stone was found dumped in Coombes Wood in 1956.

Kenley Common

When bought in 1883 the Common consisted of 70 acres and lay entirely on clay soil on the plateau top. It was surrounded by land owned by George Cutt, who farmed Welcomes Farm and John Young, who owned 'Kenley House'. Byron and Cutt appear to have carved up a narrow strip of land on the west side of (the old) Hayes Lane between them – for this land was not included in the sale, but appears to have once been common land. Young certainly appropriated two acres of the original Common adjacent to 'Kenley House' that was not included in the sale of land to the Corporation. While he was alive, William Hall successfully used his court ruling of 1877 to compel Young to remove his fencing from it but, after his death, Young enclosed it again.

One of the jobs of the keeper was to impound stray cattle or sheep whose owner did not have grazing rights on the Common. The keeper had difficulty knowing whose animals were entitled to graze the Common. In 1888 the lord of the manor, Edmund Byron, claimed he was entitled to graze 500 sheep on Kenley Common (70 acres) and Farthing Down (121 acres) and George Cutt at Welcomes Farm, claimed grazing for 150 sheep on Kenley Common.

Hayes Lane was an unsurfaced track at this time and people complained about the Common being rutted by 'wagons, traction engines and other heavy conveyances' owned by George Cutt. He denied he was responsible blaming the damage on a general increase in local traffic – but he had to remove two manure heaps from the Common and 'disused duck ponds' were filled in. The Golf Club eventually took on responsibility for having the turf rolled in the spring.

The Corporation obviously felt that the Common was a bit too open and windswept for in 1888 it planted two circular clumps of trees and two more in 1893. These trees were felled in 1917 when the Common was requisitioned for an Aircraft Acceptance Park. The events of 1917 and the use of the Common as an airfield are told in other chapters.

In 1919 the War Office approached the Corporation saying it wanted to keep part of the Common as an aerodrome but would give an equivalent adjoining area in substitution. Local people petitioned the Corporation to use its influence to persuade the War Office to hand back the Common . This led to a meeting at Guildhall in 1920 between the Head of the Air Staff, Sir Hugh Trenchard, and representatives from the Kenley residents, the Coulsdon & Purley Urban District Council and Corporation officials.

The end result was that the RAF kept its airfield (including 51 acres of former common land) and the Corporation was given 61 acres of farmland to the east overlooking Whyteleafe as substitute common. No building was to be allowed on former common land and it would revert to the Corporation if no longer required for military purposes. The airfield would not be used for civil aircraft and would be opened on public holidays. These arrangements were made official under the terms of the Air Ministry (Kenley Common Acquisition) Act 1922.

To celebrate the compromise, trees were planted on the Common on 31 December 1920 – the first in what was intended to be an avenue, added to each year. It was to be called 'Oscar Berry Avenue' after the Chairman who negotiated with the Air Ministry. It is not known whether the planting was kept up.

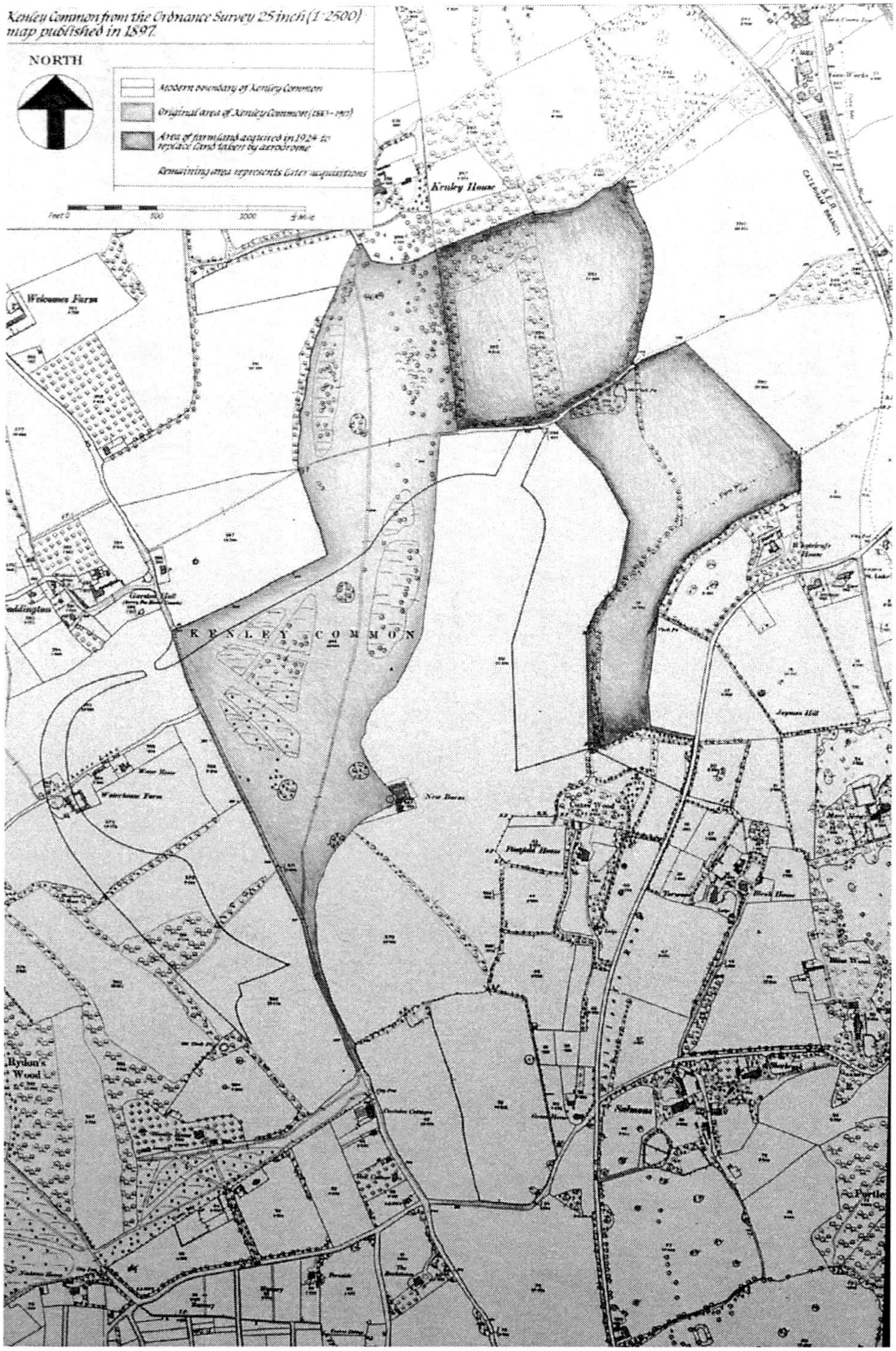

Kenley Common showing the original Common acquired in 1883 to the west. The substitution land, overlooking Whyteleafe in the east, was handed over to the Corporation in 1925 to make up for the area of Common kept for an airfield after WWI. The modern boundary of the Common, showing land added after this date, is also plotted on the Ordnance Survey 1:2500 map published in 1897

The Corporation began work adapting the land for public use in 1923 – fencing and hedging the new boundaries, putting ploughed land down to grass and clearing bushes (scrub) from the steep chalk grassland overlooking Whyteleafe. The Air Ministry paid for this work. The land was officially handed over in 1925 and became part of the public open space.

The northeastern section of Kenley Common and Whyteleafe taken from the air in 1949. The northern extension of the main runway and wartime buildings were later removed. The woodland closest to the main runway was coppiced during the war to give more space for take off and landing. The grassland, especially of the nearest field (Hilltop) is being invaded by bushes since it stopped being managed by grazing or cutting.

The events of World War II in relation to the airfield are described elsewhere, but the war also greatly affected the Common. Woodland at the northern end of the main runway was grubbed up or coppiced in 1939-40 as the new fighters needed more space for take off and landing. Some tall trees overlooking the valley were also coppiced, where trenches, dug by Local Defence Volunteers in 1940, and gun positions were established. All entrances to the Common were closed in 1940, and remained closed until 1947/8 as the long process of derequisitioning and restoring the Common took place.

Riddlesdown

In 1883 the Common consisted of 79 acres, the parish boundary marking its northern limit. The London, Brighton and South Coast Railway Company had already served notice on Edmund Byron for three acres of this land for its railway. This passed to the Company in 1888. In 2000, the railway land on the north side of the track was sold to the London Wildlife Trust for a nature reserve.

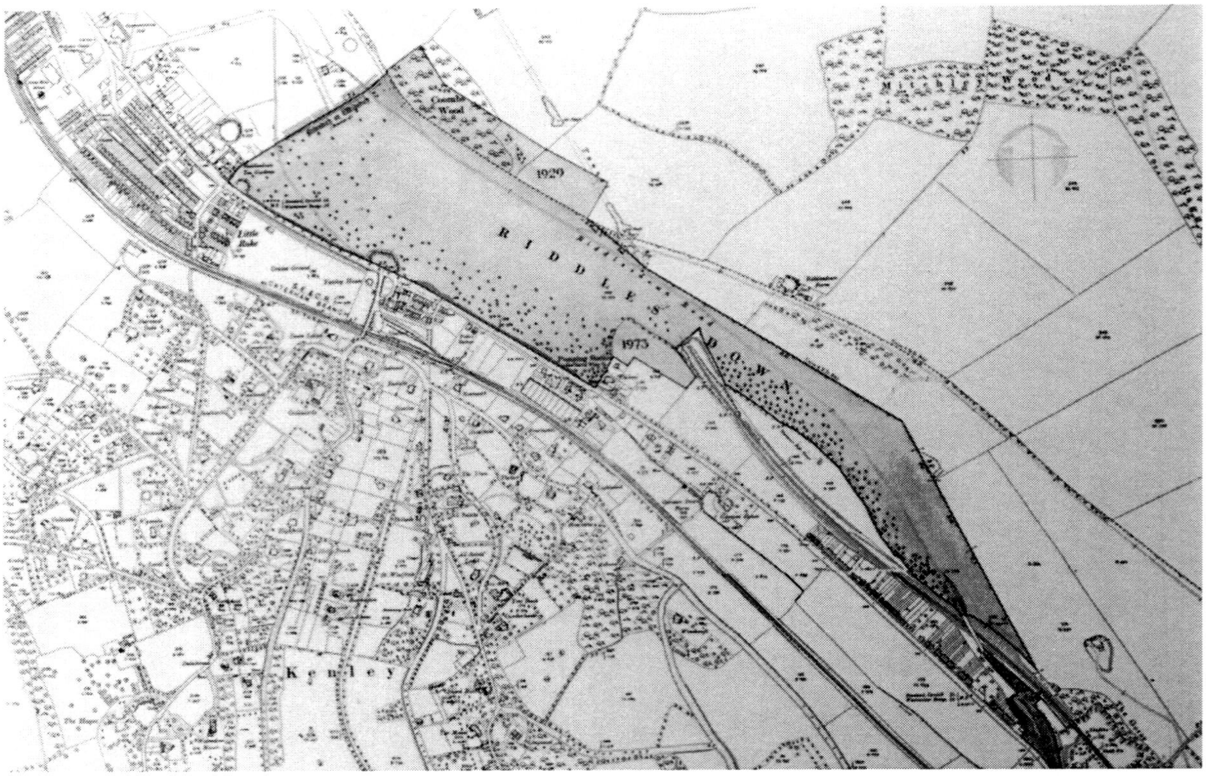

Riddlesdown – acquired in 1883 – plotted on the Ordnance Survey map of 1912

Riddlesdown seen behind the station master's house at Kenley Station. The downland is predominantly open with a few bushes

***c.*1906**

Postcard courtesy of Roger Packham

KENLEY COMMON AND RIDDLESDOWN

The Common included two chalk pits by Godstone Road – a small one opposite Little Roke Road and a larger one opposite Hayes Lane and *The Kenley Hotel.* The Corporation started fencing the larger one in June 1883 but, before it was completed, a child fell over the edge and later died of its injuries. This provoked another letter from William Hall and led to two workmen being employed to warn people off until the job was finished.

The pits were used as a source of chalk by local people and by the council which also used it to store road building materials. In 1898 Coulsdon Parish Council was given permission to put 'a hose cart shed for the purposes of storing fire extinguishing appliances' in the pit opposite Hayes Lane, at the rate of one shilling per year. This pit was also used as a place to sell refreshments and for public toilets. In 1941 Surrey County Council constructed a large air raid shelter there. After the war the tunnels were used by a mushroom farmer and, in 1967, an optical lens manufacturing business moved in, making use of the low vibration and constant temperature conditions found there.

The large pit opposite *The Rose and Crown* was not acquired by the Corporation until 1995. It is not part of the public open space – access is restricted to special interest groups.

Coulsdon Parish Council marked Queen Victoria's Jubilee in 1897 with a bonfire on the highest ground at Riddlesdown.

In 1927 Mitchley Wood Estate began to be developed and, to prevent the Common's high ground becoming overlooked by housing, part of Coombes Wood and the adjoining meadow 'the Donkey Field' were bought and added to the open space in 1929. The Bull Pen, between the railway and Garston Lane, was added in 1973.

In 1940 Local Defence Volunteers dug trenches and in 1943 virtually the whole of Riddlesdown was requisitioned. It was derequisitioned in January 1945 and by September the trenches were filled in and barbed wire obstructions removed.

Landscape and wildlife features

The landscape we see today is the culmination of all that has gone before. It has been shaped by physical (geology & climate), chemical (weathering) and biological processes working over time. People's influence is all-pervasive and even apparently natural features like grassland and woodland have been subtly altered directly or indirectly by mankind.

The same scene in 1993.

Riddlesdown has become a wood, bringing about the extinction of its characteristic downland flowers, butterflies and other insects

Photograph courtesy of Andrew Scott

Grassland is not 'natural' here, i.e. it cannot be maintained without people's influence, for it changes over time to woodland by the process of natural succession. Grassland is subjected to a continual rain of mainly wind- or bird- borne tree seeds that establish and, unless their development is stopped by the grassland being grazed or cut, grow into woodland. For at least two millennia grassland has been kept open and maintained as grassland by commoners' livestock, rabbits (introduced by the Normans), deer and small mammals. Although hundreds of sheep were pastured on Kenley Common in 1888, Mr Stubbington of Roke Farm only claimed grazing for 25 on Riddlesdown. Clearly the number of livestock on Riddlesdown was not enough to stop the downs scrubbing up with bushes because Thomas Wright noted in the mid 19th century 'its carpet of green sward, [was] speckled with innumerable little groups of dark shrubs' (probably juniper and yew).

Commoners' grazing probably ended on both commons about the time of World War I. Burning was used to control the spread of scrub on the steep downland above Whyteleafe Hill between the World Wars. It was reported that during the War thorn bushes got out of hand on the Commons because they were closed and no work could be done to control them and grazing by wild rabbits was insufficient (although residents complained about the number of rabbits on Kenley Common in 1940).

In the early 1950s Mr Jones grazed his Jersey herd at the end of Golf Road on Kenley Common. Myxomatosis killed rabbits on both Commons in 1954 and they have not yet returned. From the 1950s grass was cut by tractor and where possible baled for hay. Between 1968-70 about 15 acres of scrub were bulldozed and burnt from the plateau top at Riddlesdown and another 15 acres from the grassland overlooking Whyteleafe on Kenley Common, in a major effort to restore lost grassland. In 1989 the clock turned full circle with the progressive reintroduction of grazing animals owned by the Corporation to parts of both Commons. Sheep and cattle are being used to restore and conserve the grassland in a way that is more beneficial and sensitive to the needs of wildlife than can be achieved by mechanical means.

Without doubt the rarest and most important habitat found on either Common is the chalk grassland, for this habitat is restricted to NW Europe and even the small areas of the Commons are nationally important. Unimproved downland is famed for the variety and richness of its colourful flowers and insects. Unlike most agricultural land, the Commons' grassland has not been enriched by chemical fertilisers or treated with herbicides or deep-ploughed. So archaeological features and wildlife have survived. On both Commons one can find 30-40 species of plant per square metre in the best downland. It is mainly because of this value that Riddlesdown is protected as a Site of Special Scientific Interest and that the same protection is proposed for the grassland in the north and east of Kenley Common.

The richest chalk grassland is found on the steepest slopes where the soil is thinnest and most impoverished. The dark blue flowers of hairy violet, pink, white and blue forms of common milkwort and nodding heads of cowslip bloom in spring. In common with many plants these flowers need small bare patches of soil for their seed to germinate and establish. Sheep and cattle create exactly these conditions and these flowers are certainly increasing where grazing was re-established.

Grazing suppresses the growth of vigorous grasses allowing less competitive flowers to coexist so grazed areas tend to be richer in types of plant. Grazing removes vegetation slowly and selectively compared with the brutal sweep of the mower that chops up everything instantaneously and nothing can escape. Grazed areas therefore tend to support a greater variety of invertebrates than cut grassland. For example, it is noticeable that the hay meadows are eerily silent in July before the cut whereas lightly grazed areas are alive with singing grasshoppers – the timing of the mowing prevents them from completing their life cycle.

Grassland flowering reaches its peak in June. Many species are found only on the chalk including rough hawkbit, greater knapweed, wild carrot, small scabious, hawkweed oxtongue and autumn gentian, as well as three aromatic herbs – marjoram, wild basil and very small amounts of wild thyme. On Riddlesdown tall delicate sprays of common dropwort are widespread, intense blue heads of round-headed rampion and tiny white

Sussex cattle were reintroduced to Main Common, the northern part of the original Kenley Common, in 2001. Grazing by commoners' sheep and cattle had kept this area open for centuries.

Photograph: Andrew Scott

flowers of squinancywort are rare and flowers of the biennial early gentian are occasionally seen. Several chalk plants found here, particularly on banks or the steepest slope, are food for scarce butterflies. Horseshoe vetch supports a flourishing colony of the chalkhill blue butterfly – the pale, powdery blue males can be seen in July and August (not to be confused with the bright blue wings of the smaller male common blue, found on both Commons). Common rockrose is the main food plant for the brown argus – a small brown butterfly that is easily missed. The much smaller small blue feeds on kidney vetch and has its stronghold in the quarry opposite *The Rose and Crown* and the railway cutting.

A characteristic sight in grazed grassland are the mounds made by the yellow meadow ant. These are visited by the green woodpecker who feeds on them and emits the familiar 'yaffle' when disturbed.

Wingless female glow-worms emit a ghastly green glow at night to attract flying males. They are seen regularly on the chalk downland at Riddlesdown but rarely on Kenley Common. Larvae of these beetles feed on snails, but they must struggle to consume the largest British land snail found here – the Roman snail.

On Kenley Common, where scrub was removed to restore chalk grassland in the 1990s, man orchid appeared and, following grazing, the nationally rare white mullein flowered. This plant's seeds had lain buried in the soil

Jacob and Southdown sheep on Hilltop, Kenley Common, in autumn 1998. Note the anthills that are characteristic of unimproved grazed downland.

Photograph: Andrew Scott

since the land scrubbed up some 50 years before. In June, sainfoin makes a vivid splash of pink on the chalk. It is also found more sparsely on Riddlesdown, occurring on both Commons where scrub was cleared in the 1960s – possibly having been introduced in a seed mix at that time.

Common spotted, pyramidal and bee orchids are found on the chalk – the last two being confined to it but many plants have less specific requirements and grow on more fertile neutral soils too. These include oxeye daisy, common bird's-foot-trefoil, meadow vetchling, tufted and bush vetch, common knapweed and greater yellow-rattle. Greater yellow-rattle is rare in Britain but common in some areas of the Commons.

On nutrient-poor acidic grassland, largely restricted to the original area of Kenley Common, may be found yellow stars of tormentil, tiny white flowers of heath bedstraw and heath grass. Though the range of flowers is smaller than on the chalk or neutral soil, these specialised plants and associated insects are found nowhere else locally.

The open grassland habitat can be extinguished in a matter of 40-50 years if scrub is allowed to expand through inadequate control or neglect. In the early stage of scrub invasion, while bushes remain scattered, most of the grassland species coexist. The richest scrub is found on the chalk where the predominant shrub, hawthorn, is joined by much smaller amounts of purging buckthorn, wild privet, dogwood, spindle, wayfaring tree and whitebeam. The bushes provide food, shelter and nesting habitat for invertebrates and birds in particular and their berries and autumn foliage add vibrant colour to the landscape. Male yellowhammers pick isolated bushes as perches for their song: 'a little bit of bread and no cheese'. Juniper, on Riddlesdown, is a nationally rare colonising shrub. Unfortunately, this rich phase is short-lived, and only small amounts of young chalk scrub may be found on either Common.

Soon after the canopy of bushes merges, the ground becomes heavily shaded and grassland species become dormant. Bushes become overtopped by colonising oak, ash, cherry, etc., which begin to replace the original woody shrubs. One of the few plants favoured by the increased shade is the nationally rare green-flowered helleborine which is found on Riddlesdown. Juniper was once abundant on Riddlesdown but today only a handful of bushes survives and the specialised insects which lived on it have become extinct (except for one species of shield bug that adapted to another shrub found in neighbouring gardens). Interestingly, dormice appear to have a foothold on Riddlesdown – characteristic feeding marks were found on hazel nuts here and several animals dropped in to the engineering business in the quarry through a ventilation pipe! The young scrub woodland which covers so much of this common is poor in characteristic woodland flowers found in 'ancient' woodland.

Ancient woodland may be recognised by flowers such as bluebell, wood anemone and yellow archangel and, not surprisingly, tends to contain some old trees with rot holes to attract hole-nesting birds such as nuthatch and greater spotted woodpecker. Coombes Wood on Riddlesdown, most of the woodland on the north and north-east side of Kenley Common – Pitlands Wood – and a small fragment next to the rifle range in the south-west is of this type. This woodland was managed as coppice-with-standards in the mediaeval period.

The arid desert environment of the concrete and tarmac runways provide specialist niches for plants such as the stonecrops, storksbills and whitlow grass.

SOURCES

Corn, Coal and Finance Committee minutes and papers

DAWE, D (1968) 'The Lord Mayor opens Coulsdon Common' Bourne Society *Local History Records* Vol 7

HAWKINS, Roger

PACKHAM, Roger

Chapter 21

Murder, Suspense, Mystery and Ghosts

by Colin Burgess

Most communities through the years have traumatic events that are frequently remembered in conversation. Some of those that happened in Kenley have been well documented—

The Sussex Agricultural Express in January 1854 reported on two inquests on **Harriet and William Attlee** and their three children at Waddington. They had died in rather mysterious circumstances and the body of Harriet was later exhumed amongst rumours that she may have murdered the rest of her family. However, it was established at the inquests that the family had not taken 'any foreign substance' and in fact they had all died of typhoid. Mary Bashford, their lodger was the main witness and it appeared that Harriet had been obtaining contaminated water from what was little more than a puddle opposite their home, even though there was a good supply of water only 60 yards away. The inquest heard that the family lived sometimes on boiled turnips and butter, bread and butter and tea. They had died after being nauseous for two or three days.

A snowy scene in Hayes Lane, near the scenes of a number of the incidents in this chapter. The forge on the right.

Photograph: E Straker 18 Dec.1866

Courtesy of Purley Library

Events nearly 50 years later in 1898 dragged Kenley into the international limelight. In March that year American editor and author **Harold Frederic** of 'Homefield', Valley Road, fell ill and later died. The inquest opened at *The Kenley Hotel* but moved to the new Commemoration Hall for more space. There was a long list of witnesses giving details that were rushed to British and American newspapers.

Harold Frederic first fell ill in March 1898, he suffered a stroke on 13 August and despite the medical attention lavished on him he died on 19 October. After the stroke, a friend Dr Nathan Ellington Boyd had seen him and he called in the local GP, another friend of the patient Dr Robert Brown of 'Yateley'. He had explained to Kate Lyon, Frederic's mistress, that with care and rest the patient had a good chance of survival. Friends rallied round – Mr & Mrs Crane from Oxted had sent a servant, Adoni Ptolemy, to help; Dr Montagu Murray, lecturer in pathology at the Charing Cross Hospital, saw the patient and male nurses were engaged; Dr Ludwig Freiberger (MD Vienna MRCS MRCP) paid a number of visits. The medical profession spoke with one voice about the treatment – no alcohol, no smoking, a light diet and plenty of rest.

However, Kate Lyon was a Christian Scientist, and in her wish to be of real help she wanted him to have non-medical help and she sent for Mrs Athelie Mills for moral support. The witnesses at the inquest were called to ascertain whether Frederic acquiesced in Mrs Mills' beliefs or not. After the coroner's summing up that death was from heart disease and rheumatic fever, he discussed whether the lack of medical help contributed to death. He concluded that Miss Lyon and Mrs Mills were responsible and they were accused of manslaughter. There were two subsequent trials, and evidence gradually piled up that Harold Frederic was an active, forceful, intolerant personality, irritated, aggrieved and perhaps frightened by his illness. He sought any likely remedy but was, however, determined to enjoy his pleasures to the last. In the end there was insufficient evidence against the ladies and they were discharged.

The Commemoration Hall at the bottom of St James' Road, where the inquest on Harold Frederic took place

Postcard courtesy of Roger Packham

In 1922, the wife of **Revd Gordon Tombe** of Sydenham had a dream that their son Eric was buried at 'The Welcomes' and called the police to search. They told the police that in the dream Mrs Tombe heard a voice saying, 'Oh let me out!'. She felt he was shut up somewhere and could not escape. At first the police took little notice, then Revd Gordon Tombe went to Scotland Yard. Chief Inspector Francis Carlin, one of the 'big four' at Scotland Yard and one of the founders of the present day CID, organised a search at the ruins of 'The Welcomes', where Eric and a friend Ernest 'Bill' Dyer had lived. Apparently, Dyer and Tombe had burnt the farm down to claim insurance money.

On a warm September day in 1923, a team of plain clothes policemen sweated profusely in rolled up sleeves and unbuttoned waistcoats as they toiled away with picks, shovels and buckets to uncover an old cesspit. It was 18 inches across at the top and sealed with cement and under it lay 4 ft of concrete masonry blocks and drains from the stable block. It was afternoon before the detectives discovered what they were looking for. A human shape was squatting in sitting position beneath a blue overcoat and despite the dirt and decay, it was evident that the skull had been smashed. That it was a murder was fairly clear.

The remains were those of Eric Gordon Tombe, the best friend of Dennis Wheatley, the author. Tombe and Wheatley were bound together by their experiences of fighting in the Western Front in World War I.

Dyer was a gambler and adventurer who played the horses. Tombe was good looking, with a keen sense of humour and a self-confessed hedonist, who believed in the pursuit of pleasure by whatever means. His 'means' were as a gentleman criminal, which started with stealing his parents' silver and blossomed when he and Dyer dreamt up a scam with which they defrauded the Air Ministry.

DAILY SKETCH, FRIDAY, SEPTEMBER 14, 1923.

CLOSING SCENES IN FAHMY MURDER TRIAL DRAMA

DAILY SKETCH.

20 Pages

No. 4,520. Telephones: London—Holborn 6510. Manchester—City 6501. LONDON, FRIDAY, SEPTEMBER 14, 1923 (Registered as a Newspaper.) ONE PENNY.

KENLEY DRAMA: DREAM REVEALS MYSTERY OF BURIED SON

The fire-charred ruins of "The Welcomes," the house at Kenley, Surrey, where the police discovered in a well the remains of Eric Gordon Tombe, a partner of Ernest Dyer, who shot himself at a Scarborough hotel last November to avoid arrest. Inset is the dead man's father, the Rev. Gordon Tombe, of Sydenham.

Ernest Dyer (left) and Eric Tombe, his partner. Dyer is stated to have travelled to France and made use of their resemblance to obtain monies.—(Daily Sketch.)

An exclusive picture of Mrs. Dyer, the wife of the man who shot himself in a Scarborough Hotel when the detectives arrived to arrest him. The death of Tombe was discovered by a dream.

Ernest Dyer (left) and Eric Gordon Tombe in happy days.—(Exclusive.)

Supt. Carlin (right), one of the "Big Four" at Scotland Yard, is investigating the mystery with Detective-Inspector Hedges.—(Daily Sketch.)

Detectives were busy yesterday still searching the well for further clues to the mystery.—(Daily Sketch.)

Hugh Shepheard-Walwyn

The coroner's court came to the conclusion on 25 September 1923 that Ernest 'Bill' Dyer had wilfully murdered his companion Eric Tombe. He was later traced to Scarborough and in a struggle with police when they tried to arrest him, he shot himself.

Sadly over the years there have been other suicides in Kenley itself. In 1892 it was reported in the press that **Robert Whitford**, aged 22, who was a medical student, committed suicide at 'Hillside House' after failing his examinations. Also in 1892 **Mrs Beadle** of Kenley attempted suicide. Barbara Cooper remembered that three days after the beginning of World War II **Hugh Shepheard-Walwyn** of 'Dalwhinnie House' shot himself. He was a writer and an excellent naturalist.

During the last war **an author** was posted to man the guns around Kenley aerodrome, about where the observatory is today and having undertaken the basic duties of cleaning and checking that all was ready if a German aeroplane came within range, his mind turned to other things and the storyline for a book began to develop.

When the first words were written he sent the script to his wife in East Anglia via the service mail to be typed. When it arrived it was heavily censored with black pen, so the next time he posted the letter from a post office letterbox in Hayes Lane. His wife soon had it typed, then travelled to London by train and they met at Kenley Station where the author would check the typescript. On a nice day they sat on the seat on the platform but if it was cold or damp they went into *The Kenley Hotel.*

The book was soon finished and when it was published, it went around the world, became very popular, was serialised in American newspapers and is credited with improving opinions of Britain at a delicate stage of the war.

The author was **Bombardier Ralph Hammond Innes** and the book was called *Attack Alarm.* If read, it does not take much imagination to understand the parts of Kenley and Caterham that were in the author's mind at the time of writing.

The Bourne Society carried out archaeological excavations at the site of the present Wheat Knoll where once **Watendone Manor** stood in 10 acres of grounds. When the house was built, it was claimed that human bones had been found so when it was demolished over half a century later excavations were carried out there and revealed that it was the site of the Domesday church of Watendone and there was a cemetery about one acre in extent – with bodies buried at more than one level and all placed with their feet towards the east. The skeletons at the lowest levels were set in orderly rows at intervals of about two to three feet.

There had long been rumours about **ghostly monks and nuns** in the area which gave rise to some interest and speculation.

In a house in Welcomes Road, claimed to be on the site of an **old monks' walk**, the delightful perfume of narcissus was said to waft through one of the rooms. Not only were the owners aware of this peculiar phenomenon but numerous visitors would comment on the 'lovely scent' and would be puzzled when it changed to that of candle grease. In the same house, built in the 1880s, footsteps were frequently heard in the evening walking straight through the house, as if the walls were not there.

It has not been unknown for a **phantom nun** to be seen carrying a pitiful bundle resembling a baby and the flint cottages opposite Old Lodge Lane were believed to be built on a monastery on the outskirts of the ancient village of Watendone. When Garston Hall, in Old Lodge Lane, near the junction of Hayes Lane was demolished, the remains of an old tunnel were discovered.

There had been several reported sightings of a ghost known as **'The Grey Lady of Kenley'** in the area of Hayes Lane and Old Lodge Lane. Just after World War II the tenant of Welcomes Cottages was awoken by her baby screaming. She ran to the bedroom and was shocked to see a misty shape in the form of a woman bending over the child's cot. As she comforted the baby the ghost just faded away. One day Mrs Howland, then owner of Welcomes Farm, happened to look out towards Barn Cottages in Hayes Lane when she saw a figure of a lady in a grey gown in the front garden. Mistaking it for Mrs Fretwell, the mother of the owner of the cottages, she waved and called out a greeting. It was only when the shape faded away that Mrs Howland realised that she had been another witness of The Grey Lady.

It is believed that along Pondfield Road next to the school there used to be a row of poor cottages. It is there that there used to be a story of another ghost, this time an old lady who used to be seen regularly at the junction of Hayes Lane and Pondfield Road. When the pond there was filled in the apparition stopped.

SOURCES

ANDREWS, E (1982) Bourne Society *Local History Records* Vol 21, pp 32-36

Caterham Free Press 23.4.1892 and 21.5.1892

HAMMOND INNES, R *Attack Alarm* ISBN 616921X

SAALER, M (1967). The Search for the 'lost' Village of Watendone', Bourne Society *Local History Records* Vol 6 pp 3-6

Sussex Agricultural Express 7.1.1854 and 28.1.1854

The Daily Sketch 14.9.1923

Park Road (formerly Riddlesdown Park Road) at the junction with Oaks Way, looking towards Riddlesdown

Postcard courtesy of Roger Packham

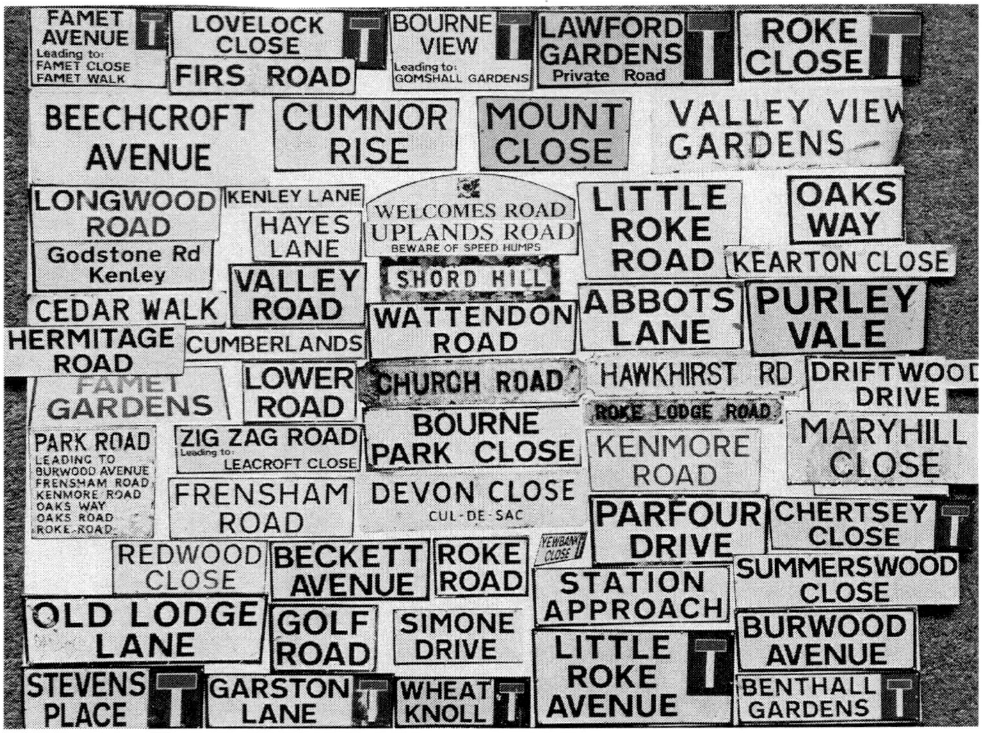

A photomontage of most Kenley street names

Grahame Brooks

Chapter 22

Kenley's Street Names

by John Bishop

Streets in most towns, villages and areas have local names that have associations with history – either in field names or in the people that lived there. Kenley is no exception.

Domesday Book provides us with tantalising snippets of our past history. St Peter's Abbey of Chertsey held Waddington, (a recent translation of Watendone), a village that boasted 17 villagers and a church. In the ninth century the village is referred to as Hwaetedune interpreted as the Anglo-Saxon for Wheat Hill or a wheat-producing village. Today all that reminds us of this ancient village is **Wheat Knoll,** a new road built over the site where excavations in 1966 found evidence of the early church and christian burial ground. **Wattendon Road** is nearby on the opposite side of Hayes Lane. **Chertsey Close** is also a reminder of Kenley's links with Chertsey Abbey.

In 1406 the tenement of Kenley was granted to a chantry in the chapel of St Mary in Steyning, Sussex. There had been a long association with Steyning and lands in Selsdon, Sanderstead and Waddington. **Steyning Close** is a reminder of these links.

A combe, from the Old English cumb, a hollow and later to mean a deep wooded valley can be linked to the name Welcombe, a valley with a well or spring and this is seen today with **Welcomes Road**, running as one would expect, through a valley that was undoubtedly wooded in the past. Welcomes Farm is also recorded in the manor of Watendone in 1545.

Portley Farm was the land of Sir Isaac Shard c1720, Abraham Shard in 1736 and William Shard in the period up to 1790. There is a possible link with this name to the road named **Shord Hill,** built next to the field called Shord Hill and the wood Short Wood. The field names: Great Abbots, Middle Abbots and Little Abbots from the Portley map also suggest that **Abbots Lane** (formerly **Occupation Road**) is so named as perhaps these fields were themselves named after the Abbots of Chertsey. Occupation Road is the temporary name given during road construction. Kenley Farm in 1762 had four fields with names such as Hawkhirst Shaw, Upper Hawkhirst, Middle Hawkhirst and Lower Hawkhirst. Today nearby **Hawkhirst Road** is a reminder of those old field names.

There are many references to Fox or Foxley in the London area and the name locally is associated with Foxley Hatch, an old name for Purley. **Foxley Road**, the unadopted road next to **Higher Drive** Recreation Ground still has its share of foxes. Both Hayes and Roke Farms have roads named after them though **Hayes Lane** (formerly Foxley Lane) was originally the major road along the plateau.

Roke Farm has a very long recorded history. Roads with the name Roke next to Godstone Road are on the site of the old farm and were named after the farm was demolished. The name is first recorded in 1367 when Adam atte Roke had a home there. Later, le Roke is recorded in the Chertsey court records. The derivation of le Roke is 'at the oak'. Kenley's very old oak trees stand near to **Roke Road** next to the railway footbridge so it is probable that at least one significant oak tree grew in that area in ancient times. The Caterham branch railway now separates Roke Road and **Little Roke Road. Lower Road** nearby lies just beneath Godstone Road.

Waterhouse Farm which was sited just to the west of Kenley aerodrome still has the remains of its approach road named **Waterhouse Lane**. Garston Farm, between the waterworks and *The Rose & Crown* is still remembered by **Garston Gardens** and **Garston Lane**, although the name Garston goes back to 1269 when Joel de la Garston had a home at the top of Old Lodge Lane. New Barn was taken over when Kenley aerodrome was constructed and there was a New Barn opposite *The Rose & Crown.* To remind us of this **New Barn Lane**, the original farm track, exists today together with **Old Barn Lane** separated by the railway.

Kenley aerodrome, so renowned for its role in World War II, is remembered for two of the planes that flew from there in **Anson Close** and **Gauntlet Crescent**. Douglas Bader, a fighter pilot famous for his ability in the air despite having two false legs is also remembered with **Bader Close**.

The Bourne waters flowing through Kenley have only two references in road names. **Bourne View** and **Bourne Park Close** are aptly named. Nearby **Waverley Avenue** is not thought to have a Bourne water connection since the flow of water has never been sufficient to make waves (until December 2000)!.

Two brothers, naturalists and photographers are associated with this area. Richard Kearton lived in Caterham and his brother Cherry lived in Kenley, first in a house called 'Shunafell' then later in 'The Jungle', and remembered in **Kearton Close**. **Beckett Avenue** is named after a former chairman of the Coulsdon & Purley Urban District Council. **Famet Gardens** and other similarly named roads on that estate have a name coined by the builder, E T Brown, which would defy the powers of logic of any treasure hunter. His family, Frederick, Annie, Mary and their father Edward Thomas provide the clue.

Property developed in the extensive grounds of large houses usually have road names that reflect the name of the house. The property developers named **Langham Dene** after the house 'Langham'. **Redwood Close** was also named after the house 'Redwood'. **Pine Close** was named by the property developers, but this time they chose a name as a reminder of all the pine trees they cut down.

Purcell Close in a 1996 development was named after Henry Purcell who died 300 years before that date. It was built next to two blocks on the station sidings named after the composers Elgar and Sullivan.

Three roads remind us that a golf course existed on part of Kenley Common . They are **Golf Road, Fairways** and **Parfour Drive**. The 19th hole is probably under the site of a house in Abbots Lane called 'Shay Wen'.

All Saints' church is approached by churchgoers up the hill, as one would expect, via **Church Road. Valley Road's** name is self explanatory, following as it does the railway and Godstone Road along the valley between Kenley and Whyteleafe. **Zigzag Road** is indeed a zigzag. **Park Road** was originally **Riddlesdown Park Road**.

SOURCES

Bourne Society *Local History Records*

The Thomson Directory

Geographers' A to Z Atlas

Rowed, Portley and Messeder maps

GLOVER, Judith. *Surrey Place Names*

Purley Local Studies Library

Chapter 23

Personalities

by all contributors

Addley, William (1817-*c*.1900) – lived at 'Forge Cottage' in Hayes Lane and was a faithful servant to the community. He attended St John's Church, Coulsdon for 50 years, blowing the organ while his daughter played and sang at the same time. He was Collector of Tithes for 40 years, assistant overseer for 30 years, collector of taxes for 29 years and schoolmaster at St John's Church School for 18 years. He took the census in 1851, 1861, 1871 and 1881 and was an authority on commoners' rights. He retired from parish affairs in 1897 aged 80.

Barnard, Capt Franklyn L B, OBE AFC (d.1927) – He lived at 'Windyridge', Hayes Lane and made the first flight for the Instone Air Line on 13 October 1919 fresh from the great war. He won the *King's Cup Air Race* in September 1922 for Sir Samuel Instone and was the very popular winner of the final *King's Cup Race* from Croydon in 1925. When he was killed on 3 August 1927 he was the chief pilot for Imperial Airways and died tragically whilst testing the Bristol 'Badminton' biplane.

Beckett, E H, JP (b.1864) – E H Beckett was born at Birkenhead. In 1893 he was elected an associate member of the Institution of Civil Engineers and was in practice in London from 1894. From 1907 he was managing director of Ledward & Beckett Ltd, engineers, Westminster. He lived at 'The Grange', Firs Road. He was chairman of the Coulsdon & Purley UDC 1926-27.

Bélanger, Roy (1943-1995) – Roy Bélanger was booking office clerk at Kenley station for about 20 years. He was a friend to all his customers, particularly children – for example when a train was cancelled, he would telephone parents or he would drive the children to another station so that they would not be late for school. His office was full of *wellies* to combat the floods at the bottom of Kenley Lane. He ran the local Railway Travellers' Club, was chairman of the Roke Park (Kenley) Football Club and group administrator to the 7th Purley (All Saints' Kenley) Scouts for 20 years.

Roy Bélanger

Blenkinsop, Benjamin, JP (1830-1902) – He was a director of the Hand-in-Hand Insurance Company of the City of London and lived at 'Shord Hill', Kenley Lane – which was built for him – from 1889 until his death. He left over £25,000 in his will.

Broadhurst, Air Chief Marshal Sir Harry, GCB, KBE, DSO, DFC, AFC (1905-1995) – Sir Harry lived at Welcomes Farm in 1947 when he was in command of No.6 (Eastern Reserve) Group Air Transport. He was son of Capt. Harry Broadhurst of Emsworth, Hampshire, and married Jane Townley of Crickhowell in 1946. He joined the RAF in 1926, became group-captain in 1944, air commodore in 1947 and air vice-marshal in 1949.

Brown, Dr Robert, MA MB CM (Glasgow) (d.1919) – Medical practitioner, public vaccinator 8th District, Croydon and churchwarden; he lived at 'Yateley House', Hayes Lane. He was a very dour Scotsman, who was the first man in Kenley to have a motor-car – a Wolseley. He actually had two in case one broke down! His wife, Helen, who died in 1910, had a stained glass window in her memory at All Saints' Church but it was destroyed in World War II.

Claysey, Ron (1907-1980) – He was a locally well-known representative for the Provident Clothing & Supply Company in the 1950s and 1960s. He lived in Roke. Money was collected by him for a variety of goods which he delivered to local families. Payments were collected weekly, often from the jug or teapot on the mantlepiece when no one was in. Ron was secretary of the Kenley British Legion for many years.

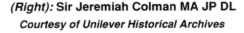

***(Above):* Ron Claysey and his daughter**

***(Right):* Sir Jeremiah Colman MA JP DL**

Courtesy of Unilever Historical Archives

Colman, Sir Jeremiah, MA JP DL (1859-1942) – Sir Jeremiah lived at 'The Towers', Hayes Lane from 1886-1888, when he moved to Gatton Park. He was son of J Colman of Carshalton Park (died 1885) and was educated at Cambridge. He was Chairman of J&J Colman Ltd, mustard manufacturers. He was High Sheriff of Surrey 1893-94, one of HM's Lieutenants for the City of London and Master of the Worshipful Company of Skinners 1899-1900. He was one of the best known growers of orchids in the world and president of Surrey County Cricket Club. He had a famous collection of cricket pictures and some were exhibited at the Tate Gallery in 1934.

Coombes, Captain William (*c*.1720-1790) – The tenant of Welcomes Farm from 1779 had been captain of a succession of brigs trading to South Carolina and later to other destinations such as New York. It was not until 1785, when he was in his mid-sixties, that the captain was able to retire and turn gentleman farmer. The last years of his life were devoted to his sheep. He died in 1790 and was buried in the old parish church at Coulsdon, where the ornate lead plaque on his grave was recently uncovered.

Cousins, Harry – Harry Cousins ran the general stores at 133 Godstone Road from 1941 to 1945. He was also the local chimney-sweep, trading under the name Bliss, and using a motorcycle combination with the brushes in the side-car. Harry and his wife Emma moved to Lower Road, Roke in 1945.

Cushing, Peter (1913-1994) – The actor and filmstar was born at 11 Godstone Road, where he lived for several years. The family moved to St James' Road before moving to Caterham. He was educated at Purley County

Grammar School. He made his stage debut in 1935 and film debut in 1948, and excelled in the roles of Baron Frankenstein and Count Dracula.

Diver, Ebenezer MD MRCS (b.1839) – He was a churchwarden and Kenley's first doctor until about 1897. He had moved from Caterham to Godstone Road in 1876, naming his house 'Yateley' after a village near Sandhurst, Berks, where the eldest of his 10 children was born and the location of his first practice.

Drew, George (1789-1862) – Formerly from Streatham, he lived at 'Kenley House' from 1853-61. He was a solicitor and a director of the Caterham Railway Company, for which he did much of the legal work in connection with land purchase for the railway line through Kenley. His son, George Henry Drew (born 1817), was also influential in the development of the area, building 'Whyteleafe House' in 1859 and living at 'Beechhanger Court' in 1875/76 in Caterham.

Galbraith, Judge James Francis Wallace, KC JP – He was a member of the Chancery and Company Bar. He was educated at Oriel College, Oxford and lived at 'Monkswood', Kenley. He was president of Kenley Bowls Club from its inception and vice-president of other sports clubs in the area. He was a supporter of Boy Scouts, Girl Guides and the RSPCA.

Gardner, Councillor H G, OBE FRGS (b.1867) – For 30 years he lived on and off in Kenley in Lady Lawrence's bungalow, but he was born in Surbiton. He made banking his profession and went abroad in 1891, working mainly in China. He served on many public and charitable bodies and was chairman of the China Association. He was awarded the OBE for his war service.

Gardner, William George (1839-1930) – William Gardner was the founder and driving force behind the celebrated Gardner's Pleasure Grounds, Riddlesdown, which started in 1892. He had previously started his own foundry and the locomotive for the pleasure grounds was made there. His wife, Henrietta (1839-1909), came from Monmouthshire and was a staunch Wesleyan. Her grandson later recalled that whilst Henrietta was attending her temperance meetings, his grandfather would quite likely be in *The Kenley Hotel.*

Gillespie, S B, MBE JP (1890-1954) – A civil servant in HM Stationery Office, he was awarded the MBE in 1950 in recognition of his services. He became chairman of Coulsdon & Purley UDC, was a magistrate and founder member and secretary for seven years of Whyteleafe & Kenley Residents' Association.

Griffiths, Sir William (1895-1952) – Born near Merthyr Tydfil, he graduated as a metallurgist from the University of Wales. He worked at the Woolwich Arsenal Research Department and later joined the Mond Nickel Co Ltd as manager of R&D Department, rising to become the company chairman and managing director. He was vice-president of the International Nickel Company of Canada Ltd and president of the Institute of Metals. He lived at 'Highclere', Hayes Lane and was knighted in 1946 for his wartime work

Hall, William – was living at 'Little Roke House', Hayes Lane in 1876 and was a director of the St Louis Beef Canning Company. He will be remembered for his law suit against Edmund Byron which ultimately led to the acquisition of the local commons by the City of London. Hall owned some local farms and his brother James of 'Oaklands', Hayes Lane, was also involved with the legal action.

Hawkins, William Francis Spencer, CB (1896-1979) – William Hawkins lived at 'The Oaks' in 1961. He was a signals officer 1915-19 with 27th Division Artillery and 80th Infantry Brigade in Salonika, and the British Army of the Black Sea, mentioned in despatches twice. He became a partner with Bird & Bird, Gray's Inn in 1921. He was master of the Supreme Court (Chancery Division) 1933-59 and chief master in 1959-69. He was a member of Coulsdon & Purley UDC, a JP for Surrey and chairman of Wallington Petty Sessions from 1958.

Hecht, Hermann (1923-1985) – He lived in Zigzag Road. Browsing the stalls in Portobello Road in the 1950s, Hermann Hecht came across a small projector with a few glass slides. This was to lead to a lifelong study and the writing of the definitive work in 1993 – completed by his wife and published posthumously – of *Pre-Cinema History*. This book is an encyclopaedia and annotated bibliography of the moving picture image before 1896. He taught at Croydon College from c.1966.

Hills, Sam (1796-1873) – Born in Godstone, Tom Hills was appointed huntsman to the Old Surrey Hounds at Garston in 1816 and has been described as the 'best huntsman who ever lived'. He held the post for 45 years except for a break between 1840-1843 when he was dismissed for refusing to submit to more rigid discipline. He was skilled at boxing. His son, Sam, succeeded him as huntsman and between them they held the post for 76 years.

Holland, Thomas (b.1886) – Mr Holland was headmaster of Roke Central School. He was born at Clay Cross, Derbyshire and was articled to an architect and surveyor. After three years he decided to take up teaching instead. He was appointed to Roke Central School in 1926. He wrote many school stories including 'Bully Austin'. At one time he was president of Surrey Teachers' County Association.

Hubback, Sir John Austen (1878-1968) – Lived at 'Pen-y-Bryn', Hayes Lane. He was educated at Winchester and Kings College, Cambridge. He entered the Indian civil service in 1902, became governor of Bihar and Orissa 1936-41 and was advisor to the Secretary of State for India 1942/7. He married Bridget Royds in 1906. He devised a method of measurement of crop yields, which was adopted all over India as the standard.

Kearton, Cherry (1871-1940) – Cherry lived first at 'Shunafell' and later at 'The Jungle'. Cherry's brother, Richard, came from Yorkshire to work for Cassells and contributed many natural history articles to Cassell publications. When Cherry joined him, he took relevant photographs with a five-shilling Kodak camera. Cherry later became a photographer in Africa, India and America, pioneering photography of big game in its natural habitat. The brothers wrote a number of books full of superb photographs. They lectured all over the British Isles, to the Royal Family and the president of the United States.

Cherry Kearton

Kerans, Commander John DSO (1915-1985) – He lived at New Eastcot House for a short while. He was best known for freeing the Royal Navy frigate HMS *Amethyst* from the Chinese communist authorities. In April 1949 she was on her way to Nanking via the Yangtze River when she was fired on and held. Captain Kerans managed to get on board and after three months he decided to 'make a run for it'. The ship reached safety without casualties. Captain Kerans was awarded the DSO. He retired from the Royal Navy in 1958 and was elected MP for Hartlepool.

Kershaw, Henry Edward – He lived at 'Viewfield', Park Road, from 1900 to 1907 (renamed 'Beechcroft' in 1910). In 1900 he became the first mayor of the Metropolitan Borough of Shoreditch.

Key, Roger 'Tiny' (1904-1968) – He lived in Kenley from the early 1930s until the late 1960s. Tiny was the local rodent operator for the Coulsdon & Purley District Council. His jolly nature, diminutive stature, with the poisons for his work carried in a small suitcase, made him a well-known figure throughout the district!

Lawrence, Dowager-Lady Harriet Katherine CI (1820-1918) – She died at 'The Hayes', aged 97, as widow of the first Baron Lawrence, GCB GCSI, governor-general of India 1864-69, who died in 1879. She was the daughter of Revd R Hamilton of Cloncha, Derry and great-niece of 11th Baron Blayney. She married Lawrence in 1841 and was sister-in-law of Henry Lawrence, defender of Lucknow. Her daughter, Hon. Maude Lawrence was born in 1864.

Sir Joseph Lawrence JP

Lawrence, Sir Joseph JP (1848-1919) – He lived at 'Oaklands'. He was MP for Monmouth 1901-1905, sheriff of the City of London 1900-01 and one of His Majesty's Commissioners of Lieutenancy for the City of London. Sir Joseph was chairman of Coulsdon Parish Council for seven years, a member of Surrey County Council and gave £6,000 to build the Commemoration Hall to celebrate the Diamond Jubilee of Queen Victoria in 1897. He was chairman of the Linotype & Machinery Company, twice president of the Association of Lancastrians and a captain in the 40th Lancastrian Rifle Volunteers from 1873-78. His wife Margaret came from Southport, Lancashire. He was one of the principal and earliest pioneers of the Manchester Ship Canal.

Maw, George (1832-1912) – He lived at 'Benthall', Zigzag Road from 1886 until his death. The house was named after 'Benthall House', Shropshire, where he had established a flourishing tile industry. He was a noted geologist, chemist, artist and botanist and in 1871 he undertook a journey to Morocco and the Great Atlas. He demonstrated the former existence of glaciers at the latter and later introduced exotic plants into English gardens. His eldest son, George Hornby Maw (born 1862) married Evelyn, daughter of William Pugh of 'Bod-Dyffryn', Valley Road, Kenley.

Tommy Mayhew

Mayhew, Tommy 'Jammy' (1888-1976) – He was pest controller for the Highways Department of Coulsdon & Purley District Council in the 1950s and 1960s.

McBain, James Anderson Dickson, CIE (b.1869) – Retired to 'Hill House', Kenley. He was born at Arbroath, educated at Arbroath High School, went straight into business and was soon working abroad. He became general manager for India, Burma and Ceylon for the Sun Life Assurance Company of Canada. He received the CIE (Companion of the Order of the Indian Empire) in 1916 and the Durbar Medal and became Mayor of Bombay in 1917.

Mears, Ray (b.1964) – The TV personality lived in Kenley. In the 1980s many Scouts from the 7th Purley troop benefited from his skills when he was their instructor. Ray was greatly influenced by the North American Indian survival techniques. Television soon discovered Ray, who appeared on *Tracks* and was then given his own series *Ray Mears' World of Survival*, followed by the very popular *Extreme Survival*. He has written a number of books including *The Survival Handbook* 1990.

Mitchell, B E, MA – He was born at Brighton and educated at St John's, Cambridge. He taught for four years at Perse School and 14 at Newcastle-under-Lyme. He had been head of Purley County Boys' School for 13 years when it moved from Roke to the new buildings at Old Coulsdon in 1933.

Morgan, Sir Charles Langbridge CBE (1855-1940) – Charles Morgan was born in Worcester and taken as an infant to live in Australia. He returned to England *c*.1871 to study engineering. He and his family came to live in

'Cullesden' in Firs Road *c.*1890, moving to 'Woodhurst' in Welcomes Road *c.*1903. His wife Mary died 7 October 1906. He was a past president of the Institution of Civil Engineers, director of the London, Brighton & South Coast Railway and Director of Willey & Co, engineers. He was created CBE in 1918. He was a Lt Col. in the Royal Engineers. Sir Charles, who was knighted in 1923, retired to Hove. He made generous contributions to Kenley Memorial Hall, see Chapter 12.

Sir Charles L Morgan CBE

Courtesy of the Marchioness of Anglesey

Morison, Hector JP (1850-1939) – Lived at 'Beechcroft'. He was president of the East Surrey Liberal Association. He was born in Scotland and married Josephine Ashton of Manchester. He worked on the Stock Exchange. He was a JP for 27 years and was the oldest member of the Croydon bench. He was a governor of Whitgift School and served one term as an MP from 1912 for S Hackney.

Moss, Harry (1892-1958) – He was born in Leicestershire but moved south to Kenley in 1912. He married Mary Hammond from Ferring in West Sussex and lived for the rest of his life at 15 Little Roke Road where he built up his business of tree felling, coppicing, gardening and general handiwork. He became a well-known character in Kenley with his white horse Winston.

Harry Moss with his horse Winston

O'Connor, Des (b.1932) – The singer and entertainer lived at 'Old Place' in Uplands Road until his divorce in 1969. His ex-wife was reported to have been shocked when visiting her old home some 30 years later, to find the half acre rear garden had been sold off as part of the Benthall Gardens development.

Pattison, Mrs Dorothy (d.1979) – She lived in Church Road and she and her husband, Professor Pattison, were co-opted to the Residents' Association Committee in 1945, which she served as an officer or committee member for all except three years until ill-health forced her to resign in 1976 – 28 years in all. She held a seat on Coulsdon & Purley UDC from 1953 until 1964.

Popper, Professor Karl Raimund (1902-1994) – The distinguished, world renowned philosopher was born in Austria. Much of his career was spent in England, where he lectured at the London School of Economics and other educational institutions. In later years, heads of state and foreign royalty would visit his home in Welcomes Road, which would occasionally necessitate the closure of the road as a security precaution.

Price, Cecil Herbert Thornton (1851-1920) – He was born in Stoke Newington, became a shipping insurance broker and later a wine merchant of the then well-known firm of White & Price, 57 Mark Lane – a business that had been run by his father before him. He lived for at least 36 years at 'Copenhagen House', Kenley Lane – later known as 'The Ivies' and then 'White House'.

Jack Railton with his grandchildren

Railton, Jack (1890-1979) – He lived all his life in Kenley and was a dustman for over 40 years. On retirement he took the job of 'Lollipop man' at Kenley Primary school during the 1960s and 1970s. He will be remembered with great affection by the many children from the school.

Rowe, Revd C V (b.1884) – He was educated at Manchester University and ordained in 1908. He held three curacies before coming to St James' in 1922. He raised £7,000 for the completion of the church.

Shepheard-Walwyn, Hugh W (1879-1939) – He was born in the Peak District and graduated from Oxford University. He was a master at Winchester. Fellow of the Entomological Society in 1898, naturalist and photographer, he lived at 'Dalwhinnie' – later 'Acorn House' – in Hayes Lane. He was the author of a number of natural history books including *Nature's Riddles* published by Cassell & Co. For 22 years he kept a herd of Japanese deer in his own adjacent wood. He was a churchwarden and in 1930 was admitted by the Bishop of Southwark to the Diocesan Order of Readers.

Shilcock, Revd Sidney Isaac Welbank lived at 'Woodleigh', Kenley Lane and 'Wellbank', Hermitage Road. He was headmaster of St Winifred's School from 1896 before moving to be rector of Titsey. He married Eva Winifred Spence in 1887 at Kenley Church.

Simpson, Margaret Mary Crawford, FRCS (née Louden) (1910-1998) – An eminent surgeon who became a Fellow of the Royal College of Surgeons in 1938. She lived with her husband at 'Longwood' until it was sold for development in 1987. Summerswood Close was built on the site.

Skeats, Mrs Grace Ethel, JP – lived at 'Ridgehurst', Uplands Road. She was born at South Norwood, daughter of George Thomas of the London Stock Exchange, and was educated at Croydon High School. She became chairman of the Women's Municipal Association in 1915, was elected to Surrey County Council in 1919 and became the first woman alderman of Surrey in 1935. During the war she was commandant of Voluntary Aid Detachment.

Smith, Mrs Walter Heaton – Mrs Heaton Smith, wife of the popular Kenley doctor FRCS (Edinburgh) of 'Yateley House' was Molly Carew, the famous Australian composer of 'Love's a Merchant', 'The Piper of Love' and other successes.

Smith, Walter (1853-1915) – Headmaster of Kenley National School for over 30 years from its opening in 1885. He had earlier been master of Earl Brownlow Memorial Schools, Totternhoe, Beds and Fetcham School, Surrey. Mrs Smith taught the infants and gave sewing lessons. Walter Smith kept a meticulous log of every aspect of school life which showed that the school was often complimented on its standards. In 1897 the school had around 200 pupils. He and his family lived in the school house, which survives at the end of Garston Lane.

Squire, Leonard Harding MA (1854-1918) – He was born in Kentish Town. His mother was Julia Pepys, distant relative of the diarist and he became the first vicar of Kenley, where he remained from 1889 to 1918. A stone let into the wall of All Saints' was formerly part of the synagogue of Capernaum brought from its ruins in 1889 by Revd Squire. In 1920 some clergy desks and choir stalls were installed at the church in his memory. He was a noted Egyptologist.

Stewart, Allen, RA (1865-1951) – Allen Stewart lived at 'Bonally', Valley Road, in 1926. He was an artist in oil and watercolour. He exhibited at the Royal Academy from 1892. He painted *The First International Golf Match, Leith Links 1682,* when the Duke of York (later James II) partnered John Paterson, the cobbler of Canongate and the best golfer of his day and won the match for Scotland v. England. The picture is now in America. He was on the staff of *The Illustrated London News* for some years and accompanied King Edward VII on his Mediterranean cruise.

Tufnell, Carleton Fowell (1856-1940) – Lived first at 'Iver', Firs Road and later at 'Watendone Manor', Hayes Lane. He was an Etonian, Lloyds underwriter and a churchwarden. His wife laid the foundation stone of Kenley Memorial Hall. In 1929 Mr Tufnell invited members of the Purley Natural History & Scientific Society to his home where they viewed his famous collection of walking sticks and fire insurance signs. He played county cricket for Kent in 1878-79 and wrote a book in 1889 called *The Cricketers' Form at a Glance* with five folding charts. He was captain of Kenley Cricket Club 1895-1902 and his sons were cricketers.

Albert ('Bert') Wilkinson

Wilkinson, Albert (1909-1980) – After World War II he lived in Kenley for 40 years with his wife Mary. He was resident pianist at *The Kenley Hotel* and *The Rose & Crown.* He played for many wedding receptions and parties and for many years was Father Christmas at the All Saints' Christmas Bazaar. He was a special constable attached to Kenley Police Station in the 1950s.

Willis, Harry, JP (1889-1968) – He was a civil servant who lived at 49 Beverley Road and was a founder member of the Whyteleafe & Kenley Residents' Association. He was its longest-serving member – 37 years – and was its president in 1963. He was elected to Coulsdon & Purley UDC in 1944 and maintained his seat until 1958 when he retired. He was chairman 1955-56.

Woodland, Edmund (Teddy) (1839-1919) – He bought Welcomes Farm in 1902, where he was stud owner, trainer and horse breeder. He was the father of Percy Woodland (1882-1958), who achieved great fame – riding his first winner aged 13 he went on to become one of the greatest ever riders. He was champion National Hunt jockey in 1903, riding 54 winners including the Grand National on 'Drumcree'. He was placed 2nd in 1905 on 'Nappertandy', then in 1913 won again on 'Covertcoat'. Teddy Woodland had previously lived at Tollers Farm, Coulsdon and is buried at St John's.

Worth, Harry (1917-1989) né Illingsworth – The comedian was born at Tankersley near Barnsley and lived in Valley Road for about two years in the 1960s. After working as a miner, he made his BBC TV debut in 1948 and appeared in variety theatres and music halls. He was instantly recognisable as his bumbling TV persona extended to his private life. He performed his 'plate glass window act' in the window of Pudney & Sims car showroom to the amusement of passers-by but not, it is understood, to the owners!

Young, John (1814-1893) – He lived at 'Kenley House'. He was the son of a brewer and maltster from Bedale in Yorkshire. He had moved to Upper Stanford Street, London, set up business as an Australian merchant and married Louisa Jeffree in May 1840. They had four daughters and two sons. In 1865 he acquired the 100 acre Kenley Park Estate, which included Hayes Farm. He was founder member and director of the Caterham & Kenley Gas Company and went on to become a JP and a guardian of the Croydon Union Infirmary. He was a fine horseman and an active member of the Old Surrey Hounds.

THE BOURNE SOCIETY

The Bourne Society was founded in 1956 and takes its name from the underground streams which follow the lines of the A22 and A23 roads, meeting in Purley to flow northwards and join the River Wandle, which flows into the Thames at Wandsworth.

The objects of the Society – England's largest local history society – are to extend the knowledge of local history in Caterham, Chaldon, Chelsham, Chipstead, Coulsdon, Farleigh, Godstone, Kenley, Purley, Sanderstead, Whyteleafe, Warlingham and Woldingham, and to ensure the preservation of records and objects of historical interest. The Society's Membership Secretary, Mrs. J. Emery, 118 Coulsdon Road, Coulsdon, Surrey CR5 2LB, will be happy to provide details of membership and subscription rates. The Society's telephone number is 01883 349287.

The Bourne Society is a registered charity, and as well as general work it has active special-interest groups in archaeology, industrial archaeology, landscape history, photography and pub history. Regular meetings, events and outings are arranged. A wide range of publications are produced, including a quarterly **Bulletin** and annual *Local History Records* which are sent free to members. For prices and current availability contact John Tyerman, Publications Co-ordinator, 60 Onslow Gardens, Sanderstead CR2 9AT, telephone 020 8657 1202.

Some recent publications —

Books:

Village History Series. Vol. 1–Purley, editor Andy Higham (1996); Vol. 2–Caterham, editor Gwyneth Fookes (1997); Vol. 3–Sanderstead, editor Joy Gadsby (1998); Vol. 4–Warlingham, editor Dorothy Tutt (1999); Vol. 5–Coulsdon, editor Ian Scales (2000); Vol. 6–Kenley, editor Grahame Brooks (2002); Vol. 7–Chaldon in preparation for publication in 2002.

The Way We Were – A Bourne Society Book of Days by John D Matthews

A Surrey Childhood in the 1930s and 1940s by Muriel Neal

Villagers – Five Shillings by Harley Sherlock

A Celebration of the Bourne

Rosie Remembers by Rosie Watts née Huggett

Leaflets:

Getting to know our Downland Villages – No. 1. Sanderstead (1997); No. 2. Godstone (1998)

Postcards:

Ancient and modern views of places in the Bourne Society area are available from East Surrey Museum and local stationers.